GOD IS IN AFRICA

MARTIN FALARDEAU

Translated by:
Remy Godin and Martin Falardeau

Edited by:
Jennifer Lachance

Cover pictures by:
IanZA and Pexels on Pixabay.com

Copyright © 2018 Martin Falardeau

ISBN: 978-1090795304

DEDICATION

I would like to dedicate my second book to all the inhabitants of Burkina Faso who have shown me a living spirituality and have fortified me in my journey to my Father's divine will. Without even knowing it, they were a great source of inspiration for me and my family. They taught me how to be bold with the Holy Spirit, in order to advance the Kingdom of God. Since my arrival in Burkina Faso, God has shown me that he will use this country greatly to show his glory to the rest of the world. This small, landlocked country will have a great role to play and will be an example to follow for all Christians on the planet.

I would like to express my deepest thanks to God himself for, without divine intervention in my life, I certainly would not have become a missionary in West Africa.

I also thank Pastor Tiken Akomatsri of the International Centre for Evangelization in Dedougou. From our first meeting, he immediately felt that God was working with me and asked me to pray for the sick and the people in need, though he did not know me. He knew that the Lord was going to use me and helped me in the prayers of healing and deliverance.

TABLE OF CONTENTS

FOREWORD

I am pleased to write the Foreword for this book entitled "God is in Africa" by Martin Falardeau. I am one of translation editors of this encouraging and inspiring book. I was honored to be involved, not only as a service directly to God, but I felt a sense of urgency getting this story translated from French to English, with the goal of dramatically extending its reach. "God is in Africa" is much more than another story following the travels of a missionary family - it is a glorious testament of what God can and will do with radical obedience, a servant heart, and simple desire to serve.

Martin's bold foray into missionary ministry in Africa reveals an extraordinary, in depth look into the supernatural world of a yielded servant of God in a mission field, wildly different from North America. Literally, walking you away from the tame, almost complacent, ministry atmosphere of Canada, to a country and people steeped in Satanism, sorcery and black magic, deeply in need of salvation and deliverance.

I have great admiration for the journey and courage of this humble servant. This book provides a very simple yet overlooked revelation of the most powerful way to position yourself to be used mightily by God and advance his Kingdom – humility. It gives the reader a profound, yet accessible understanding of how to be yielded to God, following his spirit and just how much he is able to use you from this position. Make no mistake - if you hunger to be used by God and question just how much he can do through one person - you will find this to be an excellent hand on field manual to purely God lead ministry.

In conclusion, I know Martin's transparent and articulate story will educate, enlighten, and inspire your faith in so many ways, as it did me. It will deepen your understanding, not only of God's love for people and the power he makes available through a humble heart, but also the startling lengths to which the enemy will go to stop God's servants. The warfare is more real than you can imagine or certainly expect to be prepared for. A vast amount of the missing information in my knowledge base concerning hands on deliverance, healing and battling spiritual attack from the very real powers of the enemy, have been filled in thanks to Martin and I am eternally grateful. I am confident any readers will benefit richly as well.

Jennifer LaChance

i

INTRODUCTION

"And he said to them: Go into all the world and proclaim the gospel to the whole creation. Whoever believes and is baptized will be saved, but whoever does not believe will be condemned. And these signs will accompany those who believe: in my name they will cast out demons; they will speak in new tongues; they will pick up serpents with their hands; and if they drink any deadly poison, it will not hurt them; they will lay their hands on the sick, and they will recover."

-Mark 16:15-198 (ESV)

There is no guide or manual that explains in detail how to do the work of a missionary in Africa. Each day is different and brings a lot of adventure and adventures as wacky, as they are serious. Nowhere is it written that it is easy to be a missionary these days. Nowhere is it said that the people around us will support us all along our journey. There is no proper preparation to be a perfect missionary. When God implants a mission in our heart, we must simply leave everything and follow him every day without ever deviating from his will and guidance. We must not look away and try to refuse the call of God because the Father will do everything to push us in the direction he desires for our lives.

"And that servant who knew his master's will but did not

1

get ready or act according to his will, will receive a severe beating."

-Luke 12:47 (ESV)

To follow the call of God that drove us to leave everything in our country of origin and to go to a country in West Africa was a true test of faith. When God asked Abraham to sacrifice his son Isaac, it was terribly hard and painful for Abraham to obey this call of his Creator. The feeling of sadness and the worry of not knowing what will happen afterwards had to make his legs limp as he walked over to the place that God had indicated to him.

It was an incredible ordeal for a man, but God saw all the trust that his servant Abraham had in him. He was willing to sacrifice his own son because he knew that God had something better for him otherwise, he would never have asked for such a thing.

Faith is to be sure, that the insurmountable ordeal that God puts on our road is simply to give us even better afterwards. Whether it is a personal experience, a fortification of our faith or to offer us his blessings on a gold platter, he is always at the rendezvous to fill us when we obey his will. He is a loving father who does not want our misfortune, because if he did, he would never have sent his only son to save us. What's the point of saving men you want, only to see them in misery afterwards? He is a father who does not abandon his children but only wants to see them succeed, in victory.

It is certain that to answer a call from the Lord requires a great deal of faith and unwavering confidence in our Creator, but the blessings that ensue are truly wonderful. On the other hand, it is very important to know that the path to the will of God is always dotted with many pitfalls. These obstacles often challenge us because the enemy does not want us to succeed in the mission God has given us.

It is the role of the enemy to do everything to block us. He is very cunning and acts in a subtle way, by sowing doubt or fear in our heart to keep us away from the Word, from the double-edged sword. It has always been so since the creation of mankind. Just look at what he did to divert Adam and Eve from God's blessings, to keep them away from the peace and tranquility of the Garden of Eden. He sowed doubt in the heart of Eve, in order to control her more easily and cause her to rebel against her Creator. Satan acted intelligently to achieve his ends, by sowing doubt in what God had told Adam and Eve.

"Now the serpent was craftier than any other beast of the field that the LORD God had made. He said to the woman: Did God actually say: You shall not eat of any tree in the garden? And the woman said to the serpent: We may eat of the fruit of the trees in the garden."
-Genesis 3:1-2 (ESV)

Then Satan continued the discussion with Eve to bribe her even more. He wanted to keep her away from God because he knew that Adam would also succumb if the woman spoke to him.

"But the serpent said to the woman: You will not surely die. For God knows that when you eat of it your eyes will be opened, and you will be like God, knowing good and evil."
-Genesis 3:4-5 (ESV)

Satan had just contradicted God and now Eve had enormous doubts about her Creator. She doubted so much, that she no longer believed in him.

"So, when the woman saw that the tree was good for food, and that it was a delight to the eyes, and that the tree was to be desired to make one wise, she took of its fruit and ate, and she also gave some to her husband who was with her, and he ate."
-Genesis 3:6 (ESV)

Eve had so much doubt, that she now found the fruit was pleasing to the sight. Not only that, but it was mostly valuable in her eyes. She had an object of distraction that diverted her gaze from the face of God. The Creator no longer had first place in her life. It is Satan's way of acting, his strategy to keep us away from God. He has and will always do so. By installing doubt in people's minds, he can easily distance them from God using distraction.

He's still doing it today. Just look at the world we live in. There are many distractions everywhere that keeps us away from the Word of God. When I was still in Canada, I never realized how distracted I was in my personal relationship with my Savior.

Entertainment is everywhere - Internet, television, video games, etc. Since I have been in Burkina Faso, I have learned to get rid of these distractions of the world to focus on the Word of God. After being totally rid of what turned me away from my Lord, I received the gifts of the Holy Spirit forcefully and began to perform miracles by the name of Jesus Christ.

"For you have need of endurance, so that when you have done the will of God you may receive what is promised."
-Hebrews 10:36 (ESV)

I felt a great power in me and I know that God is acting with strength and power in Burkina Faso.

God is in Africa!

BURKINA FASO

It was the night my wife, my son, and I headed to the counter of United Airlines. I still remember the face of despair that the employee had at the counter, seeing us approaching proudly with our 19 suitcases. Although she seemed discouraged, she gave us excellent service. Unfortunately, our excess baggage cost us a surplus of $2700. Canadian dollars.

This expense made a big, but necessary dent in our budget. We were bringing a lot of gifts for the Christmas celebration to come, and lots of items and tools that we could sell or exchange once at our destination. All our luggage was meticulously organized for several weeks, to not exceed the maximum weight and dimensions per suitcase, required by the airline. Once we finally got rid of all our suitcases, we were left with only our carry on which allowed us to walk freely in the Edmonton International airport.

We were excited to leave Canada, not only because we were going to travel, but mostly because we were responding to the call of God. There had already been several months since the Lord had told me to leave everything and move to West Africa to serve him. I did not know our final destination, but the Lord had shown me that we would celebrate the Nativity in Africa.

Christmas should be a family celebration; we made the decision to go to Dedougou in Burkina Faso to celebrate with my wife's family. From there we will wait for the Lord to tell us our final destination in order to work for the advancement of his kingdom. We were not ready for such a trip considering, we may or may not return, but we had obeyed our King of Kings. No Canadian church wanted to help us financially, not even a small amount of money, simply to encourage us. It was God who sent us and he had said several times to trust him because the money would come from everywhere and he would provide for all our financial and personal needs.

"Do not be like them, for your Father knows what you need before you ask him."
-Matthew 6:8 (ESV)

"And my God will supply every need of yours according to his riches in glory in Christ Jesus. To our God and Father be glory forever and ever. Amen."
-Philippians 4:19 (ESV)

We had done as Abraham; we put all our trust in God without even knowing in which country he wanted us.

"Now the LORD said to Abram: Go from your country and your kindred and your father's house to the land that I will show you."
-Genesis 12:1 (ESV)

There was a lot of excitement in our hearts, but also a bit of concern, as we were making a great leap into the unknown. Our trust in God was the only thing that gave us a positive hope in our future. The Lord now had full control over our lives and we could no longer go back. Our eyes were fixed on him and him alone.

Our flight had several stopovers – a quick stop in Denver,

Colorado, a second stop in Newark, New Jersey and one in Brussels, Belgium, before being able to set foot on the ground of Ouagadougou, the capital of Burkina Faso. It was a long journey that would exhaust us completely, but necessary to accomplish the mission that God has asked us to.

We were now approaching the secure area of the airport for US flights. Since the September 11 attacks in New York, the United States had upgraded its security system for all flights entering their territory. This new measure could seem grueling, but also gave an extra sense of security. Several travelers complained that entry into the United States had now become very complicated, but they often forget an important detail - this country had been heavily attacked and had to protect its population.

If a person had nothing to be worried about, they would pass freely, but if you had a criminal record or were trying to do something illegal, the agents would prevent you from entering the United States. It's their country - not ours! Getting a visa and traveling to another country was a privilege granted by this country. They could refuse who they wanted since it was their country and not ours. They had to protect American citizens first and foremost.

Contrary to what you might believe, we also had problems passing the security check. They had searched all our hand luggage, emptied our pockets, and asked us to go through the specially designed scanner to see if we were hiding something on us. Afterwards, they kindly informed us that they had detected a drone in my son's luggage, so they wanted to check it. They quickly noticed that it was just a cheap toy that could only be used to entertain children. We had obeyed all their requests and having found nothing illegal, they let us enter the US secure area. It was as simple as that, they had all the rights in their country.

Inside the secure area, we found a place at a table to enjoy a small snack before taking our flight. After this delicious meal, we heard the call for the boarding of our flight by the speakers of the area. What amuses me a lot every time I take a plane is to see all the people who got up quickly to be the first to go on board when their seats were already reserved. I always let them pack in like sardines in a box and wait only a few minutes for the line to drop. I still find my seat empty and, if there was no more room for my little suitcase, I simply put it under the seat in front of me.

I did not need to force through all those strangers who absolutely wanted to be the first to enter the plane, when there was not even a prize to win for the first place. Was it just a matter of personal pride? I did not know, but I let them go if it amused them so much. We were now all comfortably seated in our respective seats and the plane took off towards Denver, Colorado.

After only a few hours, the plane landed at the Denver airport.

This airport was impressive because it was built completely lengthwise. Only one corridor stretching as far as the eye could see.

There were airport employees on small electric vehicles that carried older travelers and all those who had difficulty walking long distances. I had asked one of these drivers if our next boarding gate was a long way off and he had kindly offered to drive us there.

He had heard my accent and wanted to show us the kindness and welcome of the American people. We all boarded for a free ride in the only corridor of the airport. The driver was really friendly and he amused my son so much by making him laugh. He led us down directly to our gate and we warmly thanked him for the ride.

We then noticed a little pizzeria next to our boarding gate so we bought a few pieces to taste it. It was rather impressive for a small airport restaurant. We tasted our succulent pizzas while watching the travelers who were constantly circulating in front of us. We even saw several cowboys since we were in Colorado.

The call for boarding sounded and we still waited for the crazy race for the imaginary prize of the first person seated on the plane to be completed. We waited for our reserved seats, still available even after the mad race of other travelers. The plane was taking off in an intense fog, preventing us from seeing the city of Denver. It saddened me a bit because I really wanted to see this remarkable city. A sense of despair invaded me because I realized that I would probably not return to the United States. Even worse, perhaps I would never see the country where I was born, Canada, ever again. Only God knew our future. We flew towards an absolute mystery, but our full confidence allowed us to act without looking behind us.

"In returning and rest you shall be saved; in quietness and in trust shall be your strength."
-Isaiah 30:15 (ESV)

A few hours later, the aircraft stopped on the tarmac at Newark airport.

We quickly found that our next flight was in a few minutes and we had to go through the entire airport to our boarding gate. It was kind of fun to see all these people from everywhere in front of us. There were people of all races, all colors, and all styles. There were also people of different sexual orientations; gays, lesbians and even transgendered people walked without being ashamed. It had become normal in the minds of people to see this kind of man dressed as women. Despite their accoutrements, it is obvious that they were men simply by looking at the thick makeup they wore with pride on their faces. What a shame! I was almost nauseous passing by them.

The enemy has totally won the West by making everyone believe that it was normal to be like these people. I remember telling my wife that I no longer recognize the world in which we lived. This world was no longer mine because of the perversion. The only thing I could do for them was to pray that the light of the Lord would open their eyes and repent of their sins before the return of Jesus. I was totally saddened and devastated by what I saw.

When we arrived at our boarding gate, a voice was heard announcing that our flight was delayed for a few hours to allow airline employees to conduct a check on the aircraft. We sat down and had a snack and some refreshments. My wife and son dozed off a little bit to regain strength while I kept looking at the people around me.

Several memories came to mind. Disturbing things I had seen on television, the Internet and in local news. Things like a young homosexual man who sued a Christian school in Alberta. The school refused to register him because his sexual orientation was not consistent with the Book of Christians, a wedding cake maker was in the Supreme Court of United States because he had refused to make a cake for a lesbian couple, an American pastor who was being insulted and spit on while he evangelized in a park. Christian churches that began to celebrate gay marriages inside their walls, parents who agree to change the sex of their children, and the transgendered people who walk in all schools in order to divert the children of God...

That's when God interrupted my thoughts and said, "Don't worry about it, these things must happen." I had just come to understand why the Lord sent us to Africa - God will act mightily in Africa because it is an example for the whole planet. I even believe that the work of God will begin with Burkina Faso. A small, landlocked country that will stand out by its powerful faith. It will be a light for the world.

"The saying is trustworthy: If anyone aspires to the office of overseer, he desires a noble task. Therefore, an overseer must be above reproach, the husband of one wife, sober-minded, self-controlled, respectable, hospitable, able to teach, not a drunkard, not violent but gentle, not quarrelsome, not a lover of money. He must manage his own household well, with all dignity keeping his children submissive, for if someone does not know how to manage his own household, how will he care for God's church?"

-1 Timothy 3:1-5 (ESV)

The voice in the loudspeakers called for the boarding of our flight a second time. I snapped out of my thoughts and woke up my little family to board the plane. We had a flight of more than 6 hours to do before we had to land in Brussels in Belgium. Immediately after take-off, my wife and son fell asleep deeply. For my part, I did not know how to explain it, but I could not close my eyes. I kept thinking back to what God had said to me, "...these things must happen." They had to happen because they had been prophesied by Jesus himself.

"Then they will deliver you up to tribulation and put you to death, and you will be hated by all nations for my name's sake. And then many will fall away and betray one another and hate one another. And many false prophets will arise and lead many astray. And because lawlessness will be increased, the love of many will grow cold."

-Matthew 24:9-12 (ESV)

"I tell you, he will give justice to them speedily. Nevertheless, when the Son of Man comes, will he find faith on earth?"

-Luke 18:8 (ESV)

These verses of the Gospels of Matthew and Luke had just given me the answer to what God had told me. This question of Jesus, "Will he find faith on earth?" clearly shows us, that upon the return of our Lord, faith will be very rare, as in the times of Noah where only eight people were saved from the waters.

"Just as it was in the days of Noah, so will it be in the days of the Son of Man."

-Luke 17:26 (ESV)

Let us not forget that at the end of time, many will have forsaken their faith and turn to the pleasures of the flesh and this world. They will give up for fear of confronting the torments of

Christians because of the name of Jesus. God had just told me that all these things were part of his plan, in preparation for the return of Jesus. Let us all be ready for his return and never extinguish the oil in the lamp that the bridegroom gave us. Let us constantly follow our great Shepherd.

"When he has brought out all his own, he goes before them, and the sheep follow him, for they know his voice. A stranger they will not follow, but they will flee from him, for they do not know the voice of strangers."

-John 10:4-5 (ESV)

All my reflections and biblical research made the long hours of flying pass very quickly. Again, my family and I thought we could see Brussels from the air but the clouds and rain ruined everything. With the fog in Denver, the night in Newark and now the clouds in Brussels, I began to believe that God did not want us to look at the West but that our thoughts were only for Africa.

Since the flight from Newark had been delayed, we were now very tight for time and had to go as fast as possible to our next gate. We rode aboard a shuttle that drove us to the right place. It was impossible to be mistaken since the waiting area was full of dark-skinned travelers. I knew that they were Africans as soon as I saw a black woman not watching her child running around because she was too busy talking on the phone, in a language I didn't know. A white woman would have been in a panic and would have yelled at her child to come back to her.

When they announced boarding, all Africans rose and jostled to enter first. The funniest thing about all this was that airline employees called passengers by boarding area, but most Africans were still lining up, only to be told that their boarding pass did not show the right zone.

Instead of moving aside and making room to those whose area matched, they stood there blocking everyone, just to wait for their own area to be called into the speakers. I expected this kind of situation since it was not my first trip to West Africa. We entered the last because I did not want to be part of this madness.

Not just madness at the gate but also madness in the aisles inside the plane. Everyone blocking the aisle just to chat with a long-time acquaintance, taking an hour to try to put a carry-on baggage too big for the luggage rack over their heads or just to going to the toilet. You should not risk losing the first imaginary prize for the mad race at the entrance of the plane. I had travelled to Burkina Faso in 2001 and Mali in 2004 and nothing had changed. The same crazy race.

The flight between Brussels and Ouagadougou took place without any problems. My body was beginning to feel heavy with jet lag and fatigue, so I fell asleep for almost the entire duration of the flight. Unlike all of our other flights, there was beautiful sun in Ouagadougou which allowed us to see the whole city from the top of the air. My son was near the window and he looked carefully at what was to become his new country.

I did not worry at all for him because he is a very intelligent child who adapts quickly everywhere. He was used to big moves because God had called us to leave Quebec to settle in Alberta. Emmanuel did not speak English at all, but he learned very quickly and made a lot of English-speaking friends. He had adapted to Fort McMurray and Edmonton, as if he had already lived in these two cities in Alberta. Now he looked through the small window of the airplane and eager to discover a country of Africa.

He was already asking me a lot of questions about the Burkina culture and whether he would be able to make friends quickly. I started to laugh and told him that since he was a Canadian; all children would want to be his friends because he would be the center of attention. A smile appeared after hearing this encouragement from me. The aircraft touched down to finish its race near the airport entrance. At the time my feet touched the land of Burkina Faso, a little anxiety crossed my mind. There were more deadly attacks in Ouagadougou, so I wanted to be as fast as possible to get to the hotel to feel safer.

In fact, I wasn't worried about myself, but I was thinking mostly about the safety of my wife and my son.

We all went through the security checks for entry into Burkina Faso without any problems. The policemen that were present instilled a strong sense of security in our hearts. After all, the army and the police of Burkina Faso have an excellent reputation throughout Africa. Picking up all our suitcases was a terribly frustrating adventure. We asked for help from a few employees who were helping the travelers on the spot. They did a remarkable job.

When we were counting the suitcases, there was one missing. I told myself that one suitcase on 19 was not so bad. Especially if one takes into account the fact that at the airport of Ouagadougou, the suitcases often disappear magically and they hardly ever find them. I wanted to make my declaration of loss of luggage at the counter, but the employee seemed to make a total mockery of it. I had to completely let this suitcase go, because I would never see it again.

The policeman at the exit asked us why we had so much luggage. I told him that Christmas was approaching and that we had a lot of gifts for my wife's family. He let us go and then we finally got outside to find it was already night time. I had not realized that we had been at the airport for so long. Before we left Canada, we had booked a hotel room, as well as a driver to greet us at the airport, but no one was waiting for us except a few taxis waiting for clients.

Rosalie had made another plan, just in case the driver did not show up; she had asked her brother Gilbert to join us at the airport to help us with the suitcases. Gilbert was there! We decided to take the three taxis that were available, to drive us with all our luggage to our hotel. We had agreed on a price then these three very nice men tied our suitcases on the roof of their vehicles and drove us to our hotel. They even helped us to transport the suitcases inside the hotel. Rosalie, to thank them for their kindness, gave them a generous tip and then let them leave.

We had booked an air-conditioned room with two double beds

at the hotel, but when I learned that this room was on the second floor and that we had to pack all our bags using the hotels only staircase, I was so discouraged. We had to take each suitcase, holding it in front of us, since this staircase was just wide enough for one person. Imagine a Canadian who was leaving the cold, to arrive in a very hot country and, on his very first day, work hard in this heat already. No need to explain that my whole body was covered in sweat. The shower was really excellent after all this hard work. We had a little chat with Gilbert, and then the time had come to rest.

The next morning, Gilbert and Rosalie left to find a car that could suit our needs in this new country. Rosalie had already booked a van for all of our luggage but there was not enough room for all of us. My son and I stayed at the hotel to enjoy a bit of the outdoor pool and cold treats to cool off. Rosalie and her brother came back, aboard a Toyota Avensis car. To be honest, as soon as I saw this car, I did not like it but Rosalie seemed so excited and happy with her purchase that I did not want to spoil her joy.

Being Canadian, I was not used to see old vehicles worn like this. I wondered how it could still drive, but I relied on Gilbert's word since he is a trained mechanic. In West Africa there are a lot of cars like this. The Burkina citizens call them "France Farewell" - old cars the French no longer want, often requiring a lot of repairs so they get rid of them, by sending them to Africa. Too old or too costly to repair, they leave them in the hands of Africans, who fix them with what they have on hand.

Often, they have parts that they have made themselves, sometimes of dubious quality or just plain dangerous, but it somehow works well. They are very resourceful people and it is amazing how they manage to organize themselves with the little they have.

I commend them greatly for this quality of resourcefulness. In the case of Westerners, when something goes wrong, they got rid of the item and buy another one, instead of finding a way to revive their old cars, appliances, televisions, and so on. They like filling garbage cans and landfills, better than recycling. The law of least effort!

So we could practically say that France was using West Africa as a dump, by sending all their useless junk there, instead of finding a more environmental solution.

After scanning the car, we sat at the hotel restaurant to eat a good meal. In the evening, we bought local SIM cards to use our Canadian cell phones in this new country. We also gave a phone to Gilbert because he was providing incredible help.

The next morning, the driver came to join us at the hotel because it was the day of the big departure to the city of Dedougou in the province of Mouhoun. We carried all the luggage down the small staircase and deposited them in the Nissan pickup. The driver made sure everything was securely fastened because we did not want to lose a single suitcase on the road. I was riding in our new car which was driven by Gilbert, since I hated driving to Ouagadougou. I was afraid especially after seeing all the intense traffic on the streets of the capital.

The cars were cutting in endlessly, others were running crosswalks, even when the traffic light was red, others were turning in forbidden places, others were cutting motorcyclists and bicycles that were rolling around in dangerous ways, etc. It was crazy driving in this city where the accident rate was terribly high. I preferred to leave the wheel to a man who had the proper experience to drive in this intense traffic where everyone had a driver's license, but no one knew how to drive. My wife and my son had boarded the van and we began our journey of several hours to our new house in Dedougou.

While we were still in Edmonton, God had shown me in vision that we would be staying in a house where there was a lot of green color. I couldn't figure out if it was the paint that was green or something else, but I knew the green color was very present. Despite this vision, I was very concerned about our finances and a question often came to mind, "Where are we going to live and at what cost?" I decided to put all this in prayer and ask God to help me get rid of these worries by showing me the answer to this question. The next morning, a friend of Rosalie's, a resident of Lincoln, Nebraska, USA, had heard about our divine mission and she had been committed to leaving us her house, for free, for as long as we needed.

I was so happy with this news that I lifted both hands in the air and I thanked the Lord for his answering so fast. We would have one less expense to make. This house was going to be our home for the entire duration of the mission in West Africa.

We stopped for a few moments near the Catholic cathedral in Ouagadougou to buy the famous Ouaga meat sandwiches and some sweets for the road. We filled up the fuel and then we finally left the capital of Burkina Faso. Gilbert was driving very fast on the highway, but we were still getting passed by other vehicles going faster than us. We ran into several police checkpoints on the road. I liked to stop for ID checks because it gave me a sense of security.

The town of Koudougou was finally before us. I remembered a bit of this city, since I visited it regularly in 2001 and 2002 to go to Ouagadougou to do my internship reports. I was a little saddened to see that the city had not changed, except that the road tar was totally damaged, almost impassible in some places. I had the impression that the Koudougou Town Hall had done absolutely nothing during all these years. All buildings and streets were abandoned. I was just hoping that Dedougou had not made the same blunder, but it had grown greatly since my last visit.

We drove through Koudougou without stopping because the hours passed and we did not want to drive at night. Several attacks and attempted terrorist attacks took place at nightfall in the villages surrounding Dedougou.

I absolutely wanted to be at my destination as soon as possible but when a woman was part of the trip, it was impossible to be on time. After Koudougou, Rosalie wanted to stop everywhere to buy fruit, vegetables, and pottery craft in Tcheriba.

All these stops delayed us considerably and the night found us still on the road. Joy filled my heart when I saw a huge blue bus filled with policemen overtaking us. I asked Gilbert not to lose sight of this bus, to always stay close to them. If a road cutter (road hijacker) was presently on the road, he would immediately be taken by all the policemen who were in front of us. Unfortunately, in several West African countries, road cutters remained an almost uncontrollable problem.

These bandits placed tree trunks or other large objects on the road to force the travelers off the road. Afterwards, they stole anything they could take with a firearm. Many times, they were coldly killing innocent people just to get some bank notes. I had never had the opportunity to fall on road cutters but my ears heard several mishaps involving them. I did not want to be part of one of those mishaps. These policemen before us had comforted me, without even knowing it. When I told my fear of road cutters to a few people, they all told me that I just had to trust God. They were absolutely right, but to that I replied, "When Jesus was facing great fear, as at the time of the crucifixion, what did he say?"

"The spirit indeed is willing, but the flesh is weak."
-Matthew 26:41 (ESV)

So, it is normal for man to have fears and anxieties occasionally, but we must not keep this fear too long because it will harm our faith. As soon as we are afraid of something, we must ask God to help us to confront it, to give him all fear to his mighty hands so that he can take care of it himself.

We were starting to see posters on the side of the road, so we knew our final destination was approaching. I was very happy to finally see the lights of the city of Dedougou. Gilbert led us to the house that was offered to us for free.

The house was in a neighborhood called "The Living Forces." It was a new development, as most houses were not yet fully built. Gilbert stopped the car in front of a driveway and a guard named Prosper came out through the door to greet us. He was hired to monitor the house so that no one would come and vandalize it because the home had no permanent resident.

When we entered through the entry way, one thing struck me - there was absolutely nothing green in color. I turned to my wife and told her that it was not the house I had seen in my vision. "God has planned another house for us, not this one!" We decided to move into this house because it was too late to look for a new home. We put all the suitcases inside and, despite the exhaustion of the road trip; we tried to settle down comfortably in order to spend our first night in Dedougou.

I hung mosquito nets in the rooms, made the beds as best I could and pulled out some clothes and towels for the shower. I dreamt of a good shower for several hours, since there is a lot of dust in the area of the province of Mouhoun. Unfortunately, when I got undressed and walked in the shower with the soap in my hands, I realized that the water was not coming out. I tried in every way possible but nothing wanted to come out. I was told that there were often water cuts during the heat period but we were not yet in that period. I was extremely disappointed and very uncomfortable having to lie down with my wife without being washed and cleaned. We were so exhausted that we all slept like this, hoping to have a shower the next morning.

Just as the sun came up, I ran into the shower. I could finally remove all this dust and this old sweat from my body but I was totally mistaken - there was still no water. At that time, I wondered how I could spend another day without washing myself. I made the decision to clothe myself in new clothes and wait until the evening, hoping that the water will come again. The keeper of our new home came to see me and informed me that the water came very seldom in the area of the Living Forces. He offered to bring us water cans from the fountain near our residence. The only problem was that it wouldn't be until the evening. I figured better than nothing, so I accepted his offer and we spent a whole day without being able to wash.

The good thing is that we didn't need to go out of the residence since we had to empty our suitcases to settle in.

The more I looked inside the residence, the more problems I found. This house had been badly built or erected too quickly. We could see many traces of flooding on the interior walls and the ceiling showed signs of mold. Some doors and windows were closing poorly and some electrical cables were bare and expose on some walls yet they were connected to the electrical circuit of the house.

I showed all this to my wife, explaining that this house was very dangerous. Not only was there a risk of being electrocuted, but also of flooding during the rainy season. I realized that this house had may have been lent to us free, in the hope that we would spend a fortune to repair all the problems related to a botched construction. Moreover, this house did not correspond to the visions that God had shown me - there was nothing green, neither inside nor on the exterior of the residence. Rosalie was not accepting what I was saying since the owner was a great friend, so she decided we should stay a few more days.

In the evening, Prosper, the keeper, brought us several cans filled with water. I finally managed to take a good, or rather an excellent shower. I had forgotten how much the sensation of water flowing on the skin could be so enjoyable. At that moment, Prosper had become my favorite keeper! Afterwards, we all went outside to eat delicious Guinea fowl, grilled on coal embers. A memorable evening in good company, with my favorite keeper. That night we went to bed very late because my wife's friends and family had come to greet us.

The next day, Rosalie noticed that this house was not ideal for our family when she noticed the phenomenal number of cockroaches and other insects in our kitchen. These critters were everywhere, even behind our brand-new refrigerator. We were terribly discouraged and made the decision that we had to find a new home. Gilbert, Rosalie's brother, began to search for a house for rent that could work for us. He contacted us in the evening saying that he had found a beautiful residence and we had to visit it immediately otherwise someone else will take it. It was already night but he still came to take us with our car and drove us to area 2 of Dedougou.

I didn't want to visit it with Gilbert and my wife because I knew very well how things worked in Burkina. When a white man shows up to buy or rent something, the prices are mysteriously increased for no reason. So, I decided to wait in the car. After a few minutes, my wife returned to the car and asked me come immediately with her. She did not want to explain to me why she was so cheerful, but I really wanted to know. When we crossed the doorway, I immediately saw green everywhere. The outdoor courtyard was full of green plants and trees, including small mangoes, papayas, bananas, shrubs with flowers, huge ferns, etc. I felt like I was seeing the vision that God had shown me before we left Edmonton. It was so beautiful.

A man stood in front saying that he represented the owner of this House. We talked a bit and then informed us about the monthly rental price.

The price exceeded our budget and I tried to negotiate a little downward, but the man asked me to come and see the interior to find out the quality of this house. I followed him and he was right! This house was beautiful and its rental value exceeded the asking price. There was air conditioning, fans and a shower with toilet in all the rooms, a huge living room and a large dining room. Everything was impeccable! I stopped trying to negotiate and I accepted his offer without hesitation. I still remember what Rosalie had said to me, "If God has shown you this house and he has sent us here, he will provide for all our needs!"

"And my God will supply every need of yours according to his riches in glory in Christ Jesus."
-Philippians 4:19 (ESV)

On Sunday, December 24, 2017, we first set foot in the Church International Center of Evangelization of Dedougou. The service was incredibly more intense than any service I had seen in Canada. During the praises, the women danced and walked round in the rows and they encouraged others to join the dancing. The songs were very rhythmic and it was impossible to stay without clapping hands or dancing.

We felt a spiritual presence so intense that our heart was burning with passion and love for the Lord. My wife could not hold back and she joined all the other women who danced incessantly.

Everyone seemed filled with a powerful joy that there were no words that could adequately describe it. It was alive! Afterwards a man went up to the stage and made some announcements about the activities of the Church. The pastor finally arrived on the stage and took the microphone to ask everyone to thank the Lord and pray aloud. Once again, I was impressed to see all these people glorifying our Lord with their arms in the air and tears in their eyes. Some also kneeled and prayed forcefully.

All those voices praying in tongues sounded like a sweet music. I could imagine the Lord listening and appreciating all the love that his people showed him. I closed my eyes and began to pray in tongues to accompany these singers of divine intercession. These prayers lasted several minutes and the pastor began to shout "Hallelujah!"

All the faithful replied at the same time, "Amen!" The pastor started again, "Hallelujah!" And he received the same answer. "Hallelujah!" And another "Amen" resonated in the church. I felt really good in this house of the Lord. The preaching of the pastor was about the birth of Jesus. Probably like all the pastors of the planet since we were at the time of the Nativity (Christmas).

At the end of the service, everyone went out the back door while the pastor passed through a door on the side of the stage, which also went outside. People greeted each other outside and shared the latest news about their family, their work, etc. They all came to greet us, in order to find out where we had come from and why we were in Burkina Faso. An intense human warmth showed us that they were a large family, a lot like at the time of the apostles of Jesus.

We were all brothers and sisters who fraternize together in love. Since I was white, the pastor had noticed me and came to greet us. As we shook hands, we both felt that we had already known each other for years. It was as if we were long lost brothers.

We talked a little and then he showed me his office at the back of the courtyard. Several people were waiting for the pastor's arrival to receive prayer. "These people need healing prayers because they are sick," said the pastor. "Go pray for them so they get healing." What? Me? - I had never prayed or ever attempted to do a healing prayer before.

I didn't know how to do it and now the pastor wants me to pray for all these sick people. In spite of my nervousness, something in my heart made me answer, "I'm going immediately!" I did not want to do it but a force pushed me to walk to the pastor's office and pray for all those desperate people seeking for divine healing. The pastor did not know me and he asked me to pray for the sick. Perhaps he had received a message from God about me? Maybe that's what God wanted me to do in Africa? Nevertheless, I was walking towards these sick people.

The first woman, Alarba, had a little baby in her hands and asked us to pray for her child, who could not sit down because of a birth defect.

The doctors told her that her child had to undergo an operation to correct this problem; otherwise it could get worse. It started really bad for me. Me, who did not know how to pray for the sick and this was my first case? A child with a birth defect that had to be operated on quickly? Will I be up to the task? I took a deep breath and put everything into the hands of the Lord - "Lord, it is you who sent me to this country, far from my home. I obeyed you without hesitation. Now I am the one who needs your help because I am in a situation that exceeds me as a man. For you, this situation is nothing. Help me to do this so that your name is glorified. If it is really your will then I will be more than victorious. Amen."

Now I felt ready to face the greatest challenges of the world.

So, I put one hand on the child's head and the other on the bottom of his back and prayed as I had never prayed before.

"Lord, King of Kings, to you be glory and honor. I thank you for the woman who came here before you because she trusts that you can act and heal the child you gave her. I also know that you are the God of the impossible and that you can heal this child. Use me as your work tool, use my hands to act with power and drive away this defect. Your word of truth tells us that, where there are two or three people, you are present. So, you're here with us. Your word of truth teaches us to ask in thy holy name and you are righteousness and good to offer it to us."

Then I asked for healing in the name of Jesus. "I know you're listening and hearing my prayers. I also know you're answering prayers. Thank you for answering. I thank you for the healing of this child. Let all glory and honor come back to you. Amen."

"And whatever you ask in prayer, you will receive, if you have faith."
                                                            -Matthew 21:22 (ESV)

After praying, I felt a little strange. A little doubt was going through my mind. Will this child be cured? If there is no healing, what will people say about me? I looked at the mother of the child and told her, "The Lord will heal the child but you must thank the Lord every morning for healing, even if you see no change because he acts in his own time and not according to the time of men."

She thanked me and left with a smile on her face that showed that she was happy with the prayer I had just done. Without really knowing it, Alarba's smile had scared away all the doubts I had in me and I began to pray for all the other sick with full confidence in God. After all, what I had said in my prayer for the child was perfectly aligned with the word.

"For where two or three are gathered in my name, there am I among them."
                                                            -Matthew 18:20 (ESV)

"Truly, truly, I say to you, whoever believes in me will also do the works that I do; and greater works than these will he do, because I am going to the Father. Whatever you ask in my name, this I will do, that the Father may be glorified in the Son. If you ask me anything in my name, I will do it."

-John 14:12-14 (ESV)

I knew now that I was doing the will of my heavenly Father. All these people had come to see the glory of the Lord and witnessed it. They all left happy because some were cured, others had just received a fiery love in their hearts, others were comforted, etc. The Lord was in the process of acting forcefully. I warned everyone to thank the Lord every day for what he did in them. I didn't want them to glorify me, but glory only came to the one who healed - Jesus.

On the evening of the same day, we moved into this splendid house and we then received the family members of my wife for the great celebration of the Nativity. The joy was at the gathering since we were doing exactly what God had asked us to do when he said, "You will celebrate the Nativity in Africa!" I was in the process of reconnecting with the beautiful African family that I had not seen for several years. They all remembered me, even those who were very young. It was really great to see in full health.

I was especially happy to see my wife's mother again. Despite all these years, she had not aged and always seemed to be the same age. She was physically fit. In Burkina, the festivities during the Christmas period do not last only a few days - it's every day!

We had the family for supper every night until after the celebration of New Year's Day. We had to pay for food, drinks, as well as make some gifts. We all knew that this period would cost a lot, but we had to do it because they had not seen us for years. We had to recover all the lost years, in some way. Every night we had tea, the African way. We would sit on a bench together and talk about everything and nothing, while a man was preparing tea. The careful preparation of the tea required unusual patience, as it could take one to two hours. It was more of a pretext to regroup and have a good discussion, than just drinking a glass of tea.

I liked it because the long period of preparation allowed us to get a little closer to each other and to fellowship together. I already loved my new life in this wonderful country.

"But if anyone does not provide for his relatives, and especially for members of his household, he has denied the faith and is worse than an unbeliever."
-1 Timothy 5:8 (ESV)

I still can't explain the feeling I had in me, but I felt like I was finally back home. The people of Burkina Faso were really warm and welcoming and showed us that our presence was greatly appreciated. But, there was only one thing I hated - the word "Toubabou." That word meant "white" in the local language. As soon as I came out of my house, the kids kept yelling "Toubabou" for no reason. They didn't greet me, didn't want to talk to me, they were just screaming "white" loudly, for no reason.

It was like a contest for them. The one who screamed the fastest and the loudest won a prize - seeing the white man get angry. I did not understand this reaction on the part of the children and especially their parents, who did absolutely nothing to prevent this racist chant. I say racist because if a white man shouted "black" in the West, he would be arrested, prosecuted and could find himself in prison for racist mischief. But in Africa, everything was allowed to be said to white people. Perhaps that was the kind of gesture that Westerners called "positive racism." Personally, I saw absolutely nothing positive since it irritated me to the highest degree.

Hearing this once or twice a day did not bother me, but the children shouted it everywhere I went. I heard "Toubabou" all day! The first few days, I was joking with the kids. I suddenly stopped and replied, "Farafin dé!" which means, "Black child" and they didn't answer, because they did not expect to hear a white man answer them in their local language. Sometimes I could also say, "Where? I have not seen a Toubabou anywhere. Where is he?" It made me laugh to see their faces surprised by this answer because they never knew what to say.

I thought that by doing so, they would stop yelling at me, but I was wrong. It seriously started to annoy me and one day I stopped next to a child and I shouted to him sternly, "I am not Toubabou, I have a name like everyone! Damn it!"

What a stupid thing I just did. As soon as I got back on the road, the child shouted even louder the word "Toubabou" repeatedly and his friends then joined in the game. I now understood that when the "white man" gets angry they would intensify accordingly. I decided not to take note of it anymore. I didn't go back; I kept going my way without worrying about these children with a very questionable education.

My own son suffered the same abuse on the part of these rude young men. He was not white - he was biracial! My son often got angry, yelling at others, that they were blind because he had no white skin. Unfortunately, this on the part of behavior of the children of Burkina Faso is not likely to change soon, since it seems to be part of their culture and traditions. I was going to have to learn to live with this throughout my stay in Burkina. Maybe for the rest of my days...

LET THE HUNT BEGIN

The day we moved into this beautiful home, we noticed a very strange man right in front of our residence. He lived in a house without a fence around the yard. He often stood in front of the front door of the house and spoke to himself. He was arguing and talking to an invisible person only he could see. We knew he was talking to demons or evil spirits. Very often, he held a machete in his hand and brandished it as if he were threatening the invisible person in front of him.

I asked Rosalie to tell me what language this stranger used. She told me that she did not know because she could distinguish a little Moré, Dioula and another local language but he mixed all these languages together. As if he had invented a new dialect using words from several existing languages. When we arrived in his neighborhood, his demons had shown him that a divine light had just settled in the house in front of his house, so he had performed more than three days of incantations, satanic praises and various spells against us, his new neighbors. He forgot something very important - the light makes the darkness flee.

"The people who walked in darkness have seen a great light; those who dwelt in a land of deep darkness, on them has light shone."

- Isaiah 9:2 (ESV)

All the neighbors heard this man make these curses against us, newcomers to his neighborhood. He or they didn't want us in his territory. At night, people came to his house to ask for consultation from a kind of maraboutage (African sorcery), witchcraft, clairvoyance, and other works with the enemy. No wonder the demons came to yell at him in the wee hours of the morning. Everyone was afraid of him but he didn't scare me at all. On the contrary, I empathized with him and I wanted to share with him the love of the Lord. After all, God didn't set us up right outside his house for no reason.

Every morning, when I came out of my house to buy a loaf of bread from the shopkeeper, I would wave my hand as a greeting. Sometimes he also greeted me, but when his demons spoke to him, he didn't look at me. One day he walked up to my front door while I was standing outside. He walked with his machete in his hand. Many would have fled by seeing him walk with this weapon in his hand and a dark look in his eyes but not me - I stayed standing to wait for him to come closer.

The Lord had not sent me to Burkina for this man to eliminate me. I knew that God had a project for me and this sorcerer was not part of it. Like King David, who had not been afraid to confront the mighty Goliath alone, with a simple slingshot, knew that God had anointed him king and that he could not die before the will of God was fulfilled in his life.

"Then David said to the Philistine, You come to me with a sword and with a spear and with a javelin, but I come to you in the name of the LORD of hosts, the God of the armies of Israel, whom you have defied. This day the LORD will deliver you into my hand, and I will strike you down and cut off your head. And I will give the dead bodies of the host of the Philistines this day to the birds of the air and to the wild beasts of the earth, that all the earth may know that there is a God in Israel, and that all this assembly may know that the LORD saves not with sword and spear. For the battle is the LORD's, and he will give

you into our hand."

-1 Samuel 17:45-47(ESV)

The man was right in front of me and showed me his little radio that he had in his hand. He put his hand in front of his mouth to show me that he was hungry. He wanted to sell me his radio so he could buy food. I gave him 2,000FCFA (just under $5 Canadian) and I refused to take his radio. I asked Rosalie to tell him that I wanted him to keep his radio because he listened to it every day and I offered him the money wholeheartedly, and I gave him a sign by putting my hand on my heart. He understood and had a tear in his eye.

This man lived alone and no one showed him what love was. He had made a hard shell that gave the impression that he was wicked, buts deep down, his heart was sad and needed love. He left with signs showing that he really appreciated what I did for him. This was our first close contact and everything was wonderfully unfolding. I was proud to have succeeded in showing him that I was not there to harm him but to help him. When Jesus had given us the command to love our neighbor, it did not mean to love only the brothers and sisters in Christ, but to love everyone, even those who hate us, even the servants of Satan.

On the evening of the last day of the year 2017, we were all at the mother in-laws to celebrate the arrival of 2018. There were family members who were already there. While a group was slowly preparing tea while discussing everything and nothing, Rosalie came to ask me to pray for a young woman who was experiencing trials. I stood up and followed her inside of the house. The woman was nervous to tell me her story. She finally decided to tell me everything.

A few years ago, she had been forced to marry a Muslim man she did not want. It was a marriage celebrated in witchcraft. Afterwards she had begun to see satanic shadows that always came to scare her. She had fled from this Muslim family but the evil spirits continued to follow her. These spirits prevented her from having a single good restful night. Also, she had pains at the bottom of her legs and her eyes. Her eyesight had diminished to the point that she saw only the things that were near her.

We prayed to expel these satanic spirits from her life and for her healing. When I put my hands on her ankles to pray, I felt the nerves of her feet moving tremendously. I had never experienced such a thing before but I knew at least one thing - the Lord was beginning to heal her. At the end of the prayer, she told us that her eyesight had come back. She now saw very clearly, even the distant objects had become very visible. The pain she felt in her eyes had completely disappeared. She took a few steps and then turned to us and told us that the pain she had in her legs was also completely gone. She also felt her legs trembling the whole time while I was praying for her.

She had no more pain in her ankles - God had healed her!

Back at our residence, I was thinking about everything I had just done. Is it real? Did God just use me to heal a person who needed it? Did this young lady manipulate me? Did I manipulate her? Things were beyond my human understanding. Everything I had learned about human healing had just crumbled before my very eyes, since I had seen an impossible healing for human through spiritual intervention. Was God really in the process of using my hands to heal the sick? Did I have that famous gift of healing that the Bible speaks of? I do not need to tell you that I did not sleep that night! I prayed to the Lord without ceasing, asking him, if it was actually He who had acted, to continue to use me greatly for His glory and for the advancement of his kingdom.

"And now, Lord, look upon their threats and grant to your servants to continue to speak your word with all boldness, while you stretch out your hand to heal, and signs and wonders are performed through the name of your holy servant Jesus."
-Acts 4:29-30 (ESV)

On Wednesday evening, we went to the evening of prayers at the Church of the International Center of Evangelization of Dedougou. During the intensive prayers, I received an incredible vision. I saw

God sitting on his throne; his face was obscured by a very bright light. There were rivers of living water that came out under his feet and flowed on the earth and onto us.

Later, Pastor Tiken asked if a person had a vision. I wasn't sure if I should share it but I still lifted my hand. The pastor asked me to approach the front to tell my vision. I didn't want to go because I was wondering what people were going to think of me, since was new to this church and many did not know me. I gathered my courage with both hands and I went to the front. I told this vision in great detail and the people applauded warmly. The pastor has announced that this vision corresponded perfectly with the subject of his next prophetic message for the following Sunday.

Later, the pastor took over the microphone and asked if there were people who wanted to have more children. My wife and I stood up in front since we already had a child, but we wanted to have several more. Then he asked the pregnant women to come also to the front. There were many of them.

The pastor asked couples who wanted to have children to choose a pregnant woman at random. My wife and I selected the woman who was right in front of us. Then the pastor told the couples to pray and intercede for these pregnant women until they gave birth to their baby. He wanted us to pray daily for them and in addition, to follow-up to make sure they were okay. The woman in front of us, called herself Anne and we noted her phone number in order to get news from her on a regular basis. We returned to our respective places and the evening ended with a final prayer. After several warm goodbyes, everyone had gone home. We really enjoyed our evening when, once again, we felt the Holy Spirit act with strength and power.

The next morning, my wife asked if we could go visit the pregnant woman's home we had chosen during the prayer night. She called Anne and she informed us that she was in a suburb area of the city. We agreed to go with our car and a man would come to join us in order to show us the way since in the suburb areas, there were no official roads or landmarks to find our way back. It was very easy to get lost through these houses that were built everywhere. In addition, driving in these areas by car was a feat because the roads were shrinking and getting too narrow to pass in several places.

We went to the rendezvous point and met a young man who was our guide. He rode on a motorbike and could maneuver everywhere but the car would get stuck and we had to look for another way. All our efforts were useless because we could not get to Anne with our car. We decided to leave it in front of a small shop and walked to this pregnant woman's home. Mamou, Anne's mother, came to meet us. She was a very joyful woman and very in love with the Lord. We could feel the presence of the Holy Spirit in her. She did not speak French so Rosalie had to translate all the details of the discussion. She had a very strange reaction when I introduced myself to her and she heard my name. She began to praise the Lord with all her heart.

I wondered why my name had produced such a reaction in a woman who didn't know me. Mamou then began to tell us the reason. Four years ago, she heard the voice of God asking her to intercede immediately for a Canadian who called himself Martin because he was living in terrible hardships. The voice told her that one day she would meet this Canadian in person. She then started to intercede for me. I then remembered that exactly four years ago, when I was driving between Edmonton and Fort McMurray, an evil spirit spoke to me and tried to do everything to influence me to commit suicide. Voices in my head kept saying, "You have debts! You're in debt! You are more valuable dead than alive. Your family would live better if you were dead because they would get your life insurance."

The voices told me how to kill myself - they wanted me to give a simple turn to the wheel, going in the opposite direction on the highway known as "The Highway of Death" by Albertans. This road had many fatal accidents and these voices wanted my name on the list of victims of the road. I firmly held the steering wheel with both hands but I almost gave in the demonic voices several times. These unclean spirits have practically won over me. I still remember stopping on the side of the road and called a brother in Christ to ask him to pray for me. Instead, he tried to reason with me by saying that

33

there will always be hardships in life but that happiness was always ahead of me. It was not what I wanted to hear, I desperately needed prayer because I was experiencing terrible spiritual attacks.

The enemy knew that God had a great project for me and my family so he was trying to eliminate me, so that I could not do the will of God. This African woman, whom I did not even know existed, had interceded for me and God had fulfilled her promise by allowing us to meet in person.

Anne finally came to join us. She was totally exhausted and just got up. We prayed for her so that the Lord might give her strength. The Lord showed me that she would have a boy and that he would be an athlete, a great sportsman. Anne was encouraged by this prophecy and seemed to find some strength.

We continued to pray and especially thanked the Lord for allowing us to meet these remarkable people. It was a very invigorating day for our faith.

Several years ago, Rosalie had sent a large sum of money to someone she knew of Bobo-Dioulasso to buy a land. Unfortunately, this person had spent the money without buying the land and always told us lies like - "Money has been given but the government has not yet divided the land to give it." There was always a different lie every time my wife called him to pick up the news. I never wanted my wife to send money, but she had full confidence in that person since he was a pastor. I always said, "There are those who are Christians and there are those who call themselves Christians!" It is sad, but in the world of Christianity there are good shepherds and there are also bad shepherds.

"Those who handle the law did not know me; the shepherds transgressed against me."

-Jeremiah 2:8 (ESV)

"Beware of false prophets, who come to you in sheep's

clothing but inwardly are ravenous wolves."
-Matthew 7:15 (ESV)

We forgave the debt and did not ever think of being reimbursed. This bad experience served as a lesson to us, because even a man who declares himself a "Man of God" can be the worst thief and as a result, wrongly teach the people of God.

"For those who guide this people have been leading them astray, and those who are guided by them are swallowed up."
- Isaiah 9:16 (ESV)

Only the Word of God that is pure truth. Men may be misled and mislead the people they teach, but the word remains and will always remain the main source of truth. It is for this reason that I always check in the Bible to confirm the statements of those whom we call "Men of God."

On Friday January 5, 2018, the old sorcerer who lives across from us came to see me while walking. He shook my hand and thanked me in Moré. "Barka," which means thank you, was the only word I knew in Moré. I still showed him the sign of the hand on the heart. At the same time, a woman walked down the street with a tray filled with fresh mangoes for sale. I bought a few and I offered two to the man. His eyes widened, surprised by this new gift of love on my part. He thanked me again and left home. A few minutes later, I could hear him arguing with the demons. I knew that the demons, his bosses, did not like to see that he was beginning to be friends with me. I thought I would continue to greet him every morning.

Rosalie received a call of her sister from Bobo-Dioulasso. She told her that the famous pastor who had robbed us money wanted to pay us back the whole amount. He had learned that we were in Burkina Faso and was afraid that we pursue a lawsuit against him, so he finally wanted to repay us. Unfortunately, he offered us to repay only the stolen amount, but if he had actually bought the land he was supposed to, we would have had more than triple of the sum, since the value of the land in Bobo-Dioulasso has skyrocketed since the last few years.

We decided to accept the offer to avoid endless legal battles that could create family divisions or any other divisions. We knew that God was behind all this since we had given up the idea of ever receiving this money and then, out of nowhere, this pastor reimbursed us the entire sum.

The next day we received money by wire transfer to a branch specializing in money transfers. This amount allowed us to buy a brand-new motorbike for Rosalie because she could not drive a car with manual transmission. We also took the opportunity to buy all the school supplies for Emmanuel since he was to start school soon. He was a little nervous about going to a new school but I knew it was because this new school was African and not Canadian. He had never learned anything about Burkina Faso, its history, or geography, etc. It would be quite a challenge for him but we knew he was a very brave and very smart boy. He was going to start his school year with a huge disadvantage - he knew nothing of the country that welcomed him and he arrived in the middle of the school year.

He would have a lot of catching up to do. This money also allowed us to purchase the equipment necessary to have Internet access at home and to constantly connect with family and friends in Canada. I bought an Internet router at the Onatel Company in Dedougou. Arriving at home, I connected the whole thing but the bandwidth was so slow that I had time to drink a full coffee before I saw an Internet page appear. Onatel had ads everywhere proudly saying they were offering 3G speed to its subscribers.

What I saw was definitely not even 2G, so I brought all the equipment back to the company demanding a full refund. They immediately agreed, as if they knew I would be very disappointed with the slowness of their network. Leaving their offices, I went directly to the Orange Company to take an Internet subscription. They offered me excellent service and offered a speed of 3G+ but, after the bad experience with the competitor, I preferred to wait for the result before I shouted victory. I went home to test the network.

The speed was remarkable and everything worked fine. To this day, I am still a satisfied customer of the Orange Company. I do not want to do any advertise for this company for free but I like to encourage those who work well.

The day of the Lord finally arrived. We got up very early that morning, as there were a lot of people at Sunday morning worship and we had to arrive early started to get good seats. Latecomers were seated outside the building, in a new section that was under construction. There were walls, but no roof, windows or doors. People were just outside sitting on chairs with a canvas as a shield against the heat of the sun. They could clearly hear the service but the view was far from good. I loved to be comfortably seated indoors to have a better view of the service.

We absolutely had to arrive before 8 am in the morning to get a place inside and, above all, right next to a window. Being a new Canadian to Burkina, my body was not yet accustomed to African warmth so it was better that I was under the cool breeze of a window. Otherwise, I was sweating constantly and my shirt became like a wet rag. The African services were not like the western services. At our place, the service begins at 10 am with praises of adoration.

At about 11 am, the pastor began preaching between 30 and 45 minutes and then the service ended with some songs of adoration. At midday, most of the faithful have already left the church.

In Burkina, the praises of adoration began at 8 a.m. and stopped at about 10 am. Afterwards, the pastor was on the stage to start some collective prayers and Thanksgiving. His preaching lasted more than an hour and then the praises began again. We went out of the church well into the afternoon, often at 1 pm, since we had to take the time to greet all the faithful who had come to worship God.

This Sunday was special since it was the birthday of our pastor. For this occasion, the pastor's wife had organized a party in the courtyard of their private residence. It was a surprise party and no one said anything to the pastor. Immediately after the service, we all rushed to the private residence of pastor, hiding the cars and motorcycles at the neighbors to not spoil the surprise. An observer advised us of the pastor's arrival and we all quietly placed ourselves just behind the front door of the courtyard.

We heard him approaching and when he gently pushed the door and we all shouted "Surprise!" Everyone laughed at the sight of his face, all amazed to see so many people in his yard. He smiled and then shook his hands and hugged all the guests. Afterwards, there were gifts and a generous meal prepared by the pastor's wife herself. It was delicious to the point that people were asking for more. There was a lot of joy and pleasure. I felt that we were a true family in Christ because we were having the same type of fellowship as the Apostles did in the establishment of the first Christian churches. The day was so beautiful that my wife and I were talking all about it well after we came home.

Monday, January 8, 2018 is an important date for my son; it was his first day at the "Wonders" school in Sector 6 of Dedougou. We were going to drop him off at his school since it was far from our residence. We had opted for the car since Rosalie also wanted to be present for our son's the first day of class in Burkina Faso. He was really nervous so we accompanied him to the director's office.

She showed where his new class was and took the time to introduce him to his new teacher and classmates. He received a nice welcome which gave him the strength to enter his class. We were like tourists taking several pictures as he entered his new class.

In Burkina, the classes started at 8 am in the morning and ended at 5 pm in the evening with a lunch break between noon and 3 pm, the time of the famous midday nap. The same evening, when I parked in front of the school to wait for my son, I noticed that there was a descent ceremony of the flag of Burkina Faso. In my heart, I would not want a man to disrespect the Canadian flag, so I got out of my car and stood up to watch the descent of the flag with the children of the school singing the national anthem. Contrary to my expectations, my son really liked his day and was anxious to go back again.

On the morning of Sunday, January 21, 2018, towards the end of the service, Pastor Tiken began to pray that the people of the Church receive the fire of the Holy Spirit with power. He kept praying in tongues and asked the fire to fill the entire room. At that time, we heard a woman screaming as if someone had just hit her in the belly. I saw her manifesting in every direction, screaming and crying. The pastor came down from the stage and walked towards this woman. He put his hand on the head to pray with authority and then the woman fell, but was caught by men who ensured that she did not injure herself when falling. It was the first time I saw such a spectacle.

Some women were possessed by unclean spirits. They all had a hateful gaze towards the pastor who prayed powerfully to expel these evil spirits. Some of these women were moving so fast, as if they wanted to hit the pastor, but the men behind them were holding them. I saw that these men were totally overwhelmed so I decided to help them because I had experience as a "catcher" while I was at Church in the Vine in Edmonton, Canada. But I had never seen such intense possessions as these African women. I must admit in all honesty that many women were so strong that they could shake me pretty violently. All the other men and I were so hot, our sweaters were completely wet with sweat.

The pastor asked the musical group to start a song of praise and then the room slowly calmed down. It was very intense because we had seen the Holy Spirit act forcefully and we had seen many demonic deliverances by the pastor himself. Something inside of me told me that was what I had to do, too. I felt that God wanted me to help do deliverance. My flesh prevented me from believing such a thought, since I had no experience in this field and in West Africa the possessions by unclean spirits were much more prevalent in appearance than in the West. I did not know how to do it.

"It is the Spirit who gives life; the flesh is no help at all."
-John 6:63 (ESV)

When I came home, I couldn't stop thinking about these deliverances. In the evening, after taking a shower and lying on the mattress, instead of sleeping, I thought about everything I had seen and experienced at this church. Is that really what God wants me to do? A thought came to my mind, "If God wants me to help deliverance, he will show me when the time comes!" And I put all of my thoughts back into the hands of the Lord and fell asleep softly.

Two weeks later, during the service of February 4, 2018, while the pastor was preaching, a woman suddenly started to howl in the room. She was screaming so loud that she was disturbing everyone. Two elders came and seized the possessed woman to take her out, in the section which is not yet built. I could see them praying with authority over that woman who was on the ground rolling in every direction. My eyes could not turn away from those elders who tried to deliver her from this unclean spirit.

A voice, coming out of nowhere, said to me, "Get up and help them!" I hesitated a little more, asking myself if I really had the strength and power to chase the demons but the voice repeated again - "Get up and help them!" I summoned up all my courage, I informed my wife that God wanted me to go help the elders to chase the demon and I walked boldly outside. After all, if this voice was truly of God, I would not risk anything, since he will protect me and always be by my side when needed.

The scene was worse than I thought. The woman was rolling in all directions, screaming at the elders. There was a whitish liquid coming out of her mouth and her eyes were open so wide that I thought the eyeballs would come out of her head. She was totally enraged.

I approached with a heavy step and I violently put my hand on the woman's head and shouting in her face, "I rebuke you in the name of Jesus! This body is not yours, so I command you to leave her by the Holy Name of Jesus Christ my Lord and Savior!" The woman calmed down immediately and the whitish liquid ceased to flow through her mouth. Even her eyes were back to normal. One of the elders said to me, "Ask her her name because the demonic spirits are not able to tell the truth. It is in this way that we will know beyond a doubt that she is delivered." I asked her and she answered her real name, though she was totally confused, because she didn't understand what had just happened. She did not remember absolutely anything.

We helped her get back on her feet and the elders congratulated me for what I had just done. When I sat down with my wife, she started asking me questions since I had come back so quickly. I was still in shock and said, "I'll tell you later." I did not yet realize the full extent of what God had accomplished through me. How could a Westerner like me, order a demon to leave? Why had this demon obeyed me without trying to go after me? I was just beginning to understand that God was showing me his will for my life. Back at home, I told my wife everything and she was joyful seeing that the Lord had used me so. I remember telling her that I had approached the possessed woman with a force of authority I had never felt before. I had the impression that nothing would stop me and that I could do anything. Rosalie quoted a verse from Luke's gospel to fortify me even more.

"Behold, I have given you authority to tread on serpents and scorpions, and over all the power of the enemy, and nothing shall hurt you. Nevertheless, do not rejoice in this, that the spirits are subject to you, but rejoice that your names are written in heaven."

-Luke 10:19-20 (ESV)

At the Sunday service, February 11, 2018, Alarba, the woman who had a child who could not sit and who was to be operated on, was back from her stay in the capital Ouagadougou. After the service, she came to greet us warmly, thanking us for our prayers of healing. She told us that she went to the hospital in Ouagadougou for her child's operation. After a few exams, the doctors were totally confused. Instead of confessing that the child had a miracle of God, they were saying, "This child does not need surgery because he is able to sit now. After our exams, we found that there was a diagnostic error since this child has absolutely nothing distorted. He's perfectly healthy."

These doctors will never admit the truth - God cured this child! Is that so hard to say? These doctors who have done a lot of scientific studies that have made them forget that, behind the human flesh there is a very powerful spiritual world.

"Even the Spirit of truth, whom the world cannot receive, because it neither sees him nor knows him. You know him, for he dwells with you and will be in you."

-John 14:17 (ESV)

One thing was now certain, we had prayed for the healing of this child and God cured him totally while several doctors had demanded that an operation be done on the child because he had a birth defect. Unlike the doctors, I could scream loud and clear that my God had cured that child!

In the early afternoon of Friday, February 16th, the pastor and I, with a team from the church planned to go to Djimbara, a village at few kilometers from Dedougou, to perform an evangelization session. I was happy so I could finally see evangelism the African way. We used my own car and I was the driver for this adventure. The road was not great and I was beginning to regret having used my personal car. There were major road construction between Dedougou and Djimbara with constant off-road detours through holes and other obstacles that could destroy shocks. We had to slow down regularly to negotiate these obstacles which delayed our arrival.

We were only a few kilometers from Djimbara when we encountered a terrible accident between a huge delivery truck and a huge bus carrying several passengers. Most of the wounded had already been evacuated, but a few people were still there. We stopped to find out about the situation. The policemen on site told us that there were deaths, including the driver of the truck. We walked all around the damaged vehicles and prayed for the comfort of the families affected by this tragedy. Just to see the extent of the damage gave us shivers. I could imagine the terror of those passengers, most of whom had been sleeping when the accident happen.

We finally arrived only a few minutes late. Pastor Tiken led us to a small house where there were already several pastors. We sat down and discussed several things because a pastor had not yet arrived. When he arrived, all the pastors remained alone in the house. We had to wait outside. I could see a few people who were setting up a scene, lighting, and a sound system for outdoor evangelization. Pastor Tiken finally came out of the house and noticed that people had technical problems with the generator. It was an evangelization outside in the middle of the night, so we needed this generator but it did not give the electricity needed for all the equipment.

Everything was planned to start around 7:30 pm in the evening but nothing worked. People were leaving the site because nothing worked. We began wondering if it might be better to restart the next morning since people were all leaving and would not return. The big event finally started at 9:00 pm in the evening. There were many more curious children than adults.

I thought we would go door-to-door as we did in Canada, but in West Africa, doing an evangelization meant simply doing a normal worship with praise and preaching. At the end of his message, Pastor Tiken asked if people were ready to receive the Lord in their lives. Five people approached while everybody else was leaving the site. It must be said that Djimbara was almost a Muslim village. Pastor Tiken then said that we had to leave because it was already very late.

I did not like the idea of driving at night, as there are often road bandits in Burkina Faso, especially outside the major urban centers. These armed bandits blocked the road with tree trunks to steal and sometimes kill the passengers to eliminate witnesses. But we had an almighty God who protected us and he would prevent any unfortunate event during our return. Everyone was sleeping in the vehicle except me. This trip back was terribly long, especially since I had no one to talk to keep me up. It was already past midnight when I stopped in front of the pastor's house and I went straight home, completely exhausted.

In 2013, Rosalie acquired a half a hectare of land in a non-subdivided area in the suburbs of Dedougou. She had wanted to sell it in parcels to her brothers, but they had never given the money for the land. In more than five years, this land remained there without anyone touching it. Only God could do such a thing. In Burkina, many people try to buy non-subdivided land. Often the same land was sold repeatedly, to several different people. And if they go to court, it could take several years before the case is settled. Often losing a lot of money and still had no land in their name.

We had visited our land to find that nobody had built anything on it. There were house constructions all around but nothing affected the land. God had wanted it so. A neighbor also told us that he wanted to buy our land at any price, but never got it. He also confirmed that it was the hand of God who had protected this land for us. While we were walking on the ground, God showed me a very clear vision - we had to set up a Widows Help Center on this site. He showed me the detailed plan of the site.

I knew where we had to put widows' houses, kitchens, showers as well as, our own home. There would be a well in the center of the site, a gardening section on the left and a breeding section on the right. I saw two large mango trees in the center that made shade for farm animals. I could see our future home and, behind the house, was a very large table where I saw several brothers and sisters enjoying a meal in the festivities. The Lord also asked me to create a business plan for this Help Center.

I spent several days composing an official document for this great project but I kept praying for the people around me.

During the service of February 18, 2018, the Lord spoke to me during the preaching of Pastor Tiken. I clearly heard the voice saying, "Today, you will go to the four corners of the field to pray. You'll pour oil on the four corners." I didn't understand what was going on but I felt that I had to obey the Lord's request. I explained to Rosalie that we had to go and pray as soon as possible on our land because something bad had happened or was happening.

She replied that we would immediately go there at the end of the service. Since we did not know the best way to get there, we asked Gilbert to come with us. In the non-subdivided sectors, it was very easy to get lost and difficult to find your way. When the pastor had finished talking, we all went out of the church quickly and left by car to get us home. The voice had said to pour oil on the four corners, so we had to take our flask of olive oil used during prayers of healing and deliverance. Gilbert came to join us at home since we all left with the car towards our land.

When we arrived on the land, after looking everywhere, we had found nothing different or suspicious, but the word said to pray to the four corners. We settled in a circle around the first boundary that delineated our land. There was nothing abnormal but we still prayed and poured oil directly on the boundary. We walked to the second one. There was still nothing abnormal, but we did pray and poured oil directly on the boundary. We then walked to the third one. There was still nothing abnormal but we did pray and poured oil directly on the boundary. Then we walked to the fourth and last one that was right next to the wall of our neighbor.

To our great surprise, there was blood and feathers all over the boundary. Chicken sacrifices had been made on our land and, to see the blood, these demonic spells had been made a few hours before we arrived. Probably at the same time the voice asked me to come, pray and pour oil on the four corners of the field. We were all blown away by what we had just seen.

Gilbert informed us that our immediate neighbor, the one directly in front of the sacrifice site, was a man that loved witchcraft very much.

Without proof, we could not accuse anyone, but all the clues were pointing to this neighbor. People did not want us on this land; they did not want to have a Christian center called "Moisson de Christ" (Christ's Harvest) right next to their private residence. We all knew that it the cunning plan of the enemy for the simple purpose of discouraging us or preventing us from carrying out the will of God.

We took the hand and made a circle around the boundary. We prayed with strength and intensity to make sure that our words went to this neighbor, and then we poured oil on the boundary, on the ground around and on the wall of the neighbor. The voice was right to ask us to come to the field. I was very happy to have come to the site to counter this evil spell and thus to protect the four corners of our land with oil. We have made a final prayer in the center of the field to cover this whole site with the blood of the divine lamb.

At the end of the service on Sunday, February 25, 2018, Pastor Tiken prayed again for the fire of the Holy Spirit to come down and fill the place. I knew that all the catchers and I would have a lot of work on our hands. Again, several people were screaming and struggling in front of the pastor and we had to catch them to avoid any kind of injury during their fall. We also took few people outside to perform deliverance prayers away from curious glances. I did not know why, but the pastor called me personally whenever there was a case of possession to do.

He asked me to take care of this person over the microphone, in front of all the faithful who attended the service. Now, everyone knew that the "white man" was doing deliverance. If the pastor called him personally, then the "Toubabou" was surely a powerful demon hunter. These were the kind of comments that I sometimes heard indirectly. I did not like it since I had no power in me - it was God who was acting through me. All glory must go to him alone.

Later on, the same day, the pastor called us by phone and asked us to come and meet him the next morning at his office because God had just shown him something about us.

On Monday morning, after dropping our son off at his school, we met the pastor at his office. He told us that God showed him that we had to have a ministry within the church. He asked me to lead the Ministry of Sound, since he had received new audio equipment to replace the obsolete system they used in the church. I thought it was good because my last job in Canada was installing professional audio systems. I had the experience and several certifications recognized to do this successfully. For Rosalie, the pastor offered her the Ministry of Evangelization since she had this incredible gift in her.

Rosalie was a very warm and welcoming person who liked to hug people. She always spoke of the Lord to everyone. She was the ideal person for this ministry. Not only did the pastor offer her this ministry, but he wanted her to be the head of this ministry. She accepted without hesitation and was happy to be a part of it. The pastor informed her that he had already formed a team for her new ministry. There was a young pastor named David Sermé, a youth who was also part of the deliverance team named Roland, a young prophet named Joseph and a woman who did the preparations of the Church services named Florence. Rosalie was the fifth person on the team.

I remember that Pastor David had proposed to call this team "The Generation of Joshua for the Great Harvest". I thought that name was perfect since they were mostly young servants of the Lord. Their young age did not prevent them from being all powerful with the Holy Spirit. This team was perfect because they all had different gifts and, together, they formed the ideal evangelistic team. The church changed the name of the team to "The Core", although most of the team preferred "The Generation of Joshua". They would meet on Monday evening for intercessory prayers and evangelize different districts of the city every Wednesday and Thursday mornings.

A follow-up would be made to the people who gave their lives to the Lord and a monthly report of the situation was to be given to the pastor himself.

For my part, the pastor informed me that I would start my job in a few days since they were still waiting for the new equipment. I took advantage of this moment with the pastor to tell him about the sacrifices that took place on our land. He replied that he would like to see this land and pray on it with us. We agreed to do it the next day and we left his office delighted to finally be able to serve in the church.

The next day, the pastor came to join us at home. We talked a bit and then we left with the car to get to the land. The pastor marched on the land, praying to the Lord. I could hear him ask the

Lord to make sure that this center will be a great success and that people from all over come to receive the Divine Light. He stopped at the center of the field and told us that he had just seen something about the Help Center that we wanted to build for God's work.

I had never told him anything about the visions that God had shown me about construction. The pastor told us that he had just seen a very large table where several brothers and sisters reunited in Christ in order to enjoy a good meal, as if they were a big family. He indicated where he had seen the table. Everything was exactly the same as what I had also seen. We knew without a doubt that this center was really God's will. He wanted this center to help the most deprived widows in the Province of Mouhoun.

The following Thursday, I went to church since all the sound equipment had finally arrived. For the next two days, I connected all the equipment as quickly as possible; to be sure everything will be functional for Sunday worship. The day before the service, we made the adjustments for the sound. I personally took care of this task because I wanted everything to be perfect. The pastor sometimes came to see our progress and he loved the sound quality he heard. Everyone was surprised to see that I was installing microphone on the drum set because they never done that before. I'd say, "Wait and you'll hear the difference!"

When they finally heard the new sound of the drums, they really loved it. At the end of the day, the sound was perfect. I was well acquainted with the African mentality so I took pictures of the sound adjustments I had just made.

I knew that there were among our group, one or more "Joe know it all" as I like to call them. They are the ones who believe they know everything and never accept the advice from the experience of others. As soon as the leader has his back turned, they will change the adjustments, as they are certain they can do better. These people, I call them "Joe know it all".

I was right! On Sunday morning, all the adjustments I had made were no longer the same. A little "Joe know it all" had changed everything thinking he could do better, but his adjustments always caused sound to return in the microphones. I didn't have much time to re-adjust everything, so I put it all back according to the photos I had taken the day before. The service began and there was no feedback even if the pastor walked just in front of the loudspeakers with the microphone in his hand. I was very satisfied with the result and I was not the only one since several people came to congratulate me at the end of the service. They were all impressed by the sound quality.

I was really happy because I had just found a ministry that I liked very much and was finally being used in the church. I would love to find out who this little "Joe know it all" was who changed everything from the original adjustments, hoping to put shame on my shoulders. He had certainly arrived very early in the morning and, like an invader, had sneaked discreetly to destroy all the work I had done. Fortunately, he had failed because I had been more cunning than him.

"But thanks be to God, who gives us the victory through our Lord Jesus Christ."

-1 Corinthians 15:57 (ESV)

WELCOME TO MANGA

It had been several days since Pastor Tiken talked about going to evangelize in Manga. He informed us that the pastor of the church of Manga International Center for Evangelization had contacted him to ask for help in order to evangelize this city totally closed to the Word of God. Pastor Tiken had accepted and he selected only a few people to inform them of his intentions, since he did not want to make this case public. Manga was a small town of less than 30,000 inhabitants south of the capital Ouagadougou. It was nicknamed the city of sparrow hawks. All citizens in the country knew well the reputation of this city, because it had many very powerful and dangerous wizards who always fight against Christians.

The pastor did not want anyone to know that a team of evangelists would go out there and preach the Word of God. In the history of Manga, more than 24 pastors of several denominations tried to do the same thing but most fell seriously ill and some died inexplicably. This city had forged the very bad reputation of being totally closed to the Word and, above all, of being a slaughter city of evangelical pastors.

Nevertheless, Pastor Mamadou Karambiri of the Ouagadougou International Center for Evangelization had himself gone on site to set up a small church. He said that the world of darkness also needed the light of life as much as we do. A person had already told him that it was not good for a man of God to go to Manga, so Pastor

Karambiri immediately got up and went to the sparrow hawk city filled with the authority of Christ.

He did not listen to warnings and set up a small church there. Today, the pastor of this church seemed very discouraged from what he faced every day. He asked the help of a man of God and his team to spread the Holy Spirit and tear some people from the grip of the enemy. Pastor Tiken had told me about this trip to the south of the country but I did not know yet if God wanted me to leave with them.

I kept telling myself, "If God does not tell me to go, and then I will not go. Who am I to go against the will of God?" If I decided to leave by my own means or by my own strength, I was certain to fail and fall in front of the enemy. I had to be certain that it was my Father's desire.

One night, a voice woke me up by calling my name and asked me to go to Manga with the evangelists' team. I said, "I do not have the money to go there." The voice asked me again to leave with the team because they would need me there. I was now certain that the Lord wanted me in Manga, but my personal finances would not allow it. The money I had with me was to pay the next rent for the house where we lived. In addition, since no church or organization had helped us financially since we left Canada, I had to be very careful about our expenses. God provided all our needs but we were not rich. Despite the little amount of money in my wallet, I made the decision to obey the voice.

I knew very well that my car was not in good condition for such a trip, so I left it in the hands of Rosalie's brother. Gilbert was a mechanic and I knew he was the only one who could repair it in such a short time. Afterwards, I informed Pastor Tiken that I would be part of his team and that we could use my car. He seemed very happy with this answer. He informed me that the church was paying for a very ordinary room in a guest house, but that he personally took an air-conditioned room in a hotel. If I wanted to, he could book me the same kind of room, more comfortable with the air conditioning in the room.

I accepted this offer immediately, as the days could be very hot in the south of the country. Air conditioning became necessary, actually essential for a Canadian like me. I went back home to start preparing the luggage and everything I had to bring with me. I never forgot my most important work tool - my Bible! Without the Word of God, I could not have my double-edged sword that would allow me to fight and defeat the enemy. Only the Word could give me the strength to face the greatest challenges of this world.

I searched several times where Manga was on Internet. Since I was the new driver, I had the great responsibility to drive all my passengers to destination as quickly as possible without taking any useless detours. I did not want to drive a car in Ouagadougou so I was looking for a road that bypassed the capital of the country. I had, too often seen the intense traffic of this huge city, where it was very easy to have an accident and, more insulting still, to get lost in this labyrinth of streets. I had just found a way that would allow us to avoid the heart of Ouagadougou. I finally felt ready for this long journey. No surprise could discourage me now; at least, that's what I thought.

Gilbert had some problems finding the parts for my car but still managed to fix it. On the other hand, when he entered my yard with the car, I immediately heard the loud din coming from the engine. He told me that it was the "engine paws", the piece we normally called "engine mounts" in Canada. These pieces were either excessively expensive or impossible to find. In Burkina, car mechanics had to know how to deal with nothing. Gilbert asked a man to build engine mounts with rubber from old truck tires.

The man did it but I did not like hearing that noise because we had to drive hours to get to Manga. I did not want to make my passengers completely deaf. Gilbert had then proposed to me that since the rubber of the new engine mounts was still very hard, he would go back to this man's house to ask him if he could soften them or have some less tough ones. I didn't hesitated to accept this new proposal. He left again with my vehicle.

The next day, Gilbert came home with the car and told me bad news. I had to endure the noisy engine mounts that were already installed because the man did not have time to make new ones. The new mounts would be ready to be installed when I returned. He also confirmed that I would have no problem on the highway since at high speed the noise would be less intense. I did not have many choices in front of me. When my eyes fell on the bill Gilbert presented to me, I fell backwards. I could not believe that a car, which was in the garage every week, could still have so many problems. I paid Gilbert reluctantly though I knew it was not his fault.

This bill had cut my entire budget for this evangelistic journey. Gilbert left my home and I decided to wait until the next day to try my car on the road.

I had just woken up. I still had dark circles under my eyes when I went outside to try my newly repaired car. I put the key in the ignition and tried to start the engine by turning it. Nothing! The car had not started. I tried to turn the key again. I could hear the starter rattling but the engine refused to start. The panic was beginning to overwhelm me, as we had to leave the next morning very early. We were supposed to go to Manga on Thursday, but as a precaution against the wizards in that city, the pastor had decided to leave on Wednesday without anyone knowing.

We did not want to have an infernal welcome when we reached our destination, so we planned to thwart all the enemy projects against us, by surprising them one day ahead of schedule. But how could we surprise them if the car did not start? I called Gilbert explaining everything and he came immediately to the rescue. Opening the engine hood, he noticed that a cable was disconnected at the starter. There was no electrical contact so nothing could start. He reinstalled the cable, making sure to tighten the screw that held it. I stepped into the car and turned the key again. This time we could hear the soft music of a spinning engine, except that there was the loud noise of the engine mounts.

I went out for a test drive with the car and, indeed, Gilbert was right - the noise of the engine mounts was less loud when we drove on a highway. I was finally ready mentally and physically, to undertake this journey for the Lord. We would tear captive souls from Satan's hands and put them in the hands of God. I was already looking forward to the big start but I forgot something very important - money. In the evening, Rosalie and I calculated our finances for the month of March. We had just enough money to pay the rent for our residence at the end of the month, nothing more. Rosalie looked at me and said, "If it is God himself who asked you to go with them to Manga, and then take this money because you will need it. The Lord will provide for the rent and all the rest." My wife's faith had always fascinated me.

Sometimes in difficult moments, I often tended to get upset quickly and doubt that God was with us for this great project in Africa. For her part, Rosalie always maintained a strong faith in our Creator. It was probably for this reason that one day, while we were still in Canada, God had told me to always look at my wife's faith during the trials. He was, he is and will always be right, whatever happens. Men should always look at their wife's faith. The spirituality of women always surpasses that of men.

"Sanctify them in the truth; your word is truth."
- John 17:17 (ESV)

The next morning, the day of the great departure for this divine journey, Rosalie left me all the rent money, as agreed. I did not intend to spend everything but I preferred to have a surplus, as a precaution. She also gave me a big cooler filled with ice, water bottles and egg sandwiches she had prepared very early in the morning. She had a breakfast for everyone on our team. I put the cooler and my suitcase in the trunk of the car.

My wife and I prayed for the protection of our journey. I kissed her tenderly and talked to my son. I asked him to take good care of his mother. I told him that he was now the man of the house and that his role was to protect his mother. I sat behind the wheel and left in the direction of the pastor's residence since the whole team had to join me there. I brought a small MP3 player that I plugged into the radio of the car. This player included many American Christian songs discovered during my stay in Alberta. I had to have Christian songs in my vehicle because I was going to carry an important person - the pastor Tiken of the Church of the International Center of Evangelization of Dedougou!

When I arrived at the pastor's house, everyone was already there and prayed for the smooth progress of the trip. Subsequently, they put all their luggage in the trunk of the car. The pastor asked me if we needed to refuel before leaving and I told him that I was a person who always planned everything in advance. The tank was already full! We all boarded and left in the direction of Manga. We were four people, myself, Pastor Tiken, David, and Roland.

The pastor informed me that we had to stop in Ouagadougou to get a fifth person named Emmanuel. All the road mapping I had prepared the previous days had just been annihilated in a single second. Nobody had informed me of this important detail. I thought we were just going around the capital and not going deep into it, to take one person. And me, who did not want to drive in this intense traffic, will now have to. I decided to let things go as they came, not to wreck the trip. If I had refused to take this fifth person, the pastor would probably have resentment towards me for the whole trip.

When we left the town of Dedougou, we stopped at the first police checkpoint. They simply checked our IDs and let us go. It was pretty fast but I knew we would still have several controls like this one. Later, we came to a toll station. I got out of the car and paid the fees myself. I returned on board and continued our journey. After several stops for police checks, after several bypass maneuvers to avoid all the holes and the bad quality of the road, we finally arrived in Ouagadougou. Pastor Tiken was showing me the way to the heart of the city to pick up our fifth passenger. A few days before, there was a terrorist attack at the French embassy which caused the closure of several roads around the embassy. We had to take very tight bypasses because there were a lot of cars, motorcycles, and bikes taking the same routes. It was an ordeal for me. I did not have any driving experience in Ouagadougou.

We had finally arrived at the place where Emmanuel was waiting for us. After putting his suitcase in the trunk of the car, the pastor asked me to stop at the store of a woman he knew. He told me how to get to this new unexpected stop. At the store, we sat inside and talked a little bit with this woman. The team ate the egg sandwiches that my wife had prepared before we left.

We stayed there for about an hour and then left. Once again, Pastor Tiken asked me to make another stop in the capital. He explained to me that it was one of his pastoral friends who had just lost his father-in-law. He wished to offer his condolences in person. The cause was very noble, so I accepted without hesitation to make another detour in the capital. He told me the way to go to the residence of the pastor and prophet Augustin Kambou. I could not imagine that this other unplanned stop would be as far from where we were.

The prophet Kambou welcomed us home and offered to sit on the chairs of the terrace of his own residence. He also offered us a drink and we discussed several topics together. We had all offered him our condolences and he asked me where I came from and what I was doing in Burkina. I had explained to him that God had sent me to this wonderful country to serve him, and since my arrival he had been using me greatly with all the gifts that the Holy Spirit had so generously given me. He seemed very impressed to see a man like me respond to God's call with full confidence in all financial matters. He also said that it was very rare nowadays to see such faith in our Lord. Subsequently, Pastor Tiken spoke and thanked his friend for his welcome. We got up from our chairs after a few greetings and we all boarded the car to continue our adventure towards Manga.

We were a few miles from our final destination when I felt something deep inside me. After looking at the landscape through the window of my side door and I felt that death was everywhere around us. This feeling was so intense that I had a kind of pressure on my head as if someone were pressing the sides with his hands. I had told the pastor, "We are getting closer to the territory of death". I saw some shadows hiding behind the trees and watching over us. I began to pray quickly as I drove. I did not like that vision so I told the whole team, "Before every evangelistic outing, we will have to pray in order to securely wear the Christian's armor." They all agreed, "That, we will definitely do it!"

"Stand therefore, having fastened on the belt of truth, and having put on the breastplate of righteousness, and, as shoes for your feet, having put on the readiness given by the gospel of peace. In all circumstances take up the shield of faith, with which you can extinguish all the flaming darts of the evil one; and take the helmet of salvation, and the sword of the Spirit, which is the word of God."

-Ephesians 6:14-17 (ESV)

We stopped at the entrance of the city. The young pastor David had a bottle of olive oil in his hand. We prayed to repel evil spirits, spells, sacrifices, and everything that came from the enemy.

We also prayed that the people hear the Word of God and are touched by the light of Jesus. The oil had been poured on the ground and we had asked for the blood of the divine Lamb to flow on this city of Manga. By doing so, we ensured the best protection against this world of darkness.

"The sacrifice of the wicked is an abomination to the LORD, but the prayer of the upright is acceptable to him."

-Proverb 15:8 (ESV)

After several minutes of prayer, we drove back to our hotel. The hotel was really nice and had a big advantage, it was a little far from the main road which gave us a better discretion. The pastor and I had put all our luggage in our respective rooms and then we went outside. I noticed that there were several vultures flying in circles over our hotel. Normally, a vulture circled over a weakened man or animal about to die, but we were neither weakened nor dying. I felt that these vultures were the Manga wizards who were trying to scare us.

We went back to drop the other three passengers to their rooms. I was a little uncomfortable for them when I saw the poor quality of their hotel room compared to mine. In addition, they decided to take a single room for them to reduce expenses. The ceiling was almost falling apart, the beds seemed very uncomfortable, and all the walls were very dirty. Not to mention the horrible shower that I would never want to put a foot in it. The three young people, as we called them, had still accepted this room. The pastor asked everyone to take a few hours to rest and then we would meet at his hotel room later.

The night had already fallen for several minutes, when we all found ourselves in the pastor's room to begin a prayer session. This session was really intense - everyone prayed constantly in tongues, we became totally uncontrollable. An invisible force had invaded the room and we all felt it. This force was the Holy Spirit of God. We prayed for more than 30 minutes in the room to ask for protection on us but also for all sorcerers to be in failure in the name of Jesus.

At the end of the prayer, Pastor Tiken asked us to be ready for anything, since more than 24 pastors had come to the past to evangelize as we were going to do. They had all fallen very ill and most of these pastors had died in unexplained ways. The wizards of Manga are renowned everywhere in Burkina to be the most powerful. He strongly recommended that we not eat anywhere because a malicious person could put poison on the plates. We even had to be careful never to leave our water bottles unattended.

After the prayer, we all returned to our rooms. In my room, away from all eyes, I started counting my money. I found that I only had the money necessary to pay the fuel for our return to Dedougou. I did not have enough money to pay for food during my stay in this city. How was I going to do that? Since I had no choice, I made the decision that I was going to fast for the duration of our stay at Manga. A few days of fasting and prayer would be a good thing since I was in the land of sorcerers. My decision was made - I was going to fast for several days. I started praying to thank the Lord for my first day without any unfortunate events in the town of Manga.

On Thursday morning, for our first morning in Manga, Pastor Tiken called everyone and asked to join him in his room. He asked us to meet three times a day in order to pray for evangelism. Once in the morning, another at noon and one last time in the evening before going out to evangelize. So we prayed again in tongues with the powerful presence of the Holy Spirit. The fire was everywhere in the hotel room. When we left the room, the employees of the establishment looked at us as if we were people from another planet. They had to ask why we are praying intensely or why we need to pray at all. We all went back to our rooms where I turned on the TV but there was no channel I liked, so I started to read the Word. My eyes fell on a passage that was addressed to all members of our team.

"Behold, I am sending you out as sheep in the midst of wolves, so be wise as serpents and innocent as doves."
-Matthew 10:16 (ESV)

At noon, we were all in the pastor's room praying with incredible intensity. It was very hot in Manga so we left the front door of the room open. A simple curtain kept people from seeing what we were doing. We opened the window of the room because it was really hot. I think we have been praying for more than an hour of time that afternoon. When we got out of the room, there was debris all over the floor. We asked an employee who seemed surprised that we were asking. "But, did you not feel the whirlwind?" he asked. "A whirlwind? No," I replied.

"It was very powerful and that's the reason why there's a lot of debris on the ground. I had never seen such a thing - it started over the hotel and never changed position." he said.

Normally, a whirlwind (or tornado) never stays in place; it goes around and wreaks havoc all over its path. This one had always remained stationary on the hotel and not at the neighbors. We knew it was an attack of the enemy because it was destined for us but God had protected us. The evil spirits had just failed their first attack on the men of God.

In the evening, we had still prayed forcefully to make sure that we were serving the Christian's love and that the blood of the lamb would cover the entire evangelization site. At the end of the prayer, Pastor Tiken informed us that the pastor of the small church of the International Centre for Evangelization of Manga was coming to join us at the hotel to show us the place where the outdoor evangelism would unfold. He arrived very late from the scheduled time, as there were many problems that he had to manage on the site before he could leave. He met the whole team and then quietly approached Pastor Tiken to ask him a question, "Are you sure they are really ready for what they are going to face?"

"I brought the best!" replied Pastor Tiken

"And what about the white guy? Is he ready for all this?"

He repeated – "I told you! I brought the best!"

The pastor of Manga left the hotel with his own vehicle and we followed him in my personal car. I had to make sure I remembered the way we were going, but the darkness of the night prevented me from seeing the landmarks well. We arrived on a large vacant lot with a big scene in the center of the field. There was light with electricity coming from a generator. We could hear Christian praises as a choir was already singing on the stage. There were already a few spectators in front of the scene, including several children.

The pastor of Manga asked Pastor Tiken, "Here, you know, witchcraft is normal. It is part of the life of all the inhabitants of Manga. You must not say anything against witchcraft." Pastor Tiken looked at him to show that he was not in agreement with what his colleague was asking. He climbed on the stage, took the microphone, and said, "People of Manga! Witchcraft is not good for you; it comes from the enemy called Satan. We must reject it, deny it, and destroy it by the name of Jesus Christ our Lord and Savior!" I turned to the pastor of Manga and he seemed terribly disappointed with what he had just heard. Yet, all that his guest had said was truth. The Bible itself tells us not to ask sorcerers anything.

"And when they say to you: Inquire of the mediums and the necromancers who chirp and mutter. Should not a people inquire of their God? Should they inquire of the dead-on behalf of the living?"

-Isaiah 8:19-20 (ESV)

All the rest of the evangelization took place without any problems or malicious intervention. At the end, the pastor called on stage all those who wanted to give their lives to the Lord. Many went up to receive the only savior, while we were at the bottom of the stage to perform spiritual deliverance on people struggling with spells or demonic spirits. The Holy Spirit was acting with strength and power before our eyes. There was a great deal of deliverance and a few Muslim women, having come out of curiosity, remained surprised at this spiritual power. They were looking at the people they knew fell to the ground with uncontrollable tremors and letting out terrible howls, only to end up in tears of joy because they had just been delivered by the name of Jesus. It was a unique evening for all of us.

We were sitting in the car to return to the hotel and we continued to talk about everything that had just happened on this evangelization site. At my hotel room, I was reliving the experiences I had with every person for whom I had prayed and who was delivered and fortified. My thoughts were all about the incredible night I had just lived. I had never lived or even seen such a power of the Holy Spirit. I was just hoping that the next few days would be as, if not more, intense than this one.

On Friday morning, we again found ourselves in the pastor's room for a powerful prayer session under the direction of the Holy Spirit. We still felt a powerful presence among us and a burning fire inside our bodies. At the end of the prayer, the pastor informed me that we all had to go to the little Church of Manga to pray for the people who needed it. We all left with my car at this little church. The term "little" was well chosen since it was really small.

The pastor had a great project of expansion in order to be able to receive more faithful. On site, we found that we were the only ones. The doors of the church were locked and the pastor of Manga was not there. There were already three or four people waiting for prayer. We waited for the arrival of a person who had the keys to this church. The sun was hot and we were constantly moving in order to stay in the shade as much as possible.

Finally, a man arrived with the keys and apologized for the delay. He opened the doors and we started to receive people. We were five, so we had made two groups of two persons and the pastor would receive only the most severe cases. We became a sort of sorting center for the pastor. David and I received many desperate, discouraged, or depressed people and our prayers seemed to help them immensely. I can't put all the cases in this book but I would love to write about a couple in particular. The man approached me; I had recognized him since he was a deacon in the small church of Manga.

He told that his marriage was not well at all. He and his wife have not spoken to each other for several months. He feels that his wife no longer loves him and fears losing her from one day to the next. He said that this situation was no longer livable.

I asked him where his wife was and he told me that she was with the other prayer team right behind us. "But what is she doing there?" I asked him, "You should be together and not separate!" He gave me a simple nod to say that he did not know why she was not with him to solve this problem.

I immediately got up and took the hand of his wife to bring her to a chair next to her husband. I instantly noticed that they were not looking at each other while they were only a few centimeters away. I never make a decision without hearing both sides of story, so I also heard the woman's version. They both told me the same thing - I feel that he has distanced himself and that he does not love me anymore. To that, I replied, "You know, nothing can separate what God has brought together. Many years ago, you got married for love but love is like a wood fire. If it is not maintained by putting wood from time to time, it will go out slowly. To allow this fire to burn, you have to maintain it with small gestures that will appeal to the other."

"For example, you sir, when you come back from work and you enter the house, why not bring her a flower, a jewel or a simple comment about her beauty or her smile. You, Madam, when your husband returns, ask him how his day was and whisper I love you into his ear. Men will never admit it, but they really appreciate this little gesture."

I saw them smile at last. Since they had entered the church, they had no expression on their faces. Now they both smiled. I took the man's hand and put it in the woman's hand. Then we all prayed for this beautiful couple so that love burns again in their heart as the time of their youth. After the prayer, I asked the man to look at his wife's eyes and admit that he loves her. I asked the woman to do the same thing. They both did. Afterwards, the whole team noticed that they could no longer release their hands. They were merged together again - they were one. They were so happy that I took a picture with them. After they left, we all congratulated ourselves for this great victory over Satan's attempt to separate this Christian couple.

This was the way for all the people who had come to ask for help. Some had to fight against evil spirits, others had financial problems, others were ill. Our prayers changed and transformed the people who entered this church. The Holy Spirit was acting mightily with us. We had become the personal tools of the Lord.

When we returned to the hotel, it was time to do the midday prayer so we all gathered in the pastor's room. I don't know why but this prayer session was totally different from the others. I felt my heart burning in my chest. For no reason, I started praying in English, I couldn't control myself. Suddenly I stopped right in front of the pastor and as if I was driven by a rage or a powerful force, I said, "You, you're going to be a lion for the Lord. You're going to roar like a strong lion tonight. A lot people will come to the Lord after hearing the call of the lion." Even today, I cannot understand what led me to do this. I know it was the Holy Spirit but I had never felt it pushing me to talk like that. It was not me; I was somebody or something else. The pastor enjoyed hearing such a prophecy before the next evangelism evening.

It was already evening when we found ourselves in front of the pastor's room. We decided to pray in the inner courtyard of the hotel since there were no guests on the premises. We began to intercede for the good progress of evangelization when I saw dozens of bats flying over our heads. There were many of them and they all appeared as soon as we started praying. I made the others laugh because, every time I saw one, I pointed it out and shouted, "I'm chasing you in the name of Jesus!" The problem is that they were so large that I keep repeating the same phrase, "I'm chasing you in the name of Jesus!"

The time of departure arrived and we all boarded my car to go to the site of evangelization. I had noticed a very important thing. Since our arrival, we never had the pastor of Manga praying with us. When you confront the forces of evil, you have to be prepare for the fight. You have to wear the full Christian armor. I was just hoping that he would do it at his private house before he went out. Our team, when we finished praying, we became different people.

We were soldiers, no longer afraid of anything and ready to go warzone to destroy every powerful enemy. We were empowered to the maximum to confront any natural or spiritual creature. We felt that the Lord's army of Angels opened the march before us. Nothing could stop us from advancing for the Kingdom of God.

"God is our refuge and strength, a very present help in trouble. Therefore we will not fear though the earth gives way."
Psalm 46:1-2 (ESV)

On the Evangelization site, there were more people than for our first evening. People had heard about the five foreigners of Dedougou that the Holy Spirit used greatly. Many had come out of curiosity and others came to be saved and delivered. Pastor Tiken went on stage and preached on the microphone. Towards the end of the evening, he decided to call the fire of the Holy Spirit on the entire Manga population. He prayed in tongue on the microphone and then the Holy Spirit pushed him down among the large crowd.

Normally, the pastor never came down to the crowd for a security reasons. If he did, people had to protect him to ensure his personal safety, as a pastor, he was a prime target. This time, he surprised everyone by descending himself under the impulse of the Holy Spirit. He walked among the people repeating incessantly, "Fire!" As soon as he put his hand on a person's head, that person immediately fell to the ground. All the people he touched with his hand suddenly fell down. I had never seen anything like this before.

I was still on the stage when I saw a strange man near the pastor, I shouted to Roland to immediately go and put his hand on this man's head. He came running thinking that the pastor was in danger and then put his hand on the head of the man who immediately fell to the ground. I went down to the crowd to help the team to pray for all those people who were falling everywhere. It was madness but madness from the Lord himself.

"For the foolishness of God is wiser than men, and the weakness of God is stronger than men."
-1 Corinthians 1:25 (ESV)

That evening allowed us to have more people converted than the previous one. People didn't want to let us go, they longed to taste even more the fire of the Holy Spirit on them. They had become true enthusiasts of the Lord and wanted to have a solid relationship with him. We snuck quietly to the car and left the scene, leaving the conclusion of the evening in the hands of the pastor of Manga.

On Saturday morning, we still did the mighty prayers in Pastor Tiken's room. He informed us that he felt a little exhausted and that he would like to rest a little for the evening evangelism. He would not be joining us for morning prayers to the little Manga Church. He also informed us that the pastor of Manga was very ill and that he could not even get out of bed. We all knew that it was an attack of the enemy since we had never seen this pastor pray to ask for divine protection on his life and that on his family. We were sad for him and decided to go and pray for him and his family.

Before I got out of the room, the pastor asked me if I wanted mango juice. I replied that I was fasting since our arrival in Manga and that I drank only water, so as not to dehydrate because of the heat. He replied that he was also fasting for food but that he drank only natural juice and water. I was very ashamed to admit that the real reason was that I didn't have the money to eat and that I didn't have any choice but to start a forced fast. But after a day, I wanted to fast and pray for the protection of the team throughout the duration of our stay in enemy territory. I had the feeling that God wanted me to fast and intercede in prayer. When I arrived in this city, I was so upset about this financial situation but on the second day of evangelization I really wanted to fast for the cause. God wanted me to do it in order to help me strengthen my faith in him. I had to humble myself in his presence.

As we went to the little Church of Manga, we stopped at the pastor's residence. His wife informed us that he had been very ill all night and he had not slept because of the pain and of some things that disturbed him. "Some things that disturbed him?" I thought to myself, the enemy had really attacked him and only prayer could help him. His faith had certainly faltered last few days since he had fear of these sorcerers. In his situation, it was understandable, since he often found himself alone facing these evil enemies.

Now only prayer could help him, not a doctor, not a specialist, not a clinical psychologist, but only the power of prayer.

"The prayer of a righteous person has great power as it is working."

-James 5:16 (ESV)

His wife informed us that he was sleeping, so we prayed for him by staying in the living room so as not to disturb his sleep. We wanted him to recover to come to our last evangelism night. So, we prayed intensely for his divine healing and we interceded for the protection of his family against the attempts and temptations of the enemy. The pastor's wife prayed with us and we all noticed that she was a person filled with the Holy Spirit. The prayers she made were really full of power. We had a great warrior of the Lord on our side without knowing it.

When the car arrived in front of the small church, there were already a lot of people - three or four times more than the first day of morning prayers. Inside the small church, we made the decision not to make teams of two because people continued to come into the courtyard of the church. Each member of the team would work alone which would allow us to meet four people at the same time. We were totally overwhelmed. People came and went. There were Christians of all denomination, Muslims in search of miracles and atheists who were looking for something to fill the emptiness they had in their hearts.

Once again, the Holy Spirit was acting with strength and power. There was a rain of miracles, spiritual deliverances, divine healings, and many other miracles by the power of the name of Jesus. It was soon noon and people kept coming. They had all been talking about the miracles that the Holy Spirit was accomplishing through us. The people of Manga finally saw a hope that stood before them. Many also told us that they had never seen the Holy Spirit act as powerfully before. They all left happy and in the joy of the Lord. At 1 pm, there were still a lot of people waiting outside but we couldn't go on like this all day. We were already exhausted after these three hours of prayers of deliverance in a sweltering heat.

We asked all those who were still outside to come to the evening evangelism to receive prayers and deliveries because we had to leave.

On the way back, we drove behind a white pickup truck with several people sitting in the back. We drove only few feet behind them. I kept a greater distance between us, as soon as I saw who was in the pickup. There were several sorcerers sitting in the back who threw incantations and spells all over the town of Manga. They were in the process of rehanging their hexes everywhere with all kinds of satanic objects in their hands.

We followed them for several kilometers to watch them. They were driving in the direction of our hotel but strangely turned around before our place of prayer of intercession. They went back to the center of the city, continuing the incantations. They were driving around. We knew that we had disturbed them and now they were trying to block us with their black magic but they had already failed since we had the King of Kings in our camp. Moreover, we were a team of thunder; Tiken, a pastor filled with the Holy Spirit, David, a powerful intercessor, Roland, a soldier of the Deliverance, Emmanuel, a great man of prayer and myself, and a Canadian sent personally by God. We could not have a better team to confront the servants of Satan on their own territory.

We knew now that the sorcerers had all gathered together in order to attack us in the evening. The war was now on and the next outdoor evangelization would become the great battlefield. We had to wear our Christian armor and prepare to fight for the Lord. The light was going to be victorious by the name of Jesus. The light could not lose since it always chases the darkness. When we press the light switch in our bedroom, the darkness disappears immediately. This is exactly what happens when we move into darkness with the light of Christ in us. They are afraid, they are fleeing, and they are vanishing. Without wasting a moment, we have advised Pastor Tiken of the demonic maneuvers of these sorcerers. We all prayed and interceded to counter these infernal spells and hexes implanted to prevent the Manga population from receiving divine light. The Holy Spirit was on our side and we all felt that victory was ours.

On our way out of the prayer room, which had become our upper room, the hotel employees came to meet us. The manager said, "Gentlemen, let me tell you something. For months the hotel had no customers but since you arrived here and you have prayed, we have received several reservations. We all felt that there was a force in each

68

of you and we would like you to pray for us before you leave." We confirmed that we will pray for them the next morning before leaving our rooms. I was truly amazing how God worked for these desperate people to be under the control of the sorcerers.

"So, we have come to know and to believe the love that God has for us. God is love, and whoever abides in love abides in God, and God abides in him."

- 1 John 4:16 (ESV)

In the evening, after a good nap to regain strength, we still prayed for the smooth running of our last outdoor evangelization. Several requests have been made to the Lord. For example, "Put us in the full Christian armor; Let the blood of the lamb flow throughout the site and any person who will be present, Fill us with the fire of the Holy Spirit so that we can repel the enemy's attacks, and Touch the hearts of all who will come to hear thy word". We prayed for more than an hour before taking the road towards the evangelization site. The valiant heroes were ready for the final fight. We were no longer ourselves. The Holy Spirit had just taken possession of our bodies and we had become soldiers of God. The confrontation could begin!

"What then shall we say to these things? If God is for us, who can be against us?"

-Romans 8:31 (ESV)

"For you equipped me with strength for the battle; you made those who rise against me sink under me."

-Psalm 18:39 (ESV)

"And he said, "Listen, all Judah and inhabitants of Jerusalem and King Jehoshaphat: Thus, says the LORD to you, 'Do not be afraid and do not be dismayed at this great horde,

for the battle is not yours but God's."

-2 Chronicles 20:15 (ESV)

At the site, we saw that the pastor of Manga was there and completely healed. The sorcerers had failed again in their attempt to take the life of one of us. On the ground, there were people everywhere, a crowd bigger than we seen since our arrival in Manga. Our reputation as men of God had been traveling around the city. We could feel that these people wanted to receive the joy that a relationship with Jesus provides.

They did not want to live in fear of the reprisals of the sorcerers, since they had all heard the miracles that God fulfilled. When Pastor Tiken ascended the stage, satanic praise began to resonate in the distance. All the sorcerers had gathered at the perimeter of the land to pray to their dark gods. They hoped to counter us with shouts and songs, but evangelism continued forcefully. None of the people there were listening to the sorcerers screaming. They all wanted to hear the pastor's message, to hear the Word of God. Before, they would all have fled because they were terribly afraid of these cursed sorcerers. But that evening, everyone had the courage in their hearts; all were ready to fight for the glory of the Lord.

"No, in all these things we are more than conquerors through him who loved us."

-Romans 8:37 (ESV)

The sorcerers, seeing that their satanic songs did not produce any effect on the soldiers of God, decided to confront us face to face. They approached and some started shouting insults at Pastor Tiken who was preaching on the stage. A sorcerer sat on the side of the stage and shouted insults to disturb the people who listened to the preacher's message. Another had started up the few steps of the stage to come and physically attack the pastor. Emmanuel arrived before him to prevent him from being on the last step.

Pastor Tiken turned around and ordered Emmanuel to release him because he would not be able to put his foot on the last step. We had prayed that the blood of the lamb would cover this scene when we were at the hotel, so a sorcerer couldn't put a single foot on it. The brother stepped back and left the path free to this spiritual aggressor. He looked at the pastor Tiken in his eyes with a look filled with hatred and then looked at the floor of the stage. He looked at the floor with a glance of doubt then went back down and down the steps. He left the site with his great defeat on his shoulder; he seemed completely demoralized and helpless against our God, the one and only true and worthy God of praise.

"And they have conquered him by the blood of the Lamb and by the word of their testimony, for they loved not their lives even unto death."
-Revelation 12:11 (ESV)

I was on the other side of the stage when I heard a sorcerer shouting insults close to me. He sat on the ground close to the stage and kept screaming to disturb the listeners. I looked him straight in the eyes with an authoritarian look. I pointed a finger in the air and I moved from right to left to say, "Do not do that!" I said to myself, without opening my mouth, "I chase thee in the name of Jesus!" He looked me in the eyes, as if he wanted to test me or study me. After only a few seconds, he got up, took his bike, and quietly left the scene because he had just failed his fight too. He had just discovered the power of our God. He realized that he could not do anything against the Creator.

"They have no knowledge who carry about their wooden idols, and keep on praying to a god that cannot save."
-Isaiah 45:20 (ESV)

After several unsuccessful attempts, the sorcerers had no choice but to admit their defeat and leave the place with hanging heads because the Lord, the God of Armies, had just won the great battle. He is and will always be victorious! With him, no one can know defeat and failure is not an option because success is ensured by the name of Jesus.

Evangelism continued until late into the night because a large number of people gave their lives to the Lord and a more impressive crowd demanded prayers of deliverance.

It was precisely during these prayers that I noticed a young woman who behaved as if she were possessed and two brothers of the Church of Manga were praying for her. I felt in my heart that she was not sincere and that she was faking, so I quickly approached. I raised her head and I said, "I know you're faking it." Then I turned to the brothers praying for her and I ordered them - "Let her go! Do not pray for her because she is manipulating you!" Then I went back to the scene and I saw that the brothers had listened to me and had left the woman alone. Strangely, the young woman lifted her head and saw that no one cared, so she left the premises while walking normally. Her possession had just vanished without our help since she was actually pretending to be under the influence of a spirit.

These three nights of evangelization were a great success as there had been more than 125 people who had given their lives to the Lord and Savior, an incalculable number of spiritual deliverance and the sorcerers who had all been repelled by the divine power. These new converts would certainly exceed the maximum capacity for the small Church of Manga. The pastor had to begin work to expand the place of worship, in order to accommodate these people properly. We all emerged from this adventure fully fortified and filled with the fire of the Holy Spirit. We could now celebrate this great victory of our Lord Jesus Christ.

The most interesting thing about this is that our adventure was not over yet. We still had one last morning since it was agreed that Pastor Tiken be the guest preacher at the Church of Manga for Sunday morning worship. We started the day with a prayer in Pastor Tiken's room. Afterwards, we put all our luggage in the trunk of the car so that everything was ready for our departure. At the hotel reception, pastor Tiken came to see me by giving me the bill for my hotel room. I paid for my room to the man behind the counter, and then we asked the employees to go out into the courtyard of the hotel to start the prayers.

They all wanted the hotel to have a lot of guests because they liked their work, so we prayed for this. We asked God to send Christian clients by the hundreds, so that this hotel continues to be a place of prayers as we had transformed since our arrival. "This establishment will be recognized everywhere in Burkina for these miraculous prayers and that people from everywhere will fill all the rooms available every day!" The employees were really happy with the prayer that had been made, and were very thankful, hoping that we would come back one day to visit them. We all boarded the car in the direction of the church.

We left the car in front of the wall of the church courtyard and, when we entered, we were filled with joy because of what was happening before our eyes. The church was packed and there were people outside who wanted to hear Pastor Tiken one last time. We entered and sat on our reserved seats. After the praises, the Pastor of Manga introduced his colleague for preaching. Everyone was silent and attentive to the message of Pastor Tiken.

At the end of his sermon, a deacon came to the microphone to announce that it was the time of tithes and offerings. At that time, I didn't know why but I had to heart to give money, even if I had just enough money to pay for the return fuel. The man who had the basket of tithes came before me and I hastened to put my tithe for God. It was not huge but it came from the heart.

"And he called his disciples to him and said to them: Truly, I say to you, this poor widow has put in more than all those who are contributing to the offering box. For they all contributed out of their abundance, but she out of her poverty has put in everything she had, all she had to live on."

-Mark 12:43-44(ESV)

Afterwards, the Pastor of Manga beckoned us to come and join him at the front then he asked everyone to applaud us for what we had done during these three days of evangelization. The applause was really amazing, some people whistled and shouted to congratulate us.

Pastor Tiken took the microphone and said, "I wholeheartedly desire to do something special before we leave. You're all going to pray in tongues. My team and I are going to walk among you and if we hear a person who does not pray in tongues, we will lay on our hands so that everyone prays in tongues. I want to bring down the fire of the Holy Spirit upon you all."

The pastor began to pray in tongues and then everyone began to pray. I walked through people like all members of the team and when I heard a person praying in French, I put my hands on the head of that person and I prayed that the fire would fill this body. Unlike the others, I had a small problem - I did not understand Moré, the local language, so I could not tell the difference between tongues and the Moré. I had to look at how the person was praying and detecting whether he was praying in spirit or not.

The difference became easily perceptible - a person who spoke in tongues will display a lot of passion and emotion while praying. She will cry, scream, vibrate, dance or jump under the power of the Holy Spirit. What was amazing was that everyone started praying in tongues as soon as we put our hands on them. I saw a strong man who was praying normally, and a brother of our team put his hands on him. In a split second, this muscular giant began to cry like a child and pray in tongues. He could not stop crying while having his eyes closed.

A woman I laid hands on started to yell and fell to the ground. After a few minutes, we helped her to get up and she started praying in tongues, while crying and moving her arms in every direction. I went out into the outside courtyard and people were praying too. I laid my hands on a few people who immediately started praying in tongues. Pastor Tiken laid his hands on a woman who had a distorted foot that prevented her from walking. She got up and started to walk properly. She kept yelling "Thank you Jesus!" with both arms in the air to worship her divine healer.

All these prayers in tongues were like music to our ears. We had the tears in our eyes to see how the Holy Spirit had invaded all the people who were in the church and in the outer courtyard. We all felt the unconditional love of the Lord all around us. Many cried, others laughed with joy, others danced, but everyone was filled with the Holy Spirit. The fire was now in all of us.

"For this reason, I remind you to fan into flame the gift of God, which is in you through the laying on of my hands,"
-2 Timothy 1:6 (ESV)

The Pastor of Manga approached us and informed us that it was better for us if we leave immediately in a discreet way, otherwise it would be impossible to leave early for Dedougou. He also asked us to wait for him at his private residence because his wife had prepared us a good meal for the road. We accepted and he quickly made us come out through the side door. A few minutes after arriving at the pastor's house, people from the church gathered in front of the court and wanted to see us. The pastor of Manga spoke a little with them and came to join us inside the house.

"Everyone wants you to stay longer," said the pastor. "They insist and are even willing to pay for your expenses." The offer was very tempting but we had to go back to our respective families. I was thinking about my wife who was probably bored, so I had to decline the offer. I was not the leader of this team, so I had no decision authority. I was relieved when I heard Pastor Tiken told him that he was very happy with this demonstration of love, but he had to refuse because his family was waiting for him.

We sat down and the pastor's wife offered us food to eat. Pastor Tiken and I asked if we could bring our meal with us since we were fasting until we returned to Dedougou. She understood and made us a package in order to take the whole thing into the car. The other three of the team ate this meal so warmly prepared.

The two pastors decided to make a small private meeting in another room. After a few minutes, both came back laughing and shaking hands in the living room. We said our goodbyes and then finally took the road but we still had a little detail to settle. We had to pray again at the exit of the city to ensure that the new converts remain in the Lord and that the sorcerers can do nothing against them. We prayed at the very place where we had prayed when we came to Manga. The oil sank again into the Manga ground then we got back on the road in the direction of Dedougou.

We had only made a few kilometers that several sparrow hawks stole dangerously close to the car. It looked like they were trying to smash the windshield or a side window to make us lose control of the car or cause a fatal accident. We knew it was still an attempt by the sorcerers since Manga is dubbed the city of sparrow hawks. They failed again since none of these birds of misfortune succeeded in touching the vehicle.

A few more kilometers away, two intense tornados came directly at the car to drive us off the road. I held the steering wheel firmly to not lose control. The sorcerers had still miserably failed. They were stubborn to attack us, when they had already failed in advance. No one can go after men filled with the Holy Spirit, by doing so they are directly against God. Who can think of being stronger than the Creator of mankind? This person does not exist either in the present century or in the centuries to come.

"There is none like you, O LORD; you are great, and your name is great in might."

-Jeremiah 10:6 (ESV)

We did not experience any other sorcerers' attacks for the remainder of our journey back. We stopped in Ouagadougou to drop off our brother Emmanuel and fill up the fuel. The attendant showed me the amount and I paid. I was always taking the receipt of all my expenses since I was in Burkina Faso. I did not know why I did it but I had taken this habit and I continued to do so. When I got back behind the wheel and continued our long road up to Dedougou. The first toll station was at the exit from Ouagadougou. I stopped and paid the amount required. We went on our way with the Christian songs from my MP3 player.

A few hours later, after passing Koudougou, we stopped at a police checkpoint. After the routine checks, when I wanted to restart the engine, nothing worked. I was turning the key but the engine didn't want to start.

I asked the two young men from behind to go out and push the car to start it. Finally, the car started without a problem. The pastor asked me why it was no longer starting and I explained to him that, without wanting to name Gilbert, the mechanic had done a lot of repairs on my car before and that the starter cable had to be detached again.

A few hours later, we finally arrived at Dedougou. I went directly to the pastor's residence. I had taken care not to turn off the engine and then everyone unloaded their luggage except Roland who had asked me to bring him back with me since he lived not far from my residence. It was already night and I knew he was too exhausted to take a bike at this late hour, so I had agreed to help him. We were almost arrived in front of my home, so I asked Roland if he wanted me to drop him off at his house. He replied, "No, you can leave me at your home, I will walk to my house because it is really close."

"Are you sure because I can drop you off without you having to walk?"

"Don't worry" replied Roland. "I'm going to walk."

So, I acted according to his request and I parked in front of my house. My wife was so eager to see me again, that she was still not asleep in spite of the hour. She opened the garage door to allow the car to enter. I had completely forgotten that the engine mounts were making a huge noise. The whole trip my ears just got used to this racket. Roland left on foot and we closed the garage doors.

We prayed together, and then I put oil on the front door of the courtyard and on all the accesses of the house, in order to cover us with the protection of God. I did not want to take any chance of evil retaliation against my family. I prayed for of the angels on my home and on my family. Afterwards, I sat on the terrace with my wife to tell her the story of our incredible adventure in Manga. I was like a kid telling his mom about his favorite movie. Even Rosalie seemed very happy with all that the Lord had done throughout the duration of my stay in Manga. She served me a nice hot meal then I walked in to take my shower and sleep peacefully in the comfort of my bed.

I will not surprise anyone by saying that the following morning; I did not want to wake up. I slept very late to recover from the fatigue of my great adventure in Manga. Many people do not know it, but doing prayers of deliverance without stopping can be extremely exhausting. Depending on the length of time, every person who asks for prayers drains a lot of energy. Each time, one must take authority over the malicious spirit that hides in the body of its host, to force it to flee, seeing our relentlessness.

Manga allowed me to accumulate a lot of experience in the field of deliverance and I felt myself becoming better. These demons may as well give up trying, because I will continue my work until God decides to welcome me to him in the beautiful house adorned with gold that he built me in heavenly places. I know it will be the most beautiful house since I keep walking in my father's will.

"For we know that if the tent that is our earthly home is destroyed, we have a building from God, a house not made with hands, eternal in the heavens."
-2 Corinthians 5:1 (ESV)

One thing was different when I woke up - the oil mark I made on the front door was completely different. I had made a cross with the tip of my forefinger. The oil trace must have been about two centimeters wide. Now it was clear that the cross had been enlarged, as if a person had used the palm of hand to extend the oil more than five to seven centimeters wide.

It was really visible, even though we were inside the house. I felt in my heart that it was the angels, that I had asked family protection, who had done this. I cannot explain it but I knew without a doubt that this new cross had been made by the angels of God. I checked all the other marks on the accesses to the house; they were two centimeters, same as I had done the night before. Only the one on the front door of the court had been enlarged by a divine hand. I raised my arms in the air and praised the Lord for this sign that showed me that the protective hand of God was on my family. The angels wanted to comfort me by showing me their presence around us. They knew my biggest concern was the safety of my little family.

By making this simple gesture, they took away all this fear of retaliation and fortified my trust in our father.

"But let all who take refuge in you rejoice; let them ever sing for joy, and spread your protection over them, that those who love your name may exult in you. For you bless the righteous, O Lord; you cover him with favor as with a shield."
- Psalm 5:11-12 (ESV)

My car still wasn't starting that morning, so we called Gilbert to come and fix it at home. A few minutes later his head was under the hood of the motor. After a few routine checks, he discovered that the cable he had repaired before our trip had again given way because of the vibrations caused by the new engine mounts. He temporarily repaired the cable and then asked me if he could leave with the car to change the engine mounts. That was the straw that broke the camel's back - I had enough! I could not look at this car! I hated it so much because it cost me too much in various repairs. I had no confidence in the reliability of this vehicle. Imagine if it broke down on a lost road in the middle of nowhere. What was paramount to me was the safety of my family because being lost, away from the city could be risky for all of us.

I asked Gilbert to find us a buyer for this car because I didn't want to see her in my driveway. He very astonished at this decision because, when we were in Ouagadougou, Gilbert himself had chosen this vehicle for us. I think he felt a little responsible for my frustration, but I didn't blame him at all. He could not have known that there would be so many mechanical problems simply by looking under the hood before buying it. Buying a used car always includes a risk of buying a scrap that the owner wanted to get rid of. Gilbert left with the car, confirming that he would find a buyer quickly.

Gilbert came home later in the day. He wanted to show me that the new engine mounts were much better and made less noise. Indeed, the difference was easy to distinguish. It was like night and day, but my mind was already made up - I wanted to sell this car.

A little detail bothered me again - I no longer had the rent money. My wife and I finally made the decision to stop worrying about finances and leave everything in the hands of God, since it was he who had sent us to this country. We had put this in prayer.

"Surely oppression drives the wise into madness, and a bribe corrupts the heart."

-Ecclesiastes 7:7 (ESV)

I was trying to stop thinking about all this, but questions kept tormenting me during my sleep. I couldn't sleep peacefully. I sat on the mattress and started praying in a low voice, not to wake Rosalie. I kept asking the Lord to help me because I was beginning to wonder. My faith was shaken by all these things that were happening to us lately. Even though I had seen the Holy Spirit act with strength and power, I still doubted my own father. How could I doubt God himself, the one who has always been faithful and has always provided financially since we left Canada?

I finally heard a voice that told me gently, as if to appease my fears. "Let go of this money fear, I am the one who is taking care of it now. I saw what you did to Manga and I enjoyed it. You gave despite the fact that you had not eaten anything for days. You had little but you still gave. That is why I will also give to you. Do not worry." The voice was so wonderful that I still remember all the words he had told me. I felt light now and I could finally fall into a deep sleep without any worries coming to disturb me. My father had just comforted me and would now take care of all my problems.

"Trust in the LORD with all your heart, and do not lean on your own understanding. In all your ways acknowledge him, and he will make straight your paths."

-Proverb 3:5-6 (ESV)

When I woke up, something told me to check my messages on the Internet. I took my laptop, I logged in, and I checked my email account.

I had two messages - the two messages were bank transfers by email! The amounts were large enough that I thought I was still sleeping and that it was just a dream.

God had really taken care of our finances. With this amount, we had no more worry about rent for several months. I immediately showed the transfers to my wife and we both praised the Lord with all our heart. He had shown us his presence at our side. We were actually doing his divine will.

The following Wednesday, Gilbert came to my house with a potential buyer for the car. The man came from Koudougou and, while he was passing through Dedougou, his car broke down. He had an old Mercedes and the engine was completely screwed up, but Gilbert couldn't find a new engine after several days of intense research. It was at this point that he had offered to buy a new car because the purchase of a complete engine, including the mechanic's working time, could cost him more.

He had praised my car to this stranger, telling him that it was fueled by diesel and, after repairing it himself, that it was very reliable. I handed the keys to my wife's brother so he could go for a test drive with the man to show him how well it was rolling. They came back several minutes later and the stranger seemed happy. He asked me why I wanted to sell it because it looked good. I simply replied that I no longer needed it. He then asked me if my price was negotiable and I immediately replied, "No! At that price, you won't find anything better in Dedougou." I knew it was true, especially after doing several days of research to find a car to buy before taking this Toyota Avensis. I finally shook hands with this man and Gilbert's and then they went back.

Later, Gilbert called by phone to say that the man had just agreed to buy the car at the asking price but he did not have enough money here in Dedougou. He proposed to give the half of the amount then when he arrived at Koudougou, he would give the difference. I informed Gilbert that I did not like this at all it; it seemed like a trick to get the car at half price. When he got home, he would never send us the money.

He asked me what he should do. I said, "The only way to know if this man is honest, since no one knows him in Dedougou, is to go with him to Koudougou and get the money in person."

Gilbert proposed to accompany this stranger, so as not to lose this chance to sell our vehicle. Especially after my wife and I had offered him a commission if he sold our car. That was probably the reason why he had offered our car to this man, instead of fixing his old Mercedes. So, we agreed that this man would pay us in two payments.

When I was in Burkina Faso in 2001, no one talked about credit or payments in multiple instalments. Everything had to be settled entirely when buying in money, never in credit. Today, things have changed so much. The prices that skyrocketed, as wages rose slowly. People wanted to buy several luxury items but couldn't afford to have them so they jumped headlong on the credit offers. They did not calculate how much the interest or monthly payments would cost them. They just wanted to buy the items they wanted without thinking about everything else.

Even the mechanics tools we brought in from Canada, when a man was interested in buying them, he still wanted to have them in several payments. Every time, I would refuse for the simple reason that I knew that the person could disappear with the tools, without paying us the rest. Or that he would not be able to pay everything and that was why he wanted to take on credit or that our friendship would be completely destroyed for a matter of money.

Freedom is not to have any burdens. Money is the worst burden that can destroy freedom. Let's take the example of a man who lives in comfort. He has activities, a house, a family, and a good life. One day he buys a car on credit, without checking to see if he can afford it. After a few months he has no money so he has to start to tighten his belt. He decides to stop family activities because he no longer has the means. The monthly payments are too high. His life changes because he gets stressed by finances. His anger often falls on his own family. The man is only working to repay his bills and does not have any free time. He became firmly chained to the money and has totally lost his freedom.

Burkina had become like the history of that man. The new slogan of Dedougou was now, "There is no money!"

It was very sad to see such a thing happen in such a beautiful country but it was what the people of this world call "evolution". I'm glad I'm not part of this world. Thank you, Jesus, for getting me out of this earth fiasco.

"Do not love the world or the things in the world. If anyone loves the world, the love of the Father is not in him. For all that is in the world, the desires of the flesh and the desires of the eyes and pride of life is not from the Father but is from the world. And the world is passing away along with its desires, but whoever does the will of God abides forever."

-1 John 2:15-17 (ESV)

A friend of Rosalie's had invited us to visit the church where she praised the Lord. She wanted us to meet the pastor because, she said, he was filled with the Holy Spirit and had a way of preaching that made everyone burn with passion for the Lord. It was a church of the International Christian Union located in Sector 6 of Dedougou. We decided to go to this church for one of their evening of prayers of the Holy Spirit. On the spot, we met Pastor Jonathan Dao.

He was a strong man of great stature who was really friendly. He warmly greeted us. We found out quickly that men and women could not sit together in this church, so Rosalie was sitting on one side of the room and my son and I, were on the other side. I found it a bit strange but I was not there to criticize, I was there because we had been invited. During the praises, there was a woman who would always run around the room as if she wanted to win the gold medal in the Olympic Games. Sometimes she would jump with her arms swaying in every direction. She always kept her eyes closed while continuing her exaggerated expressions without apologizing for bumping into her siblings.

I know that the Holy Spirit can manifest itself mightily in a different way for each person but, in her case, she exaggerated far too much. I felt that she only wanted to be noticed by everyone and not a manifestation of the Holy Spirit. As I often say, "It takes all kinds of people to make a world!" The pastor entered and propagated the message of God to his followers. His preaching was good - I liked it.

At the end of his message, the pastor presented my family as Canadian missionaries who came to serve God in Burkina Faso. He then asked us to come to the front to talk a little bit about us and our mission to everyone. I did not expect that at all and I was not prepared for it. My wife came to join me at the front and I told how God had touched me, the visions he showed me regularly and how he had brought us to this country. For the rest, I do not know how to explain it, but the Holy Spirit invaded me and I felt that he wanted me to talk about Manga. So, I followed the indications of the spirit and started talking about my trip to Manga.

I've told them everything - the vultures that were watching us, the whirlwind attacks, the bats that were watching us, the sorcerers who threw their incantations without effect, etc. I saw the people who listened attentively to everything I told. They didn't want to miss anything because they all knew the bad name of Manga. At the end of my story, I said, "The sorcerers of Manga have tried everything against us but have failed miserably because they do not have the Kings of Kings by their side." People stood up screaming with joy and clapping. Some shouted "Hallelujah!", "Glory to Jesus!" or "Thank you Jesus!" We felt that the Holy Spirit was putting his fire in the hearts of all our listeners. There was a power hovering over our heads.

I turned to my wife and whispered to her, "I've wanted to do this for a very long time." I approached the microphone closer to my lips and I said, "God was with us at Manga and I believe that God will work mightily in Burkina Faso. I believe that Burkina Faso will be an example to the rest of the world. Burkina Faso will be 100% Christians. Hail the Lord!" At this moment, the madness of God is endeared to everyone. They yelled louder, clapped, danced, cheered, praised, etc. We had a crowd of ecstasy in front of us. They were happy to hear everything the Lord was doing for their country, happy to see that God was in Africa!

"All the nations you have made shall come and worship before you, O Lord, and shall glorify your name. For you are great and do wondrous things; you alone are God."
-Psalm 86:9-10 (ESV)

The pastor came back to the front to thank us but people continued to praise the Lord. It was almost impossible to hear what Pastor Dao said on the microphone. So he decided to conclude quickly and asked us to come out immediately through the side door because people would not let us leave. We followed without hesitation but there was already a crowd waiting for us outside. People continued to praise God with songs, applause, and thanks. Even those who simply walked down the street, stopped in front of the church to understand the reason for all the screaming and shouting.

All this crowd made it very difficult for us to take one step, since everyone wanted to shake hands and thank us for doing God's will. All this intense joy, I could feel it deep in my heart. It was also filling me. These people touched me with their joy and their love and my body became full of rejoicing. I felt so good among them that I do not believe there is a single word that can describe everything that I felt. There was love all around us.

"Sing the glory of his name; give to him glorious praise!"
-Psalm 66:2 (ESV)

The pastor made his way to join us and said, "From today, we will work together. We will work together for the advancement of the Kingdom of God." Then he shook my hand to thank us for filling his church with the fire of the Holy Spirit. I replied that I should not be thanked, a simple servant in the service of his great celestial Boss, but he had to thank the true responsible for all this - God, the Father. We got on our bikes and managed to leave the premises to come home.

I was comfortably seated on a chair from the front terrace of our house when my phone rang.

Pastor Tiken announced another miracle of God. He had just finished a conversation with the pastor from Manga. The day after our departure from Manga, last Monday, one of the oldest sorcerers of this city of the sparrow hawks had died under inexplicable circumstances. The whole population was shocked to learn this news especially the day after we left.

Then on Wednesday another of the oldest wizards of Manga died under the same inexplicable circumstances. Following the announcement of the second death, the whole city was completely astonished to see that it was not a pastor who had fallen ill or died, but it was rather these two evil forces that fell. They began to realize that Jesus was stronger than all the satanic forces of this world.

The pastor of Manga said that more and more people were coming to his church following these two defeats of the enemy on their own territory. There was now a great awakening among the people who wanted to follow the King of Kings. We thanked the Lord together and then immediately called Pastor Dao to inform him of this great news. He was also in joy! A wonderful victory like the one God had just offered deserves praise and thanksgiving. This is what my wife and I did for the rest of the night and even in bed. The Lord deserved all our sincere thanks. Thank you, Jesus, for this great miracle. Thank you, Jesus, for spreading your mighty light that makes the darkness of Manga flee. Thank Jesus for saving these lost souls and offering them life. Death is defeated in the name of Jesus!

"He will swallow up death forever; and the Lord GOD will wipe away tears from all faces, and the reproach of his people he will take away from all the earth, for the LORD has spoken."
-Isaiah 25:8 (ESV)

"Death is swallowed up in victory. O death, where is your victory? O death, where is your sting?"
-1 Corinthians 15:54-55 (ESV)

"Our Savior Christ Jesus, who abolished death and brought life and immortality to light through the gospel."
-2 Timothy 1:10 (ESV)

The following Friday, Gilbert left with my car to go to Koudougou with the unknown man to get the money from the sale. As expected, the man had given us some of the money before they left and the rest would follow when he arrived in Koudougou.

The man picked up the money and they settled all the official documents. Gilbert took a bus back and a few hours later, Gilbert came over and handed us the money from the sale. We were delighted to see that this unknown man was very honest. We handed the promised bonus to my brother-in-law and he left immediately to rest a little. God had come to surprise us financially. It is good and wonderful to be part of the great family of the Lord. Everyone told us that it was almost impossible to sell a car in Dedougou but they all forgot an important detail - God was with us!

"The LORD is my light and my salvation; whom shall I fear? The LORD is the stronghold of my life; of whom shall I be afraid?"

-Psalm 27:1 (ESV)

ATTACKS AND DELIVERANCES

"And in the last days it shall be, God declares, that I will pour out my Spirit on all flesh, and your sons and your daughters shall prophesy, and your young men shall see visions, and your old men shall dream dreams; even on my male servants and female servants in those days I will pour out my Spirit, and they shall prophesy. And I will show wonders in the heavens above and signs on the earth below, blood, and fire, and vapor of smoke;"

-Acts 2:17-19 (ESV)

Every time I prayed for a person, for any reason, I put his name in a small notebook that I had called "intercession book". If the person was delivered or healed, I would remove them from the book so that all my intercession prayers would be for those who had not yet been touched by the hand of God. When the time to go to bed arrived, I prayed for all the people who were in my intercession book.

For some time, I have been chatting with a young woman from Haiti on the Internet. She was a Christian and had been baptized with water just recently. She told me that she often had old demons from the past who came to wake her up at night. She felt that she had lost her freedom because they were keeping her under their demonic rights. I wrote to her regularly to comfort her, by giving her advice in good standing with what the Word teaches us.

She liked to speak with me because, as soon as she saw me online, she sent me a little hello before I had time to notice her online. Since I was not by her side to pray for her deliverance, I had added it to my prayer book. I didn't know why I had to talk to her but something told me I had to do it because she needed it. The couple from Manga that got back together after several months of separation were also in my notebook so that their love is always inflamed. In short, I had several pages of filled and I added regularly because many people came to the house to ask for prayer for different reasons.

My evening prayers lasted longer and longer before I could go to bed.

"And the prayer of faith will save the one who is sick, and the Lord will raise him up. And if he has committed sins, he will be forgiven. Therefore, confess your sins to one another and pray for one another, that you may be healed. The prayer of a righteous person has great power as it is working."
-James 5:15-16 (ESV)

After fully understanding the will of God, I decided to join the Ministry of Deliverance at the church of Dedougou. On Tuesdays and Thursdays, myself and other blessed men of God, were going to church to pray for those who needed it. Some people came to thank the Lord for having delivered them, others were there to get healing, and others were waiting for a deliverance.

Once again, God was acting mightily using our hands. People left healed, delivered, and in the joy of finding a long-lost freedom. It was invigorating to see the miracles that were happening every time. God was working in an incredible way and showed us without a doubt, that Burkina Faso would be an example to the rest of the world.

"And the hand of the Lord was with them, and a great number who believed turned to the Lord."

- Acts 11:21 (ESV)

On Thursday March 22nd, in the morning, we had a very important meeting with the mayor of the commune of Dedougou. Since God wanted us to help the widows of the Province of Mouhoun, we had to do it legally in the country that warmly greeted us. We had to start an association but I had no idea how to do it because the rules of Burkina Faso are not like Canadian rules. The mayor arrived to his office and beckoned us to follow him. He asked us to sit on a sofa in his office and then we presented him the plan for the project that God had brought to our hearts. I had just spent several days putting up this business plan to indicate the strengths of this humanitarian project.

He listened attentively and was very interested in this new project. He admitted that there was a great need for this kind of assistance in the community. We asked him if he could tell us what we had to do to make this kind of project happen. The mayor called one of his work colleagues who arrived in just a few seconds. He introduced us to this man as the one who signs the deeds of assignments for the land in the un-subdivided quarters. He then informed us that the High Commission was responsible for the requests for an association declaration. This man, without being aware of it, had just helped us immensely. At the end of our meeting, we prayed with him so that the Lord always made him make the best decisions for the Commune of Dedougou.

We shook hands before leaving his office since there were already several people waiting to meet him. I was very pleased with the meeting because the mayor was very enthusiastic about the new association that would be in the community. What we did not know was that there would be many trials and walls, to try to prevent us from doing God's plan. Several people were already preparing to get in our way and do everything they could to get us to abandon this project to help widows, a project that came from God himself. Was it not what Satan has always done and will continue to do until the

Lord returns?

"Because we wanted to come to you, I, Paul, again and again, but Satan hindered us."
                                   -1 Thessalonians 2:18 (ESV)

When we get a great victory against the world of darkness, we must never forget that Satan will always try to get revenge. He is extremely vindictive and hates defeat, it is for this same reason that he keeps on striving for the creation of God since he was defeated at the Cross of Calvary. This enemy is very cunning and will do anything to counter God's plans.

After defeating Manga and executing several deliverances within the Ministry of the Church of Dedougou, I knew that these unclean spirits would try to go after me or my family.

It was for this reason that I had put the anointing oil on all the accesses of my residence. Despite all these precautions, the unclean spirits and the sorcerers have tried to attack me several times.

For example, on the day of Friday, March 23rd, when I was on my way back home walking, two whirlwinds appeared before me. The same kind of swirls that had tried to get us out of the way when we were out of Manga. I had mocked these whirlwinds by saying, "You can do nothing against me because, with the help of Jesus, I have defeated you all in Manga!"

Immediately after laughing at these tornadoes, my right foot, and only the right foot, twisted continually on stones scattered by chance on the way. With each of my steps, I had the impression that a stone appeared under my foot to try to cause a fracture of the ankle. Yet, I was looking at the ground to avoid this kind of stone. I had even seen a rock roll under my foot when I was taking a step, while it was away from me. Before I hurt myself, I decided not to lift my foot while walking. I was now kicking those stones with my foot. When I arrived home, I started praying immediately in order to ask for protection on me and my family. I knew that it was an evil attack of some sorcerer who sought revenge. He forgot one thing - to go after a child of God was to go after God Himself! And to go after God personally would bring a lamentable defeat.

The next morning, a Muslim woman who knew Rosalie came over to buy natural hair packages. Rosalie had brought a couple of high-quality hair extensions in our luggage when we left Canada. She wanted to sell them in Burkina Faso, in order to have an extra revenue to support ourselves. Sales were very seldom concluded because of the very high price. It was not synthetic hair, so quality is always expensive. The client had come accompanied by another woman whom we did not know.

As soon as she crossed the front door of our yard, a thought came to my mind - "She's a witch!" I felt that she had come with bad intentions but since we had put anointing oil on all the accesses, she could not do anything against us. After concluding the sale, Rosalie felt that she had to pray for her client.

She accepted, even though she was of Muslim religion. The witch stood there without a wink, to listen to this prayer.

We felt that she did not like this gesture on our part. She seemed very uncomfortable, as if something bothered her so much that she wanted to leave the place without delay. Without waiting any longer, she told the client that it was time to leave because they would be late and that it was already night. She just wanted to get out of our yard very quickly and used any motive to convince her colleague. The women left on their respective bikes.

Later, in the night, Rosalie had a phone call. The same client told her what happened after she left our residence. The witch had invited her to have a drink at home, so they followed each other on a motorbike. The woman passed by a very dark road and very far from the city. They found themselves in the middle of the bush, driving near a dangerous ravine. The client was so afraid that she decided to turn back. She felt that her life was at stake. It must be said that the sorcerers regularly do satanic rituals in the middle of the bush, far from the curious glances. Sacrifices can be made during these rituals. In general, they use animals but, from unofficial sources, they can also make human sacrifices.

Rosalie told her that I had felt that this woman was a witch and that she had done well to flee without hesitation. The Muslim woman thanked us for praying for her because she knew that God had protected her because of our intercession. Our Lord has no religion because he himself said to love his neighbor as oneself. Our neighbor doesn't only mean our Christian brethren but everyone, without exception. If we love our neighbor, we also have to pray and intercede for him by the mighty name of Jesus.

"You shall love the Lord your God with all your heart and with all your soul and with all your strength and with all your mind, and your neighbor as yourself."
-Luke 10:27 (ESV)

The next morning, when we had to go to church, I started to have stomach aches. I felt some kind of intense swelling inside my intestines. A terrible diarrhea had taken possession of my body to the point that it prevented me from going to church for the morning service. This diarrhea was strange because it felt like a "Mexican Turista"; I couldn't get off the toilet. If I dared to get up to go out, the stomach aches came even more intensely to the point that I could barely walk back to the bathroom. I had never experienced anything like this before. This new attack of the enemy showed me well how cunning he was.

He had just succeeded in moving me away from the Word of God on this Sunday morning. The strange thing about all this was that, around noon, when it was too late to go to church, the diarrhea suddenly stopped for no reason. Without any medication, it vanished as fast as it had come. I decided that this spell would not win over me so, failing to hear the pastor's message, I began to read the Bible and meditate on the Word. This dubious disease would not prevent me from spending time with my heavenly Father.

As soon as I opened my Bible to read, head pain began and my vision began to become murky. That was too much! I closed the Bible and started praying in tongues. No matter if I was dizzy; I got up and walked in every direction taking authority over this attack. I have ordered this evil spell to leave my body and never to return by the name of Jesus. I prayed, prayed, and prayed even more, until the sweat poured down my forehead. I knew that no medicine or remedy of human origin could intervene to help me. Only my Lord could.

"Who forgives all your iniquity, who heals all your diseases..."
-Psalm 103:3 (ESV)

When the word "Amen" came out of my mouth, I felt much better. Headache, dizziness, and vision problems were completely cured. The Lord was present so I began to thank him for his help. I opened my Bible and I finally managed to read and meditate the Word of the living God.

The following Sunday, I went without a problem to the service of the Church of Dedougou. During the service, a brother came to fetch me, in order to make a prayer of deliverance on a young woman who was heavily possessed by a powerful spirit. I followed him to the pastor's office. The heaviest possessions were always brought in front of the office, out of sight of the curious and not to disturb the continuation of the service. The woman was lying on the floor and her face was covered with tears and drool. Her eyes were completely red and she laughed with a morbid laugh.

I prepared myself in prayer before I faced this demonic spirit. I asked the Lord to grant me the authority and full armor of the Christian to carry out this fight in order to liberate this woman from the grip of the enemy.

The whole time I was doing my prayer of preparation, she was just screaming "Blah, blah, blah!" to disturb me. I put my hand on her head and I ordered this spirit to leave her immediately. Her eyes turned to me and she looked at me with a rabid gaze. She replied, "You want me to go out, but to where? Give me another body to take and I'll come out."

I started praying in tongues while decreeing that he liberated her, but he still resisted. He said, "This little girl, I won't leave her because I've been working on her for too long. If I leave, her parents will come to Jesus. If you knew everything I did to that little girl." Then she laughed again, pinching her nipples to provoke me. So, I replied with more strength, "I order you to leave it immediately in the name of Jesus!"

"Why? You're going to do the same thing you did to the two wizards of Manga?"

This statement literally shocked me. How could she know about Manga since the pastor had not yet publicly announced it? That's when I realized that demonic spirits are communicating with each other. I do not know how, but I just had a proof of that. It was disturbing to know that all the sorcerers of Burkina were probably informed of everything we had done in this small town south of the capital.

On the other hand, I had no fear; they did not scare me because the King of Kings was with me forever. Fear and doubt do not come from God; they are strategically implanted by Satan. He has always used this kind of strategy to reduce our faith and thus control us. At the creation of the world, Adam had never been afraid of anything since he was in the peace of His divine Creator. But after crunching the forbidden fruit, this sense of fear began to invade.

"And he said: I heard the sound of you in the garden, and I was afraid, because I was naked, and I hid myself."
-Genesis 3:10 (ESV)

With the Creator of mankind as a whole, how could we be afraid of anything?

"Then I said to you: Do not be in dread or afraid of them. The LORD your God who goes before you will himself fight for you, just as he did for you in Egypt before your eyes."

-Deuteronomy 1:29-30 (ESV)

After this surprising response from this possessed girl, I decided not to listen to her anymore. When she wanted to open her mouth, I ordered her to shut up. Her face was surprised by my reaction, but I didn't want to hear those lies anymore. The enemy is the father of all lies and we cannot believe anything that comes from him or from one of his own.

"You are of your father the devil, and your will is to do your father's desires. He was a murderer from the beginning, and does not stand in the truth, because there is no truth in him. When he lies, he speaks out of his own character, for he is a liar and the father of lies."

-John 8:44 (ESV)

After more than an hour of fighting against this hardened enemy, Roland and I finally managed to scare him away. When we no longer felt the presence of the evil spirit, we always asked for the name of the person before us.

In this way, we were certain that the evil one had fled, since he is unable to tell the truth. The young woman was completely lost - she couldn't remember anything. Several minutes of her life had taken place entirely in the darkness. She looked everywhere to figure out where she was and why her face was sweaty and covered with tears.

Her clothes were also very dirty as the spirit forced her to roll on the ground. We helped her get up and comforted her. Roland accompanied her to her bike, as she could not return inside the church in this situation. It was better for her to go home to rest a little after such an intense ordeal. The service was drawing to a close and I had missed the whole message of the pastor. But I was very proud to have succeeded, with the help of my Lord, to liberate this woman struggling with this powerful and cunning spirit. One more victory to be entered in the book of the King of Kings.

In the evening, Christian friends came to visit us at home and we prayed together. The evening was truly remarkable. When it was time to say goodbye, we all accompanied them outside the yard. Out of nowhere, dozens of bats appeared and flew over our heads. They were everywhere and kept coming and going only a few inches above us. My friends quickly departed, while Rosalie and I returned to the courtyard without waiting any longer.

Inside our walls, no bats dared to come and harass us. It was again, a new attack of the enemy that was certainly very angry with us since we would not surrender against his satanic army. It was because of me doing deliverance and Rosalie bringing people to the light by evangelizing them. She had this incredible gift to evangelize. No one could remain indifferent when she spoke to him about the Lord and all those blessings in our lives.

She tore the darkness from all the desperate people and showed them the way to the light, the truth, and the life. The enemy saw his power diminish in Burkina Faso and did not like losing souls of his conquest, especially against men and women.

"Be sober-minded; be watchful. Your adversary the devil prowls around like a roaring lion, seeking someone to devour."
-1 Peter 5:8 (ESV)

This was not the only attempt the enemy made to hope to scare me or make me flee away from this country. The next Monday evening, as I was watering the trees in my yard with a bucket of water in my hand, a bat appeared at my feet. It flew in circles right in front of me at the height of my ankles and then went up to my hips. It always flew around in circles, making a circle about 50 centimeters in diameter. It went up to my torso and rose again to be just before my eyes. This flying horror was constantly flying right in front of my face.

I wanted to test if the bat really wanted me or not, so I moved farther. It came to join me immediately and continued the little game of flying in front of my face. I got mad and yelled, "Get out, in the name of Jesus! Out of my sight Satan!" The bat flew over the outside wall of my property and I did not see it anymore. Throughout this little game with the bat, I felt no fear. My trust in the Lord was intense, so this enemy had failed miserably. He will have to realize one day that our God is the strongest and that he will never win.

The next morning, when my wife had just left to go to the market on her motorcycle, I was in the bathroom of our bedroom. Suddenly, a whirlwind appeared forcefully. There was only one problem in all this, the whirlwind was not outside, but it was blowing inside the house - in our own bedroom! My body was shaken severely by the mighty wind. The sheets, the pillows, and our clothes flew around. Even the curtains were raised in the air. I also heard the bedroom door closing violently, producing a powerful slamming sound. The wind calmed down and everything that flew in the air fell back to the ground.

Everything was scattered all over the floor, surprisingly the mattress had been lifted and rested, standing on the wall. I had never seen anything like this. It was really impossible to believe such a thing without seeing it. I would not stop seeing strange things in this new country. I had clearly heard the slamming door close, but when I got out of the bathroom, the door was open, as if nothing had happened.

I put the mattress, the sheets, and the pillow heads in their place, doing some housework to clean this mess.

Afterwards, I kneeled down to ask for the protection of the angels in my bedroom. I did the same thing for each of the house rooms including my son's room. I didn't want to see this kind of evil interruption in my house again. When my wife returned from her errands, I told her everything I had just experienced. She went into the room and looked everywhere to see if anything was missing. She was right to do so, since we had discovered that her night gown had disappeared. She used to leave it on the edge of the bed but it was nowhere to be found. We concluded that the whirlwind had taken her night gown, even though it seemed extremely bizarre.

Later that day, a woman named Diane came to our place to ask for prayer. Her blood pressure was abnormal and she often heard a voice talking to her. This spirit prevented her from going to church on Sunday morning, by grabbing her arm to hold her forcefully. She could not free herself from this grip and was seriously afraid of that spirit. I began to pray for her and the spirit commanded her "Leave this home immediately because he is chasing me out!"

Diane was struggling hard against that force that wanted to scare her away from me. The voice disappeared slowly to make way for an inner peace. She felt so good and she was now smiling. Before she returned home, I asked her to thank the Lord every morning for what he had just done and to read the Word regularly in order to protect herself from the next attempts of these dark spirits. I explained to her that it was very important to keep a good relationship with Jesus because the enemy could try to return at any time. Without this divine relationship, the access door to her body would remain largely open for the return of the one who controlled her before.

"When the unclean spirit has gone out of a person, it passes through waterless places seeking rest, but finds none. Then it says, 'I will return to my house from which I came.' And when it comes, it finds the house empty, swept, and put in order. Then it goes and brings with it seven other spirits more evil than itself, and they enter and dwell there, and the last state of that person is worse than the first. So also will it be with this evil generation."

-Matthew 12:43-45 (ESV)

The next day, Diane came back to thank us again. I replied to her to thank the Lord and not a man. She continued by telling us that she had spent a night of sleep in peace and quiet. She no longer felt any pain caused by her blood pressure problems. She was so happy. We prayed together to give thanks to the Lord for this deliverance and healing on Diane. All glory and honor come to him alone!

It was about 3 o'clock in the afternoon when I heard a voice telling me to go to the Maquis behind my home because a person needed to hear about the Lord. This outdoor drinking establishment was owned by a white man from France, just on the other side of a vacant lot. I had a lot of questions in my mind about this request. Was it really a request from God?

After a few minutes of reflection, I decided not to listen to it and I left with my son to have his bike repaired. As we walked towards the repair trade, a huge whirlwind passed right behind us and quickly headed for the Maquis. It stopped in the courtyard of the Maquis where I was supposed to be, and spilled all the tables and chairs. We could hear the sound of the metal tables that banged with each other. The clients of the Maquis raced outside the courtyard.

I once again thanked the Holy Spirit for telling me the right choice to make. If I had listened to this strange voice, I would probably have been hurt by one of those metal tables. Unfortunately, this was not the only time the enemy had used whirlwinds to attack us. From the next evening, a huge whirlwind appeared in our courtyard. Rosalie started to chase it with authority and it left our court.

We could see that a sparrow hawk had come out of the whirlwind and was now flying round the top of our house. It was definitely a wizard from Manga. They had not yet forgiven our little visit to their beloved city. What was I saying? How can a sorcerer who works with the enemy know how to forgive anything? As long as their heart does not open to the light of the Lord, they will never know how to forgive.

"And even if our gospel is veiled, it is veiled to those who are perishing. In their case the god of this world has blinded the minds of the unbelievers, to keep them from seeing the light of the gospel of the glory of Christ, who is the image of God."

2 Corinthians 4:3-4 (ESV)

On Friday, April 6th, Rosalie had a phone call very early in the morning. A family member informed her that her cousin, Azer, was seriously ill at home. He had a big alcohol problem for years. He could disappear for days drinking alcohol, without eating anything. Unfortunately, he had never accepted the Lord in his life because he did not like the churches, which he believed was only stealing the money of the believers. He always said, "The day I give my life to the Lord, I will be buried a few days later."

Rosalie asked me if we could go to his house and pray. Normally, I did not go to people to pray because we were entering a totally unknown territory. Entering the houses where we do not know what spell or enchantment was made in these places could be extremely dangerous. I preferred that the prayer-seekers come to my house, at home, a place anointed by olive oil, a place of peace in which the protective hand of God was present. A residence where the blood of the lamb covered every square centimeter. But this situation was different from the others because it was the family and that person was not in a position to move. So, I gave my approval and we immediately left with the motorbike.

On site, I asked for more information about Azer from the cousins of Rosalie, who took care of him in a small room. I did not want to go into this room until I could better understand the reason that put him in that situation. One of the cousins told me that he had been missing for several days, as usual.

When they found him, he was so drunk that he couldn't even talk. They brought him to the hospital where the nurses put him on intravenous in order to rehydrate his body but the doctor told them that he could do nothing more for him, only time would decide his

102

fate because his blood alcohol level was far too high.

They brought him home to try to get him back on his feet. Moreover, he had eaten absolutely nothing for more than three days and the only thing he drank was alcoholic beverages. Now, he refused to eat anything and did not even want to drink water. I asked everyone out of the room. I only wanted Rosalie and myself to be with this man. The women went out of the room and when I set foot inside, I felt the nauseating smell of death floating on the ceiling of the room.

There were black flies everywhere, as if he were already dead. He was so skinny that you could easily see every detail of his bones through his skin. His face was sometimes turning from left to right; he was trying to fight the effects of the excess alcohol that was still in his blood. The globe of his eyes seemed to come out of their orbits and his mouth was always open. I could see that he needed all the energy left in his body just to take one breath. I remembered seeing this before.

In 2001, while I was an intern in Burkina Faso, my night watchman Barry had not shown up at my house for a few days. I had inquired of several people who told me that he was seriously ill at home. I then took the big vehicle from the place where I was working and I went to his residence. His wife indicated to me where his room was.

When I opened the door, I felt this same smell of death hovering, those same flies that flew and this man who had the same appearance - skinny, hard breathing, inability to move, etc. I had brought him to the hospital and I had asked the doctor to take good care of this man and I would pay all the expenses and medications for him. After a few days, the doctor told me that I had done well to bring him to the hospital because this man had malaria, as well as severe pneumonia. He would certainly have died if he had remained day one more day.

Azer did not have the same problems in his body and I knew that the hospital could not do anything for him. Only the intercessory prayer could help him, save him and put him back on his feet. We had been praying intensely for him while using the anointing oil as outlined in our wonderful instruction manual on life - the Bible.

"Is anyone among you suffering? Let him pray. Is anyone cheerful? Let him sing praise. Is anyone among you sick? Let him call for the elders of the church, and let them pray over him, anointing him with oil in the name of the Lord. And the prayer of faith will save the one who is sick, and the Lord will raise him up. And if he has committed sins, he will be forgiven."

-James 5:13-15 (ESV)

I asked the Lord to offer him healing and to take him out of his alcoholism problem. At all costs, I wanted this man to return to life in order to repair his relationship with Jesus. He had already been a Christian in the past, but had abandoned his faith following several problems with local churches. He had utterly lost confidence in men, especially the men of God, which had annihilated his faith in the Creator. I knew that the body of Azer was very fragile, so I simply asked the Lord to give him back the thirst and hunger for him to regain strength.

At the end of the prayer, I asked Rosalie to fetch water to drink. She thought it was for me so she gave me the glass. I asked her to put the glass on the lips of Azer because he was very thirsty now. A member of the family came to help by slightly raising the head of Azer and Rosalie approached the glass from his mouth. He began to drink slowly and seemed to ask for more and more. I took his hand and I said, "Thank you brother!" I let Rosalie continue to give him water and I walked out of the room to discuss again with the cousin. I said to her, "Azer is not dead yet. He's fighting right now to survive. After our prayers, he started drinking water and he will eat later today. Give him some soup tonight because his stomach is still very fragile. We'll come back later to pray again for him." She thanked me warmly.

She had tears of joy in her eyes because the hope of seeing him standing was still alive.

In the evening, Rosalie and I went back to get the update on Azer. His cousin greeted us with a big smile because he was eating soup. She told me that he continued to drink water and mango juice. I was very impressed to see that he was also regaining strength. He no longer needed help to sit up and slowly began to speak again. His words were still mere whispering, but we felt that he was already a lot better and that he was on his way to healing. We prayed again for his complete healing while thanking the Lord for his incredible gesture.

Rosalie sat at his side and began to talk to him seriously about Jesus, the way, the truth and the life. When she asked if he wanted to give his life to Jesus, he answered weakly, "Yes". So, she asked him to pray the prayer of repentance with her. She started and he was listening to her because he still had trouble talking.

In the end, he pushed out weak "Amen" to say that he had sincerely repented with all his heart. We were all happy by this great miraculous conversion.

We continued to thank the Lord, and then a woman approached and talked with Rosalie. I did not know this person and I wondered what it was about, especially as the person pointed various directions with her hands, as if to indicate a road to take or a place to go.

I was still with Azer when Rosalie came to see me and explained to me that the son of this unknown woman had been at the clinic for several hours. He suffered strange stomach pains and the doctor could not explain the cause of the discomfort. This woman asked if we could go with her and pray for her son. After seeing the saddened face of this mother, I agreed to go. I said goodbye to Azer and said, "Don't let go my brother, you're on the road to healing. Jesus loves You! "

The small clinic was located near the Church of the International Center of Evangelization of Dedougou. There were already several people in the small room and a 16-year-old man was sitting on a stretcher along the wall.

Without disturbing the foreigners who were in the same room, I started asking a few questions to this young man named Fabrice. He told me that this was not the first time he had stomach pains but this time he thought he was going to die because the pain was intense.

He did not remember how these ailments started and cannot tell me what provoked them. Even doctors cannot explain it, because they see absolutely nothing physically wrong. I said, "This is normal since it is not physical, but spiritual." So, I began to pray for his healing and to chase away any unclean spirit that could have caused these stomach aches. At the end of the prayer, I said, "The Lord has just healed you and you will have a splendid night. From tomorrow morning, you will have to thank the Lord for what he has done. You'll have to do it every day."

His mother interrupted me to tell me that she had just received a phone call from their village. Fabrice's little sister had just fallen ill, as well. She had exactly the same symptoms as her big brother. I liked praying better for someone I could lay hands on, but there was nothing impossible for the Lord. If he wanted to heal a person, he could do it anywhere and anytime. Think of the Roman centurion who came to ask for healing for his servant. He knew that Jesus could do it without even moving from under his roof.

"But the centurion replied: Lord, I am not worthy to have you come under my roof, but only say the word, and my servant will be healed. For I too am a man under authority, with soldiers under me. And I say to one: Go, and he goes, and to another: Come, and he comes, and to my servant: Do this, and he does it."

-Matthew 8:8-9 (ESV)

"And to the centurion Jesus said: Go; let it be done for you as you have believed. And the servant was healed at that very moment."

-Matthew 8:13 (ESV)

So, I agreed to pray for the healing of the little girl who was in the village. I felt in my heart that this was exactly what the Lord wanted me to do.

Then I looked at the mother and told her that the girl was already cured. She was smiling and saying thank you very much. As I said for all the people who thanked me, "Do not thank me but thank the Lord. I am only his tool; he is the one who cures." Jesus was the Carpenter and I was only his working tool.

On Saturday, Rosalie got a call on her cell phone. Her cousin was in tears and informed us that Azer was not feeling well. Everyone thought he was going to die very soon. I got up by rejecting this negative statement and we left urgently on the motorbike. When we arrived at his home, there were women who were already crying, and then I saw that men were cleaning up the body of Azer because he had just died. I shouted, "No, no, no! Lord You can't take him, not after you started healing him!" I began to pray intensely so that life could reintegrate into his body. I also asked Rosalie to call Roland and David to come as soon as possible to intercede for this man.

A few minutes later, the men laid the body of Azer on the bed, taking good care to put a sheet over the body. Women came to cry next to the bed. I still started praying by walking in a relentless and stubborn step. David and Roland arrived almost at the same time and I quickly explained the situation to them. We all began our intercession in favor of the return to the life of this man who had just accepted the Lord. I was so enraged by all this that I prayed asking God to bring him back. "A father cannot do this to his children, I said!"

Then I heard the voice of God, who replied, "It was now or never! Otherwise, he would have returned to his old life." I denied this answer because I stubbornly wanted the opposite. I wanted to get him back to life immediately. After a few minutes, I let out a big sigh and then tears fell on my cheeks. I looked at David and Roland

and asked them to forgive me for what I had just done. I admitted that I had just put my flesh before the spirit.

God had just confessed to me that he had to take him; otherwise, he would still embrace his old life, by sinking into sin and denying God again. The Lord had just taken him before he returned to the fire of Hell. I had just received confirmation that it was presently in the hands of God, but my flesh pushed me to fight this decision of the Creator.

Yet, it was the best that could happen to him. I came over to the deceased's family and I asked them to forgive me also for giving them false hope.

Rosalie's cousin came forward and told me that there was nothing to forgive because, thanks to our intervention, he had begun to heal, thanks to our intervention; he had left us in the direction of heaven instead of going to hell. She thanked me for everything while hugging me. I was so ashamed of what I had done to this family. I had acted by my own strength and will, instead of asking what the will of my heavenly Father was. David and Roland left after long goodbyes.

As I walked away from the body of Azer, a woman approached me. It was Fabrice's mother, the 16-year-old who had stomach aches. She thanked me for her son and daughter. "The clinic released my son," she said. "He had no more pain after your prayers. And the villagers called me to tell me that my daughter was also cured without taking any medication."

"It is not me that must be thanked, but it is the Lord." I said.

"I know, but the healing came after your intercession. The intercessors ask for healing and the Lord answers them afterwards. So, thanks to you." she said.

This answer seemed trivial, but it was powerful. This woman had just fortified me with this simple answer. I felt very useful for the advancement of the Kingdom of God in this beautiful country. Since the first days of my Christian life I have wanted only one thing - to serve the Lord. I was doing it and I do not even enjoy it. I did not realize how much the Lord was propagating happiness and joy through me. Thank you, Jesus!

On Sunday morning we went to the same church as we did since we arrived in Dedougou. The praises took place in joy. The pastor would soon be on the stage to come and make his message and then Roland came to fetch me for another prayer of deliverance.

He explained to me vaguely this new case of possession but he spoke so fast while walking, that I had not heard anything except a few words… "She runs away… barefoot… hits her head…" I thought we'd go to the pastor's office, but I was wrong.

Outside, near the big empty land, there was a man who having trouble holding a young girl. She struggled so forcefully, that the man was being shaken in every way. I approached and looked at her directly in her eyes. She always closed her eyes so she wouldn't look at me. I ordered the man to let go. She stood there standing, fixed to the ground, then, without warning, she began to run barefoot on the sand and stone of the large vacant lot.

We all ran after her, but she was so fast. She stopped suddenly and bent over to pick up a big stone. Roland yelled, "Quick! She's going to hit her head again!" She hit her head a first time and then we managed to grab her. There were three of us holding her. Despite her young age and small size, she was able to shake us vigorously, to the point that we could lose our footing at any time.

She was pulling, pushing, shaking in every direction to free herself. We escorted her to the pastor's office. Sitting on the ground, she was looking everywhere for a new weapon to hit her head. She tried to use the few metal chairs that were there. After pulling them out, she tried to hit her head against the walls or the concrete floor. We always had to put our hand between her head and the wall. She shook her head so hard, that we felt intense pain on our hands.

I remember saying to myself, "But what is that spirit? Will I be able to chase it out?" I had never faced a power like that, but I was not going to let the doubt invade me or I was sure to fail. This young woman was in dire need of the Lord's help. She was maybe between 13 or 15 years. We had to intervene for she was too young to live imprisoned by an unclean spirit.

I had noticed that she had hundreds of cut and burn scars on her arms and legs. So, it was a spirit of self-mutilation that sought only one thing - to make her suffer as much as possible. She often yelled, "Let me go! Go away!"

I started asking a few questions to find out who was in her. "What's your name?" The demon replied, "Justin". I knew very well that it was not his real name because he is unable to tell the truth. So, I asked him, "Why are you trying to kill her?"

"Because she belongs to me and I can do what I want with her body." said the spirit in her.

"She does not belong to you, you stole her life! You're a thief."

"No, she let me in herself."

"Why are you trying to kill her then?" I asked him.

"Because I want her to come with me."

"Where do you plan to go?" I demanded.

He no longer answered my questions but laughed and screamed with a very scary voice. This spirit was so evil that I was wondering if it was not Satan himself. Since he no longer wanted to speak, I started praying to chase him away, but he resisted forcefully. He laughed at every action I tried and said, "It's not like that." or "You missed your shot." or "You tried hard, but you failed again". Roland also prayed with authority at my side, but nothing seemed to work against this power of darkness. It was firmly anchored in her.

After an hour of fighting, Roland went outside to continue his work in the church. In my opinion, Roland was surely completely exhausted from this fight. I was alone with this demon but I was not afraid of him. I wanted to win at all costs because we are more than victorious with Jesus. I sat in front of her and looked her in the eye. It was still laughing at me, trying to raise the hatred in my heart.

I already knew this strategy of the enemy - he was always looking to insult or mock any kind of way to put more anger in us. Once filled with this anger, our faith weakened and he could control us in the same way that he manipulated his host. I wouldn't fall for his game.

She began to undress but I stopped her every time she tried. I also knew that strategy. He wanted to get the girl completely naked when I was alone with her and then accuse me of various acts of a sexual nature against this teenager girl. Imagine if somebody arrives and sees the girl completely naked in front of me struggling while I hold her by the arms. This person would never think that I was in the process of executing a deliverance but would believe that I was trying to rape her. I continually had to stop her from taking her clothes off. I was really looking forward to Roland coming back to help me in this fight.

"Free her!" I ordered him again.

"No."

"I order you to release her!"

"And go where?"

"To your place - Hell!"

He laughed even harder to insult me. So, I said to him, "You remember Legion. Jesus sent him into pigs, who then went and drowned in the water. What a shame! Legion in pigs. That's where you're going to end up too!"

"Legion was weak. I'm much stronger than him."

"So that's what we'll see!" I said.

I got up and started interceding with authority to drive him out of this young body. It had been almost three hours since I prayed and interceded for her deliverance but nothing worked.

I had the impression that I lacked an important detail to scare him away. Which one?

I had already tried with authority and speaking boldly, as the Bible said. I couldn't understand. What was I missing to be able to help this girl?

The worship being finished, pastor Tiken passed by her to go back to his office and she tried to grab his leg but I had prevented her. A few minutes later, the pastor's wife also passed by the possessed, who then tried to grab her leg. The pastor's wife, having seen her do so, shouted to her, "I command you to cease this in the name of Jesus!" Then Roland came back and I asked him to take my place because I had to retire a little to ask the Lord how to deliver her.

I heard a voice say, "With Love". I got it! I had to show the love of our Lord and not the authority. I asked Roland what her name was. He said, "Rita". So, I approached her, I raised her so that she was standing in front of me and I hugged her. The demon hit my back and screamed because it didn't want me to hold her. Roland also begged me not to do it because he feared that it would try to bite me in the neck, but I had full confidence in Jesus. After all, it was the Lord who had told me to show her his love.

The enemy in her did not like this, he cried, instead of laughing at us. I looked at the girl and I said, "Rita, you can beat him. You have the strength and the capacity." The bad spirit was struggling more and was hitting me. I continued by showing her the love of Jesus for her. "Jesus loves you; he does not want to lose you Rita. He died on the cross for you. He said, "I am the way, the truth and the life. No one comes to the Father except through him." He's here with us, and he cries for you with compassion. He's waiting for you, Rita. Come and meet him."

The spirit howled loudly and then left Rita's body. We sat her on a chair and asked for her name. A little trembling voice echoed, "Rita". We had just released her after more than three and a half hours of hard work. I asked Roland to accompany her home on a motorbike because I did not want her to go alone on her own by bike.

Most people had already left the church. Before she left, I ordered Rita to thank the Lord every morning for what he had just done on her. She still seemed to be lost, without understanding what had happened to her. Roland left with her.

I was very happy that the Lord had shown me how to help her. The fatigue had overwhelmed me so much that I sat on a chair to regain strength before returning home.

Roland called me on my cell phone and said, "When I got her home, there was no one, so I waited with Rita for precaution. Moments later, the spirit came back into her and she was still trying to hit herself with a stone. I managed to calm her down a little by prayer but we will have to start again the deliverance on her." How is that possible? But she was well delivered few minutes before when she was in front of me. There must be another problem that we did not detect during the deliverance. We were so preoccupied by this deliverance, that we certainly missed a very important detail.

So, I asked Roland to do everything he could to make Rita come for deliverance Thursday morning. I wanted to understand what could cause such an easy return of the evil spirit in Rita's body, and especially in such a short time. God would help me to better understand this situation to be more successful against this kind of spiritual intruder next time.

The primary purpose of our presence, in addition to acting for the advancement of the Kingdom of God, was to build a center for helping the widows in the Province of Mouhoun. To do this, we would use the land that Rosalie had already bought, but we had no official document showing that this land was really ours. We had to quickly ask for the land title so that no one would attempt to steal this land from us.

On Monday morning we went to the Town Hall of Dedougou with all the required documents. We were informed that this document should not be done at the Town Hall, but rather at the tax department located not far from the Town Hall on the road to Bobo-Dioulasso. We went there and a very welcoming man told us to sit in front of his desk. He took the application file for the land title and looked at each page. I was wondering if I had completed the whole thing correctly.

The man looked up and told me that everything seemed perfect and that he would call me back when everything's ready.

Rosalie reminded him that it was God's work, while I informed him of the importance of obtaining this document before the end of April, in order to have a chance to get the project funded by any organization. He replied that this kind of request only takes a few days. We thanked him and returned home.

It was already night for over an hour, when my cell phone rang. I did not know this number and, when I took the call, I did not recognize the voice of the person that spoke. He presented himself as a brother in Christ who goes to the same church as us. His cousin was six months pregnant but she had severe pain in her belly. They were currently in the hospital and he was afraid it would be very serious. He would like us to join him in order to pray for his cousin's healing.

I looked at Rosalie and then immediately left on the motorbike in the direction of the General Hospital of Dedougou. When I was riding on the bike, the same word kept coming to my head, "Preeclampsia!" In front of the access door to the maternity department, two men were praying. One of them, seeing us, approached and presented himself as the one who had called us. He told me that the doctors claimed that her cousin had fibroids in her womb that caused the pain in her belly. They had given her painkillers for the pain to calm down and were going to release her in a few minutes. I replied to the brother that the doctors were in error because she had a preeclampsia. "What is this?" he asked.

"Preeclampsia is a serious disease that may, in several cases, cause the death of the mother or child. A caesarean section is often necessary to stop the pain of the Preeclampsia."

"It's impossible!" shouted the brother. The doctors said it was fibroids, so it is fibroids. Moreover, she is a Christian, so she cannot have such a disease.

I felt that he was really angry with my answer and he doubted that word came from God himself.

I did not insist and we began to pray for the healing of his cousin and for the protection of his child. The doctor accompanied the pregnant woman outside the walls of the maternity ward while we were still praying. The brother introduced us to his cousin and we talked a little bit with her. We could easily see that she was still under the effect of painkillers. When the other brother had left the place, the one who had called us for prayer said to me, "You were right. I beg your pardon for doubting. The doctors confirmed that she has preeclampsia."

"I do not blame you at all my brother. It was not me who was right, it was God."

We said goodbye and left in different directions. At night, before I went to bed, I prayed for this pregnant woman because I knew that the preeclampsia could also be very dangerous either for the mother or for the child.

The next day, Tuesday April 10, 2018, Pastor Tiken called me early in the morning to ask me if I would come to deliverance prayers at the church, because there was one person he would like me to take care of personally. I was just getting ready to go to church so I said I'd be there in just a few minutes.

That morning we had moved the deliverance inside the church and not in front of the pastor's office because there were too many people. The pastor came to see me and introduced me to a pretty young woman named Sandrine and asked me to take care of her case. I asked this young woman to sit down and I settled on the chair in front of her. Two older women accompanied her. I presumed it was Sandrine's mother and aunt.

When I do a deliverance, I always looked closely at the person in the eyes, to detect a nervous tic, an uncontrollable facial reaction, or any sign of spiritual possession. In the case of Sandrine, there was the fact that she did not like to be looked at directly - her eyes always looked everywhere, except at me.

She demonstrated an expression of emotional depression that she had for several years. When I asked her for her name, one of the other two women replied on her behalf.

I didn't appreciate this gesture, so I asked them not to respond for her. "What is your age?" She let out a huge sigh and her gaze turned to the left. I could clearly see that she was ashamed of something. Probably an old story from her past that she couldn't forgive herself. "Why are you here this morning?" She looked down at the ground without saying anything. I could not get anything with her, so I asked Sandrine's mother to give me some clues about her.

She informed me that several years ago, her 24-year-old daughter had returned one evening with this expression on her face for no known reason.

This expression of sadness hadn't left her since. She never managed to find out what had caused all this sadness in her. So, I decided to try to make her laugh a little. "What, can I say to Sandrine? A young woman as pretty as you should not be sad. All men must look at you when they walk near you. The other women must be jealous of you." Contrary to my expectations, she did not smile at all. She simply shook her head from left to right, while clenching her lips to show me, that it was foolish to have said such a thing. "So, you don't love yourself. Is that it?" No reaction, except a small normal blink of the eyelids.

I took Sandrine by the arm and asked her to follow me outside. She got up and we went away from the looks of the two women who accompanied her. Outside, I asked her to look at the landscape in the distance.

We could see houses, families, and children playing in the streets. "You see all these people? They are all God's creation, just like you. They were created to have a life and a family. You, too, have been created to have a life, to marry and to have children." She had no reaction, but just looked away.

So, I continued, "Would you like to get married someday?" She shook her head again to tell me that her answer was no.

I put a hand on her shoulder and I said, "Sandrine, a lot of people worry about you. It is a proof that they love you all. Jesus also loves you and does not want you to end up in this sadness or depression. Help me to help you. I need to know what happened. Trust me; I won't talk to anyone about this."

She shook her head again, so we returned inside the church, since all the others had already left. I made a prayer for her, even though I could not find the reason for her despair. I asked the mother to bring her again to the deliverance so that I would continue to work with her.

In the evening, at home, Prosper arrived on his bike for his night's work as the keeper of our house. He had attended some of the prayers we had made for visitors and had been touched. He said, "I used to always have nightmares, but since I've been working here, I've been sleeping very well, without any bad dreams." I was very happy to hear another proof that God was working with us and our entourage.

Suddenly we received a call from a brother in Christ, to tell us that he had a Samsung S8 cell phone he wanted to give as a gift, to a man of God, who needed it badly. He asked to remain anonymous.

He came to our home to give us the phone, repeating that he wanted to remain anonymous. When he left, Rosalie and I thought of the same person - young Pastor David. This man served the Lord practically 24 hours a day and never asked for anything in return. He was in the Ministry of Deliverance with me, in the Ministry of Evangelization with Rosalie, servant at the main church during evening prayers and pastor in a small church of a remote village every Sunday morning. His bike was so old and worn out that it could break down at any time. His phone was also very worn out and was beginning to have communication and display problems.

He barely had the money to put gas in his old bike to go preach to the church and to feed himself away from home. He never complained because he gave his full trust in God.

He was so in love with the Lord. I thought it was a little crazy to take this old bike for such a long ride to the middle of nowhere but he always said, "The people of this village also need to hear the Word of God."

"We are fools for Christ's sake..."
-1 Corinthians 4:10 (ESV)

We called him and asked to come and join us at home. He arrived several minutes later on his old motorcycle. He shook hands and then sat down on a chair. We told him the story of this generous anonymous donor who wanted to give a phone to a man of God in need. Without knowing that we had thought of him, David started to think of someone to give it to. We were both amazed by this gesture. He always put the happiness of others before his own.

"No David," I replied, "Rosalie and I had thought of giving it to you!" His face changed immediately, he was surprised to receive such a gift. He, who never asked for anything and never complained to anyone. I gave him the box and he opened it carefully. He wanted to savor very moment of this incredible event. He took the phone in his hand and looked at it for several minutes, without turning it on to try it.

I started to laugh a little and then I showed him how to turn it on. He asked me if I could install the Bible and some apps on the phone. "Of course, I replied!" The phone had been reset to factory settings so I reinstalled everything according to his desires to make it as simple as possible for him. He was not accustomed to an "Android" model. His old phone was an old model to call and receive calls, enter contacts and use text messages only. He left home very happy. I thank the brother in Christ who, through the gift of this smart phone, allowed us to live this memorable moment with Pastor David. God give you to the hundredfold, my brother!

"One gives freely yet grows all the richer; another withholds what he should give, and only suffers want."
-Proverb 11:24 (ESV)

Rosalie and I decided to take a day off on this beautiful Wednesday morning.

Everything was peaceful until the evening when I received a phone call from the Christian Brother whose cousin was six months pregnant. He informed us that she had just entered the hospital urgently for intense stomach pain. Without further delay, we rode on the bike and left for the maternity ward. The brother was waiting for us outside and seemed a little nervous. He informed us that his cousin had such strong pain, that he was afraid for the baby's life.

A man was by his side, he introduced him to us as his cousin's husband. We shook his hand and then we all started praying for the woman and her baby. During the prayer, I heard a voice that said, "She is not sincere in her faith, her faith is very weak. She's hiding a Quran in her house. She's hiding a Quran. If she does not repent, she will have to choose between herself and her child." The voice was so powerful that I had no doubt about the source of this revelation.

I approached the brother in Christ, to tell him everything I had just heard. He suddenly became furious to the point that he no longer spoke to me for the rest of the evening. If he wanted to tell me something, he would pass by my wife because he couldn't look at me. I found all this so childish but - "There are Christians and then there are Christians". It was an expression I said regularly, meaning that there are Christians filled with the fire of the Holy Spirit but, unfortunately, there are also those who call themselves Christians but have no relationship with Jesus. To better understand, we must read the parable of the 10 virgins.

"Then the kingdom of heaven will be like ten virgins who took their lamps and went to meet the bridegroom. Five of them were foolish, and five were wise. For when the foolish took their lamps, they took no oil with them, but the wise took flasks of oil with their lamps. As the bridegroom was delayed, they all became drowsy and slept. But at midnight there was a cry: Here is the bridegroom! Come out to meet him. Then all those virgins rose and trimmed their lamps. And the foolish said to the wise: Give us some of your oil, for our lamps are going out. But the wise answered, saying: Since there will not be enough for us and for you, go rather to the dealers and buy for yourselves. And while they were going to buy, the bridegroom came, and those who were ready went in with him to the marriage feast, and the door was shut. Afterward the other virgins came also, saying: Lord, lord, open to us. But he answered: Truly, I say to you, I do not know you. Watch therefore, for you know neither the day nor the hour."

-Matthew 25:1-13 (ESV)

The five wise virgins are the Christians filled with the Holy Spirit and the five foolish are those who call themselves Christians but have no personal relationship with the Lord Jesus.

When the doctors released the pregnant woman after having given her painkillers again, the husband, brother, and cousin left immediately after bowing to Rosalie, and only Rosalie. He did not want to say goodbye to me.

They were like children who had just quarreled - "You are no longer my friend!" I laughed at this very childish situation while returning home.

The story does not end there, the next morning, the Christian Brother called my wife to tell her all the progress of their return home. He said, "When we arrived at my cousin's house, we asked her if she was hiding a Quran in her room. She entered her room and then came out with a Quran, a prayer mat and a book of Muslim prayers. I picked it up and burned it all up. I told her that God required her to repent otherwise she should choose between her life and that of her baby. My cousin repented immediately weeping. Really, your husband was right again." After Rosalie told me everything and I gave her a sign of both hands that meant, "I told you so!"

Here is a serious problem among Christians today - they do not believe anything! When God had called us to leave everything to serve him in West Africa, we blindly obeyed him with full confidence. Our brothers and sisters in Christ, as well as the pastors, have all tried to convince us not to leave. Some said that it was not the voice of God; others said that we do not have the money to do it, others have called us demons, and many have denied us forever.

I have only one answer to all these Christians - "Christians nowadays are jealous of each other".

"But when the Jews saw the crowds, they were filled with jealousy and began to contradict what was spoken by Paul, reviling him."

-Acts 13:45 (ESV)

Imagine if Paul, the great evangelist, formerly named Saul, who responded positively to God's call to go to the Gentiles, had worried about the financial problems associated with such missionary trips? The practically insurmountable trials for the common mortals, rejections from everywhere, the many days of despair spent in the infected prisons and the daily dangers and risks to his own life? The people he met, did not believe that Jesus had turned him into a great evangelist.

"And when he had come to Jerusalem, he attempted to join the disciples. And they were all afraid of him, for they did not believe that he was a disciple."

-Acts 9:26 (ESV)

He still took his courage with both hands and left the comfort and security of his personal home. He had gone walking with a blind trust that God would be able to meet all his needs. After all, it was the heavenly Father who had sent him and a father always takes care of his children.

"For so the Lord has commanded us, saying: I have made you a light for the Gentiles, that you may bring salvation to the ends of the earth."

-Acts 13:47 (ESV)

"Do not be anxious about anything, but in everything by prayer and supplication with thanksgiving let your requests be made known to God. And my God will supply every need of yours according to his riches in glory in Christ Jesus."

-Philippians 4:6, 19 (ESV)

For my part, I could not blame the brother because to be honest, I would probably have had the same reaction. But, I thank the Lord for showing him how much he was present for the people of Burkina Faso.

Rita, the 15-year-old who ran barefoot on the empty land and who was hitting her head with a stone came to visit us. She still wore a sad, depressed face.

We discussed a little of her past in order to find out what could cause this kind of possession, which door had been opened to give access to the evil spirit in her body. Rita hesitated very much to tell us everything because she seemed to be very ashamed. She felt responsible for what was happening to her and agreed to live with this intruder in her body.

What she probably did not know was that one day, this intruder was going to kill her and drive her with him to Hell. He already forced her to cut off the skin on her arms and legs whenever she had access to a blade. After several minutes, she finally decided to tell us everything.

She was born in a remote village and her parents had never loved her. They insulted her, abused her, and beat her for everything and for nothing. The worst is that they denigrated her every day with words that destroyed the little love she had left. Words like:

"You are not good; you will never succeed in life."

"You are not beautiful so no one will want to marry you."

"We'd rather you died because we could have another child to replace you."

"You have no value in our eyes."

"No one loves you."

With this kind of negative speech drilled into her daily, Rita began to believe what her parents were telling her. Language can be a dangerous weapon. Language can worship, praise, and propagate love but it can also destroy, annihilate, and even kill a fragile person. Rita began to think that everyone hated her, so she sank into loneliness and had no hope for her future on this earth. She often cried alone in her room, being careful not to make too much noise, to arouse the wrath of her parents by her cries.

Having no one to explain her emotions and to free her heart, she had invented an imaginary friend. Unlike the human beings who abused her, this invisible being was always present at her side and listened to her without mocking her, denigrating her or denying her. Over the years this imaginary friend was taking more and more place in her life.

This friend began to be wicked and to force little Rita to do things she did not like. Her friend had now become a dangerous enemy, a demon. Without ever realizing it, Rita herself opened the door of her body to this demon.

Now, with years of playing with this little girl to earn her full trust, he could do whatever he wanted with her. She had become a slave, chained to this lying friend.

"And no wonder, for even Satan disguises himself as an angel of light."
-2 Corinthians 11:14 (ESV)

Her aunt, who sometimes visited Rita's family, noticed that the little one had scars on her body and that she always showed a sad face. Some days, tears were still on her cheeks.

Being a mother herself, she had the feminine ability to detect any emotional problems in a child. Since nothing was going on in this family, she asked if Rita could come and spend the holidays with her. After some discussions, Rita's parents agreed to let her go for a week. The girl packed her bags and left with her aunt, whom she scarcely knew.

During the whole trip, no words came out of her mouth. She seemed very far in her thoughts. When she arrived at her aunt's house, Rita noticed that her young cousin welcomed her, as if she were part of the family. He often sat next to her to chat, listen, and laugh together. Rita had never felt that kind of emotion in her body. The joy filled her and her heart had to start beating again. Even the demonic friend seemed to have fled the scene. She loved her little cousin because he cared for her, as if he knew how to treat her mentally.

But this happiness was short lived because she had to go back to the family home where her parents were waiting for her. Rita began to cry and beg her aunt to keep her. The woman asked the girl to tell the whole truth about what was going on at home. She couldn't believe what she was hearing. How could I believe such horrible things were happening in the family?

She had to bring Rita back to her parents; to keep her longer at home could bring her problems at the legal level. So, they left in the direction of the village.

Throughout the journey, Rita cried and begged her aunt whose heart was now completely demolished by her niece's pain. Before leaving the vehicle, the woman said, "Rita, I'm going to do everything I can to get you out of this house to live with me." Rita looked at her and doubted this promise since she had so many false promises in her past. She no longer trusted the word of others. Her aunt was torn seeing how her niece was emotionally affected. She left Rita to her parents and went back to her own home, thinking about this whole story. Something inside her was telling her to go back and take Rita out of her parents' clutches but she was not allowed to do it. She was tormented.

The next day, the aunt's phone rang. It was Rita who was on the other end of the line and she was crying to the point that she was barely able to formulate a complete sentence. Her aunt said, "Rita, calm down, please."

"Come and pick me up!" she screamed with such a terrifying voice, "They're going to kill me! I'm scared!"

On hearing this, the woman's heart stopped because of the

shivering caused by this plea from her little niece. Nevertheless, she found the strength to answer, "What are you talking about, Rita?" Rita's second response gave even more shivers because of the tone of her voice - "Please, come quickly! I'm scared." It did not take any more for her aunt to jump aboard her car and drive to the village to understand the reason for this disturbing call.

When she arrived at the destination, the woman entered and asked the parents for explanations. They denied everything and refused to answer several questions about certain scars on Rita's body. The woman saw that they were lying, since they sometimes showed smug smiles that showed that they were mocking her.

The woman became angry at them and told them that she would not leave this house without Rita and that, if they prevented her, she would call the police and tell them everything, without sparing any details.

The mocking smiles gave way to a hatred towards this woman who came to threaten them under their own roof. The aunt turned to her niece and said, "Go pack your bags because you're leaving with me." Despite the tears in her eyes, Rita ran into her bedroom to take as many clothes as possible. She did not want to go back to this house with this family that denigrated her, insulted her, beat her, and forced her to work incessantly.

She felt that she could finally live a life as a young teenager, like all others. When the two women left in the car, Rita burst into tears again. The emotions had to come out. Her aunt comforted her by saying, "Don't worry. You'll be safe in my house." What her aunt did not know was that the demon was always present in Rita's body and was quietly waiting for the right moment to manifest itself.

Everything was going well in her new family. Rita was happy, but when she was alone at home, the demon manifested.

The evil being made her take a knife and she began to cut her arms and legs. When the rest of the family returned home, they saw Rita standing in the kitchen with the bloody knife. There was blood all over Rita's body. She cried and said, "Help me! Help me!" Her aunt took care of her because, being a Christian, she knew that it was a demonic spirit that had done this and not the fragile little girl. The spirit was becoming more and more violent, so that Rita was not to be left unattended.

She cut her skin with any objects she could get her hands on and hit her head with stones or other solid objects until she bleed. The family did not know what to do then her aunt brought her to the church to ask for the prayer of deliverance.

The elders and several intercessors prayed several times for her deliverance but nothing worked. Her aunt began to lose hope when the Lord put me in her path. After several hours of intense prayers, the demon was chased, but he returned to Rita's body as soon as she arrived at her aunt's home.

Gathering all the details, I managed to have following conversation with the young Rita and her aunt.

By telling us about her past, we could see all the emotions that Rita had kept in her heart for years. Crying in front of us, tears were beginning to flow from my eyes after listening to her story. A little girl so fragile who carried all this misfortune on her shoulders, it was too heavy for her. She had to leave all that weight in the hands of Jesus.

"Come to me, all who labor and are heavy laden, and I will give you rest."
-Matthew 11:28 (ESV)

It was now time for Rita to get rid of this burden forever and begin to live her new life with Christ. God had just shown me how she would win her fight against that vicious old friend who was still in her. I looked Rita in the eye and said, "You have to forgive your parents for all the hardship they've done to you. If you don't forgive them, you'll never be free of that spirit. The hatred that is in you, gives access to the spirit to stay in you. You can hunt him yourself, you have the strength to do it, but you must forgive your parents absolutely."

"It is too hard." she replied, all hopeless.

"I know it is hard, but it is the only solution to free you completely from this enemy that prevents you from living normally. Don't keep that anger in you."

She began to cry again. I felt that she already knew that it was the only possible solution but she still refused to do so. If she overcame such an obstacle, she would finally be free from this cruel spirit.

"For if you forgive others their trespasses, your heavenly Father will also forgive you, but if you do not forgive others their trespasses, neither will your Father forgive your trespasses."

-Matthew 6:14-15(ESV)

"Be angry and do not sin; do not let the sun go down on your anger and give no opportunity to the devil."

-Ephesians 4:26-27 (ESV)

Rita left my home slowly, under the weight of this new ordeal that stood before her. She had to do it and I knew she would do it, since the Lord loves her and will help her to flatten all the mountains that would be in her way.

In the evening, the prayer group of Rosalie's Ministry of Evangelization came to our house to intercede on several different subjects. The greatest subject of prayer that evening was a powerful intercession for the inhabitants of Safané and for the Pastor David who travelled every week to this village to bring the Word of God. During the prayer, Roland was experiencing discomfort and was forced to sit on a chair. I noticed he was really not feeling well. He had the symptoms of malaria or extreme fatigue. He was about to fall asleep on the chair, when I got behind him and prayed for his healing.

I put my hand on his head and asked that his body be immediately filled with energy and that all discomfort and fatigue be removed. As soon as I withdrew my hand, he suddenly rose up and began to pray intensely while walking fast in every way.

He pleaded now with power, pushed by the Holy Spirit. Roland himself confessed that he felt a force filling him when I prayed for him. As soon as my hand left his head, something made him stand up and he lost control of his body. The Holy Spirit had filled him to the point that he was overflowing with energy. The whole team noticed the way that he had risen from his chair - there was nothing human in this movement, it was spiritual, it was the Holy Spirit. We had felt the fire spread in each of us.

The daughter of our sister Suzanne, a lover of the Lord, was to be married in Koudougou and my wife wanted to help organize this special event. So, I dropped Rosalie off at our sister's business, but when I saw Suzanne's condition, I knew I couldn't leave until I prayed for her. She was so totally overwhelmed by the organization of the marriage that she had neglected her own health. Accumulated fatigue and exhaustion showed on her face. She said she didn't have the strength to get up from her chair.

I knew Suzanne since my first trip to Burkina in 2001. I had taught computer science to one of her daughters. She was always happy and had a joy of living that could make even the most desperate people in the world smile. I couldn't believe she could be so devastated by exhaustion. I started praying for her. I have asked that the Lord give her all the energy she will need for this marriage in the mighty name of Jesus Christ. After saying "Amen" she looked at me with a smile and thanked me. She already felt that the energy was slowly coming back into her body.

I told her that the Lord knows how much she loves him and that he will accompany her in any ordeal. She gave me another smile and then I returned home after wishing a good trip to my wife.

On Saturday morning, Emmanuel and I had to take the bus reserved for the wedding of Suzanne's daughter. We had been to the bus stop very early because the bus for Koudougou was quickly filled with brothers and sisters in Christ. The trip was really pleasant as the passengers were constantly singing Christian songs in their local language. I could not sing with them because I did not speak their language but the melody of the voices was beautiful to the ears.

When we arrived in Koudougou, everyone was amazed by the grandeur of the wedding. The ceremony took place inside the immense Church of God Assembly in the heart of the city. There were even choreographies planned for the entrance of the bride and groom. Everything was wonderful. Afterwards, we all left on the buses to enjoy a meal in a large outdoor restaurant. There were a lot of people.

The whole thing ended at the private house, where another meal was warmly served to us. At the end of the day, the buses brought us back to Dedougou. We were all completely exhausted but filled with incredible memories.

Our sister Suzanne had taken up this challenge with great vigor and had never shown any sign of fatigue. She surprised everyone by the greatness of this marriage. Congratulations to this great lady who loves the Lord!

After receiving a new message from God revealed by Pastor Tiken on this beautiful Sunday morning, we came back home to enjoy a good meal and take a little rest because we still felt the fatigue of this long day spent in Koudougou. I never had an afternoon nap, but exhaustion forced me to rest to regain strength.

In the evening, two women came to visit us and asked for prayer. The first, named Fatoumata was a former Muslim woman newly converted to the Lord, who continued to see shadows around her. She told us that her father worked a lot with the marabouts

(African sorcerers). He liked to be surrounded by these satanic people. We prayed for her first and then she collapsed to the ground under the power of the Holy Spirit. I said, "The shadows have fled and you won't see them again. You are now free and you will spend a wonderful night under the protective hand of our Lord Jesus."

I turned to the second woman and she explained her problem to me. Several years ago, she had made a pact with a marabout. He had given her an object, a kind of fetish (satanically charged object), which she had to bury herself. She had done it without thinking and now she does not remember where she had buried it. It was therefore impossible to break this evil object which bound her to this marabout.

I began to pray for her, and as soon as my hand touched her head, she fell to the ground screaming inaudible sounds. When I asked her name, she replied, "Muhammad." I knew that the spirit in her was trying to provoke the first woman, since she was a converted Muslim. I told Fatoumata not to listen to her because the demonic spirits are all very cunning liars.

I continued the deliverance until she opened her eyes. I asked her name again, and this time she answered the truth, so I knew the spirit had left her.

We helped her up and I strongly recommended the two women to thank the Lord every morning for what he had done for them and to take time to meditate on the Word, in order to have a nice intimate relationship with Jesus. They accepted and left the place as free women.

All these prayers of deliverance began to exhaust me completely. I felt drained of my energy and even had trouble getting out of bed in the morning. So, I decided to take at least one day off to regain physical, mental, and spiritual forces. After all, God had also rested on the seventh day of the creation of earthly humanity. Even after a beautiful day of rest, I had no doubt that the next day would also be filled in prayers of deliverance.

At night, a woman called us to ask us to come and pray for her at the Great Hospital in Dedougou. We did not really know the reason for this prayer request but, when the call comes from a person at the hospital, we knew it was important.

We went by motorcycle to the scene. Djeneba, the woman who had called us, she was sitting outside the operating room with a few friends and strangers around her. We learned that she had to undergo surgery to remove fibroids from her uterus. I told my wife that I had to prepare myself before praying for her, so I moved away from the curious glances. I knew all the people sitting around the place were going to judge us on what was going to happen.

"So also, the chief priests, with the scribes and elders, mocked him, saying, "He saved others; he cannot save himself. He is the King of Israel; let him come down now from the cross, and we will believe in him. He trusts in God; let God deliver him now, if he desires him. For he said, 'I am the Son of God.'"

-Matthew 27:41-43 (ESV)

I prayed to my God and asked him to show me his will on my presence at the hospital.

"The LORD is near to all who call on him, to all who call on him in truth."

-Psalm 145:18 (ESV)

I walked praying as I always do and then I heard a voice that said, "Pray for her, and the others will come". At that very moment, I felt a force invading me from the feet to the head. My torso felt like it swelled, as if I was getting stronger and more resistant. I was ready for the fight against the disease and against the enemy. I said to Rosalie, "I'm ready, let's go!" I walked briskly and confidently. The Lord was by my side so the victory stood before me. I stood behind

Djeneba and prayed for her by laying on my hands. I asked the Lord to protect her, to accompany her and to fortify her during the surgery.

I put oil on her forehead saying, "You are now the daughter of the King of Kings. The daughter of the King is called a princess, and as a princess, you benefit from the protection of the King's army. The angels will camp by your side during the whole surgery. You will spend the most beautiful night of sleep in your life because the Lord keeps you under his protective hand." She was so happy with this prayer and the fear of this surgery had left her.

She had now confidence that everything would go well since the Creator had everything in his hands.

The curious, who had watched the prayer attentively, saw the power of the Lord. A woman named Françoise also asked me to pray for her. Back pain often prevented her from getting up from a chair and walking normally.

She suffered a lot because of the intense pain in her lower back. I put my hand on her back and prayed for her immediate healing in the name of Jesus. I put the oil on her forehead and I declared her daughter of the King of Kings. She rose from the chair and no longer felt any pain. She made several steps in the courtyard and squealed with joy as she walked normally without any painful sensation in her back.

A Muslim man named Yakuba also rose to ask me to pray for his father who was currently in surgery. His father was over 80 years old and he feared he would not wake up after the surgery. If he woke up, he was afraid that because of his age, there would be complications and that the doctors would decide to keep him for a long time in the hospital.

I asked him, "Do you love Jesus?" He answered me without hesitation, "Too much!" This response had really pleased me coming from a Muslim. His response surpassed many of the Christian responses to their faith in Jesus. I said to him, "Then I will gladly pray for your father."

"When Jesus heard these things, he marveled at him, and turning to the crowd that followed him, said: I tell you, not even in Israel have I found such faith."

-Luke 7:8 (ESV)

I started interceding for the success of his father's surgery. I did not know much detail about the kind of surgery but the Lord knew it. I have asked that Jesus himself use the hands of the specialists, so that the operation was a great victory, that the angels protect the sleep of this man and that his healing was immediate and that all the doctors on the spot are in amazement at the speed of healing of this man over 80 years old. That he may leave the hospital the next morning and that everyone is remembering this great miracle of Jesus in this Muslim family. After my prayer, the man admitted to me that he felt that he was in peace.

He had a great fear for his father's health but, following my prayer, he felt a wonderful peace invading him. He had no more fear, he trusted. I asked him never to forget to thank Jesus every morning. He said he would. "All glory goes to our Lord!"

A brother in Christ was present at the hospital and told me that he would like us to go to his home with him, because his wife had strange stomach aches and she was not the same for several weeks. I didn't like going to people's homes because we never knew what kind of evil spirit was in the person or what kind of spell had been made in the house. But in this case, I knew the brother and his wife well, so I immediately agreed to go to the residence right away.

More and more people came to ask us to pray for them, but I had to leave, otherwise we would spend the whole night in the hospital.

We followed our brother in Christ by motorcycle to his house. His wife was there on the terrace and greeted us by showing us chairs to sit. Without further delay, I asked her what the problem was. She explained to me, "It's been several weeks since I've been able to read my Bible. I open it, I look at it, but I cannot read it. Tonight, I have a terrible belly ache that keeps me awake every night." I immediately replied, "This is a spiritual problem!" I ordered her to stand up and we removed all the chairs because I knew inside me that she would fall on the ground.

The brother and his wife wondered why I did this, so I explained to them that when a spirit is in the body of a person, and we pray for deliverance, a shock occurs that makes that person fall to the ground. She doubted what I was saying because she believed what a lot of pastor teaches, "A Christian who has received the Holy Spirit cannot be possessed by an evil spirit." False! If a Christian commits a sin, he opens a door to the enemy. I asked the sister to close her eyes and the brother not to say a word or intervene no matter what happened. Prayer could begin. I prayed in tongues to prepare myself and then, as soon as I put my hand on her head, she fell to the ground.

She squirmed in every direction making noises with her mouth, "Ya-ya-ya-ya..." Her husband was completely stunned by what he saw. I put myself on my knees and asked her what her name was. She replied again, "Ya-ya-ya-ya..." I put the oil on her forehead, one hand on her head and the other hand on her belly. I cried out, "By the authority given to me by Jesus Christ himself, I command you to leave this body immediately. I order you to release her!"

At the same time, she opened her eyes and took a deep breath, as if it was her first breath after being underwater too long.

I asked her name again to be sure that the spirit was no longer in her. She answered her real name, so we helped her sit on a chair. She was so shocked because she couldn't believe what had happened. "How can a Christian like me, have a bad spirit in her body? I am a good Christian who always goes to church every Sunday, evening prayers, and vigils of the Holy Spirit. I'm also part of the church choir and several ministries. I am involved in God's work, so how did this happen?"

"You opened a door to the enemy without realizing it. He's very cunning. You said you had trouble reading the bible. It's enough to open a door because, without the Word, your Christian love weakens. I can tell you that tonight will be a wonderful night. You're going to sleep peacefully like a baby. Now try to read verses."

We handed her a Bible and she tried to read. She could do it easily now. She was totally liberated from this intruder. Her husband's face showed how he could not understand everything his eyes had seen. He knew beyond a doubt that God had just acted on his wife. He made a few steps forward and asked us to pray also for him. "For several days, he said, I also feel some slight belly aches and a spirit of sadness is in me. I get up in the morning without any energy, I spend my day at work having no energy to go on, and I come back at night without talking to my wife. I feel so sad every day."

He was right, there was a spirit behind all this, and we were going to chase him by the name of Jesus. He was standing in front and I put my hand on his head to pray. I asked the Lord to fill him with his love, so that this love poured out also on his wife. I interceded for this brother to regain the joy of life and I ordered this spirit of sadness to leave him immediately by the name of Jesus Christ my Lord and Savior.

I could see that the brother's breathing changed - every breath made his chest expand more and more. It was a sign that his sadness was leaving him and that he was increasingly self-confident. At the end of the prayer he let down a huge sigh. We asked him how he felt. "I feel so good, he said. I'm full of strength. I feel no pain in the belly and I am in joy. I don't feel sad anymore."

It was so late that we said goodbye to them warmly and returned to our house to rest from this beautiful evening of work for the advancement of the Kingdom of God.

The next evening, I wanted to hear from some people we had prayed for. We went to the hospital to find out about the woman who had to be operated on for fibroids in her womb. As we walked to the operating room, we met Françoise, the woman who had back pain. She was so happy to see us again and proud to announce that she spent her first day without any back pain.

She walked normally and could even dance and jump. She confirmed that she had thanked the Lord that morning and that she would do it every day.

Afterwards, we went to the room where Djeneba was located. She was on a bed and just waking up. She was also happy to see us again and told us that she slept very well, without being afraid of anything. She woke up very late this morning and her wound was already almost healed. The doctors were all surprised by this quick healing.

We thanked the Lord together in this hospital room. Afterwards, we went in search of Yakuba's father, the Muslim man who loved Jesus too much. Fortunately, his father had been released the same morning. That very morning, I wondered? A man over 80 years of age had been released the next morning. Françoise had inquired for us and informed us that the old man's operation had gone very well. That morning the doctors had returned to see the patient and were all very surprised to find that his wound was completely closed as if he never had an operation.

They did some routine exams and then released him only a few hours after the operation. They could not explain how a man of this age had been able to heal so quickly. "It's simple!" I replied, "We have the God of the impossible with us! Praise the Lord for all that he has done." And we have again thanked the King of Kings for all the miracles he performed through us.

"Then they cried to the LORD in their trouble, and he delivered them from their distress. He sent out his word and healed them, and delivered them from their destruction."
-Psalm 107:19-20 (ESV)

I still had two people to find out about - the brother in Christ and his wife. We went to their house but the brother was not there yet. So, we talked to his wife. She announced that she had spent the most wonderful night. She had fallen into such a deep sleep, that an earthquake would not have awakened her. She had slept like a baby and now she felt so good and happy. The relationship with her husband had been much improved. She felt like they had returned to their first encounter because their love for each other had increased so much. Her face was now resplendent with joy.

We were happy to hear that. We thanked the Lord together and that all glory and honor return to Jesus.

"But if it is by the Spirit of God that I cast out demons, then the kingdom of God has come upon you."
-Matthew 12:28 (ESV)

Friday, April 20, 2018 will always remain in my memory. During the day, a person came to knock on our door. Rosalie opened and little Rita was there, the one who had an evil spirit who was trying to kill her, by cutting all over her arms and legs with a blade and hitting her on the head with a stone. She jumped up to Rosalie to hug her and then ran and jumped up to hug me. She shone with joy and had a huge smile on her lips.

We sat down and she explained that she had managed to forgive her parents. After having done so, an intense love had filled her and, since then, she had embraced everyone she loved. I could not believe what I saw before me - it was no longer the Rita I knew before. It was a new creature, resplendent with happiness. She exuded such intense joy that she made us cry tears of happiness down our cheeks. My little Rita was finally released; she had just won her fight against the enemy. We all rejoiced in the Lord.

The next day a mighty whirlwind came into our outer courtyard and moved all the patio chairs. Rosalie and I chased this enemy's attack into our own yard and the whirlwind suddenly ceased. When we looked at all the damage, we saw that Rosalie's night gown was hanging on the top of the courtyard wall.

This gown had disappeared when a whirlwind had appeared in our bedroom. Since that day, we had never found this gown. Now it was strangely appearing following the passage of this new whirlwind.

We knew that the sorcerers had stolen Rosalie's gown to put on a spell and had returned it to us hoping that she would wear this again. I took a stick to remove the gown from the top of the wall; we put oil on it and burned it completely until there was nothing left. The enemy would not win against us. We will not be victims to his attempts to divert us from the will of God. He failed miserably!

We rented a house that we had to pay every month. So, I went to our landlord to pay for the month of May. He was a Muslim man, very sympathetic with everyone. On the spot, I noticed that he was not doing very well, intense sweating, dizziness, fatigue, and heartache. He told me that he had a dream at night, "A man in black came to put poison in the dish I was eating. I ate this poison and, when I woke up, I had a terrible heart ache." I asked him if he wanted me to pray for him. He accepted, and then I immediately set to work. I called for divine healing on this man and I ordered the evil spirits to leave him without any delay in the name of Jesus.

After the prayer I could see that he seemed much better so I asked him how he felt. "While you were praying for me, he said, I saw a man in white approaching me and he delivered me by removing the black man from my body. I felt that it was Jesus in person, who was there by my side. Now I don't feel any heart discomfort or dizziness anymore. I am very well and I have a strange feeling of peace in my heart." I asked him to thank Jesus every morning for what he had done and, one day, the Lord would show him the truth about God's wonderful free gift of salvation. I finally paid my rent and went back home.

Two women were sitting on the terrace waiting for my return home. Rosalie had already served them a drink, so I sat on a chair right in front of the women. They were Janet, 17 years old, and her mother Mariam. The mother told me that Janet's grandparents and her dad had very close ties with marabouts and had made pacts with these satanic sorcerers.

The mother believed that these spells had fallen on her daughter because one day the marabout had come to the grandfather's house and he had forced Janet to wear a scarf on her head. Inside the scarf there was a little black bag with something strange in it. The marabout forced her to wear it every day without ever opening the bag. Since then, Janet always had a very bad headache and sadness had invaded her. The grandfather had given her clay pots full of fetishes and a bottle with a suspicious liquid.

The mother, who was a sister in Christ, as soon as she learned this act of marabout on her daughter, removed the scarf from her head and tried to burn all the satanic objects from this sorcerer.

Nothing wanted to burn. She had tried everything, but the fire was still hot and nothing was consumed. The grandfather had taken all the fetishes and pots with him, to make sure that nothing would be destroyed. The mother was desperate seeing her daughter in this state and was very afraid for her daughter's life.

Like Satan, the marabouts always promise beautiful things in exchange for money. But what they never say, was not the money that interested them, it was the souls of the innocent people. Let's never forget that their boss, the Devil, is the father of lies.

These African marabouts always give fetishes, objects, or statuettes that have been bewitched with satanic prayers and mantras. By accepting this gift, it is like signing a pact with the servants of Satan. They can manipulate their hosts as well.

To deliver a person with this kind of spiritual attachment, it was absolutely necessary to break this link and then to destroy all the fetishes and objects that could restore the link with the marabout.

Deliverance can be done quickly but, on rare occasions, spells can take much longer to break, especially if they have been implanted for several years. In general, the person connected to the marabouts always ends up crazy; she walks completely naked in front of everyone, speaks to herself for no reason, does not manage to speak intelligently, or acts in a very strange way. All ties created with marabouts always end badly if they are not broken as quickly as possible.

The whole time the mom was telling me this story, Janet did not say anything. She had not even moved. I looked at the mother and said, "Don't worry, she will leave here free of all ties with the marabout." I asked Janet to stand up and I started praying for her. By putting the oil on her forehead, the young Janet fell asleep. Her head turned constantly from left to right, as if the spirit refused to obey the order to leave her. I put one hand on her head and the other on her belly and I authoritatively ordered this impostor to leave her alone and never come to harass her again. Some sounds came out of her mouth but were incomprehensible. After a few minutes, the spirit left her; the links with the marabout had just been broken. Janet looked around everywhere, without understanding where she was.

I said quietly, "Don't worry. It is quite normal to be a little lost since you were under the influence of an evil spirit. Now you're free." I turned to the mother, who was already crying with joy because she saw that her daughter was beginning to change for better. She finally demonstrated different emotions from this longstanding expression of sadness. I explained to the mother, "Your daughter is delivered, but never forget to thank the Lord every day. Moreover, to make sure that this spirit never comes back, you must bring me all the objects that this sorcerer had given her. We will destroy them all in order to completely annihilate the link between your daughter and this servant of Satan."

"We had already tried but nothing would burn." she said with dismay.

"Bring them tomorrow to the prayer of deliverance at the church and I will destroy them. Believe me, they'll all burn!"

The two women left my home, after long goodbyes. I was very

141

happy to see that the Lord was very helpful in healing these destructive attacks.

"The seventy-two returned with joy, saying: Lord, even the demons are subject to us in your name!"
                                                              -Luke 10:17 (ESV)

The next morning, I went very early to the church's prayer of deliverance. Janet and her friend Astride, a 13 years-old, were already there with two big bags in their hands.

Janet told me something really incredible, "Last night we went to the grandfather's house to take the fetishes and the pots. The grandmother refused to give them to us and she called the marabout to chase away the prayer you had made on me. But when the grandfather arrived in the room, he saw a powerful light shining all around my body. He felt an incomparable peace and love that hovered in the house. The marabout arrived and the grandfather kicked him out of his house, shouting that he was an impostor and that he did not want to hurt his little girl. Then the old man picked up all the objects of the marabout and handed them to me and said to do what I had to do with these evil objects.

I couldn't believe he'd changed that much. He himself worked a lot with the marabouts and the witch doctors, but last night he was a different man before us. He confessed that he did not know what prayer had been made about me, but knew that I was now protected by a God more powerful than any gods of the sorcerers."

"Glory to God!" I cried!

They opened the bags and I could see the clay pots filled with various satanic objects. I asked them to follow me out of the church land to destroy them. I dropped the two canaries on the ground and Janet showed me the famous scarf she was forced to wear every day.

I rolled it out and there was a little black bag in it. Inside this bag was a piece of paper folded into several parts. I unfolded it to discover a message written in an unknown writing.

No one around us could translate this message. I prayed for the total destruction of these satanic objects and threw oil on both pots. I used the paper with the strange message to light the fire. Everything that was in the two clay pots burned beautifully, including the bottle that contained the suspicious liquid. Janet was happy to see that everything was so easy. When the fire stopped, I took the pots in my hands and smashed them against big stones.

I turned to Janet and said, "You're free!" She was smiling. It was the first time I saw her smiling.

Janet's friend, Astride also asked me to pray for her. She had seen the positive changes in Janet and wanted to be delivered from the connection to the marabouts.

Her parents also made pacts with these sorcerers and the spells fell on her. Pastor David and I prayed for her and she rose up with a joy in her heart. I said, "You saw how I destroyed Janet's fetishes. You must do the same thing to permanently destroy the bonds that bind you to this sorcerer." She accepted and left with Janet.

Rita also came to the prayer of deliverance because she wanted to thank the Lord for everything he had done in her. She was glowing with joy and it was really beautiful to see her smile. I prayed with her to thank the King of Kings. Pastor Tiken passed behind us and stopped by my side, to find out who the little girl was and why she was smiling like that. "You don't recognize her?" I asked.

"No. Should I?"

"It's little Rita - the one who would run barefoot on the vacant lot and hit her head with stones."

"Rita!" exclaimed the pastor, looking at her more closely. "It's amazing how much you've changed! You've become so beautiful!"

The pastor congratulated her warmly and complimented her on her new conversion. When he walked away from us, I said to Rita, "You see, even the pastor didn't recognize you. Now you are a new creature in Christ and everything you have done or been able to do in the past must remain in the past. Your old body is dead and buried so we don't have to dig it up for any reason. You will be an incredible witness to all those who are trapped in darkness. You can show them that it is possible to get out of it." She gave me a friendly hug and then left in joy.

Another person came to see me, Sandrine, the one who was in a state of emotional depression. She always had the same expression of deep sadness on her face. I knew that she was hiding in her heart; an emotional trauma connected to an event in her past, but didn't talk to anyone about it. In fact, she didn't want to talk to anyone at all. I always had a friendly and gentle approach, even if her gaze showed that she did not agree with me, I complimented her on her beauty, her intelligence, and her size because she was very tall.

I asked her the same question, "Would you like to get married someday?" I saw her lips move, as if she wanted to talk to me, but no sound came out. "Excuse me Sandrine but I did not hear" I replied. This time, I clearly heard a weak voice say "Yes."

"Do you have any children?"

"No," she said again with a faint voice.

"Do you love Jesus?"

"No."

This answer surprised me since she was still at the prayer of deliverance, with me the church but she did not believe in Jesus. I didn't believe her because most of the people who say they're atheists lie. They try to make everyone believe that God does not exist but, deep down, they all believe that he exists.

If God does not exist, how can you fight against a person, a being, or something that does not exist? I stayed with her, until the end of the time allocated to deliverance, to continue to discuss, without seeing any positive progress.

I had the impression that she did not have the will to make it out, that she wanted to remain in this sad and desolate state. She remained in the same state as she was when she arrived. I had at least a little consolation, she was beginning to talk to me, and she trusted me. Maybe...

"If you are willing and obedient, you shall eat the good of the land but if you refuse and rebel, you shall be eaten by the sword for the mouth of the Lord has spoken."
- Isaiah 1:19-20 (ESV)

On Wednesday morning, a woman came to speak with Rosalie. She was accompanied by a little girl who had a huge belly. It looked like she had a soccer ball in her belly. Her belly button was completely out because of the inner pressure in her belly.

It was horrible to see a little girl in this situation, especially since children of this age could be very mean to others. She certainly had to hear a lot of insults about her belly. We asked his mother to explain the reasons for this physical deformation.

She replied, "One day, her belly started to inflate for no reason. The doctors never found out what she had. They don't have the ability to explain it." I then stood up from my chair and put one hand on the head of the girl and the other hand on her belly. I asked her not to worry and I prayed for her healing. When I withdrew my hands, I felt that the Lord would bring healing to this little girl. I told the mother, "Jesus will cure her in a few days. You'll see the difference by tomorrow morning." She thanked us warmly and left our court.

In the evening, a woman named Pauline came to ask for prayer. She had "night husbands" who always came to haunt her while she was sleeping. We started praying to chase that spirit off of her.

To my amazement, this spirit was manifesting very quickly before us. He used to call himself Awa and really hated me. We could see hatred in Pauline's eyes. I asked, "Do you want to hit me?"

"Oh Yes!"

"You know, you're not the only one who wants to hit me but you can't do it."

We continued to pray and Pauline fell to the ground and was delivered by the power of Jesus.

Our keeper, Prosper, had a little sister named Nyangalie. She had lower back pains and was going to try to get her BAC for the third time. BAC is a French school degree that gives you access to a lot a great jobs in Burkina. BAC is a very difficult test and few people succeed. The Lord informed me that she wanted to work in the field of health. She confirmed it without hesitation. I put one hand on her head and the other on her back. I began to intercede for her divine healing. Rosalie put oil on Nyangalie's forehead while I continued praying for her back.

I finished my prayer by interceding for her success at the BAC. I said to her, "Tonight you will feel your back cracking, but don't worry, it'll be the sign that the Lord is healing you. Tomorrow morning, you'll be completely cured!" She raised her arms in the air to thank the Lord. Then I continued, "For your BAC, I want you to look in the mirror every morning. You look at the person you see in the mirror and point her out by saying - you are more than victorious!" She thanked me and left. The next day, Prosper informed me that his sister had felt her back crack and then had fallen asleep peacefully without back pain. This morning she woke up in great shape and had no lower back pain. She had recovered her trust in her and felt in her heart that she would pass her BAC this time. Glory to God!

Rosalie's brother, Gilbert, called us in the middle of the night to ask for help at his garage. We went as fast as we could, as soon as he called. He was standing there waiting for us.

He joined our meeting and informed us that he believed that a spell was hovering on the ground of his garage. His employees had discovered on several occasions traces of sacrifices and broken eggs on the ground. In addition, when a person was standing at a place of the sacrifice, she had severe headaches and dizziness. He believed that a fetish or satanic object had been buried at this precise spot on the ground.

It was time for me to be in prayer. I spilled oil on the exact spot that caused headaches and, on the corner, where the broken eggs and traces of sacrifice had been discovered. I prayed forcefully while walking in every direction shouting the name of Jesus.

I said loud and clear, "Let the blood of the divine lamb fully cover this land and if a sorcerer, marabout or fetishist tries to set foot here, his legs will break on the field in the name of Jesus. Only what comes from God can set foot here." After the prayer, I asked Gilbert to go to the place where he had headaches. He stayed there for a few minutes and felt no pain.

I pointed to the place where the eggs were broken and I told him, "If a person with bad intentions comes here, you will find him crying on the ground because he will have both legs broken." He replied, "Amen!"

I heard a voice in my heart that said to me - "Exodus Chapter 22 verse 20" God had just given me a word for Gilbert who opened his electronic Bible on his cell phone and began to read it.

"Whoever sacrifices to any god, other than the LORD alone, shall be devoted to destruction"
-Exodus 22:20 (ESV)

We were all very impressed to see how exactly this verse

corresponded to the situation. We could see that Gilbert's faith had just been mightily fortified following the reading of this verse. He now trusted that the mighty hand of the Lord, the God of Armies, provided protection, and security on the ground of his garage.

The following Sunday, we were sitting at the church as we always did, when little Rita came running up to hug us. She was so happy to see us and to show her joy to everyone around her. During the service, Pastor Tiken called Rita and asked her to come and join him at the front. She approached with a little shyness and then the pastor explained her story. The pastor had completed the testimony by saying, "See now how she is happy and in the joy of the Lord. I prayed for her and I managed to chase that powerful demon that was in her." I was very happy for Rita because I had told her that she would be a great witness for others but I expected at least that the pastor would give my name.

He had just said "I succeeded" but I was the only one who had prayed on Rita for weeks. She had been delivered at home and not at the church. I must admit that I was expecting a bit of that. After we returned from Manga, the pastor had done the same thing. He had never said who had prophesied over him about the roaring lion, when he knew very well that it was me, because I was the only one who spoke English in the group that was there. He could not have forgotten who had prophesied about him that day. And now he could not have forgotten who had presented to him Rita at his office after her deliverance because he had not even recognized her.

"Do not be arrogant toward the branches. If you are, remember it is not you who support the root, but the root that supports you."

-Romans 11:18 (ESV)

Rita's aunt came to see me after the service. She was very angry at what she had just heard from the pastor. She told me that the first time she had asked the pastor to intervene for her niece whom she loved as her own daughter, Roland had entered the pastor's office, and he had asked him to say that he was not there. Roland, a very honest young man who did not want to lie, said, "The pastor asked me to tell you he was not here." The pastor had refused to pray for little Rita and had not never done anything to help her. Now he publicly took all the glory of this deliverance.

I told the aunt that both of us knew the truth and that, in any case, I did not want to be glorified for this deliverance.
All glory came back to our Lord.

In the evening, Fatoumata, this Muslim woman converted to Jesus and who had asked for prayer, came to give us some news. She was proud to say that her own father had abandoned all the marabouts and the fetishists after seeing how happy his daughter had become after accepting the Lord Jesus in her life. She had become a light for her family; she would bring them all to the only truth - Jesus, the one and only Savior. We have all praised the Lord for this incredible act within a Muslim family. I knew that God would act mightily in Burkina Faso.

Later, Pastor David's mother called us to inform us that Anne, who was pregnant, had just entered the hospital urgently, because the contractions had begun. I had prophesied about this woman by telling her that she would have a boy and that he would be a great athlete.

We left in the direction of the hospital. On site, the mother was there and told us that the doctors had confirmed that she would give birth that night. God revealed to me a word of knowledge which I repeated to the mother, "She will not give birth tonight because this is not the time. It's too soon! The baby is doing well and he will be born in full health." We had entered Anne's maternity ward to pray for her health, and we had asked the local nurse about the results of the ultrasound. "It's a boy and he's doing very well!" she replied.

"And the mother, what about her?"

"She's fine too, we'll just keep her here for the night, and then she will be released tomorrow morning. She will not give birth right away because it is too early."

I knew it! We went outside to announce it to the mother then we greeted everyone to return home. The Lord had already answered the prayer we had made for Anne. Now we could go and rest for the night.

The following Monday, Anne's mother called us to inform us that her daughter had just entered the hospital to give birth. We went right away, but I still said it was too early. The child would not be born right away.

The mother told us that the nurses had said she was going to give birth soon. I replied, "Who are they to say the opposite of what God reveals to us?" At that time, a doctor came into the room and said, "We will release Anne in a few minutes because the birth has not yet arrived. It's too soon!"

We had prayed again for the health of Anne and the child she was carrying, and then we returned home to find a woman waiting for us at the door. It was the mother of the little girl who had a belly, as big as a soccer ball. She just wanted to thank us for our prayers because since the day of prayer, the belly of her daughter had decreased considerably.

The child was much better and she was on the road to complete healing. We thanked the Lord together. Glory to Jesus!

"That evening they brought to him many who were oppressed by demons, and he cast out the spirits with a word and healed all who were sick. This was to fulfill what was spoken by the prophet Isaiah: "He took our illnesses and bore our diseases."

-Matthew 8:16-17 (ESV)

CHRIST'S HARVEST

It was barely 4 am in the morning when my cell phone rang. Rosalie's brother needed us because his wife's brother was very ill. The family feared for his life. Since he lived in a non-lot and it was very easy to get lost, especially at night, Gilbert came to join us at home to be our personal guide. We followed him with our bike. At the family residence, since it was very hot that night, a mat had been put outside on the ground so that everyone could sleep in the coolness. A pastor was already there and I knew him since he had already spoken against me. He told everyone that I was just another fake missionary who would not stay in Burkina. Probably another Christian jealous of the gifts of others. Yet he should know that the Holy Spirit gives gifts to whoever he wants.

"Having gifts that differ according to the grace given to us, let us use them…"

-Romans 12:6 (ESV)

"All these are empowered by one and the same Spirit, who apportions to each one individually as he wills."

-1 Corinthians 12:11 (ESV)

The young man was lying on the mat and turned from left to

151

right while holding his belly. The mother informed me that he was like this for a few days. They were in the hospital more than once but the doctors couldn't explain the cause of this intense pain that kept him awake. I began to pray for him in spite of the presence of this pastor, because I was there for the sick only. I put oil on his forehead and I also asked him to drink some and then I asked the immediate healing of this young man in the name of Jesus. The young man had fallen asleep since all the pain had dissipated. Since he was better and he had finally fallen asleep, we left to try to get some sleep before facing a new day.

Two hours later, while I was at the morning prayer of deliverance at the church, little Rita came to see me and she hugged me every time she saw me. She was always overflowing with joy. She announced wonderful news, "I want to be baptized!" Thank you, Jesus! The little fragile woman who had lived in darkness for years, now wanted to be baptized and to follow the real Savior. My heart was so filled with happiness that I informed Pastor Tiken without further delay. He congratulated Rita for this great decision.

We all thank the Lord for this miraculous conversion. Only he could snatch that little girl from the enemy's claws. I firmly believe that she will be a great servant of the Lord and a great worker for the advancement of his kingdom.

Sandrine also came to prayer, still wearing her sad face. She sat in front of me and I started to talk a little bit with her. A one-way discussion, since she always answered yes or no only. She didn't want to say anything more.

I still felt like she had no will to get out of this depression, so I asked her to do something very important for me. She always looked at me with the same sad look but this time her eyes were fixed on me. I knew she was intrigued. "Since you don't want to tell me what caused your sadness," I asked her, "I'd like you to put it in writing. It will be easier for you to empty your heart on a paper rather than to a man. Do you want to do this for me?" She stayed a few seconds without saying anything and then replied faintly, "Yes."

"Then I'll let you go home and come back next Tuesday to see me with a full written description. If I know your story, I'll be able to help you."

She blinked her eyes to tell me that she agreed with this request. I was really glad she agreed. I prayed a little for her then she returned with her mother waiting outside.

The pastor came to ask me for a little request. He wanted me to go to a woman who had a problem with a spirit in her house.

Normally, I never went to people, but this request came from the pastor himself. When I arrived at the scene, the woman, who seemed completely overwhelmed by what was going inside her home, gave me some details about the situation. In the middle of the night, she often heard a person walking in her house. This intruder played with the plates, utensils, and chairs of the dining room as if he wanted to eat a meal.

Sometimes she felt a presence in her own bedroom and felt like a man watching her sleep. She was really afraid of this intruder, as he was also bothering her children. He was moving things and dropping a metal chair on the floor to wake the children. As soon as I entered the children's room, I felt the presence of this intruder and I understood who he was. I could see it. I explained to the woman, "This man is the former owner of this house. He died but did not leave the house. He does not intend to take either of you or your children. You have nothing to fear from him."

"You know," she replied, "I think you're right. The presence of this man began after the death of the owner of the house. And, indeed, he was not a bad man. He liked us."

"I can get rid of it if you want."

"Yes," she said. "I don't want to be scared any more at night."

I took some oil and started praying in the children's room. I put few drops of oil on the walls, the doors, and the windows, asking that the blood of the lamb should cover these places and that everything not from God no longer has the right to be in this room. I did the same thing in the master bedroom and in every room in the house. After putting the oil at the front door of the residence, I saw through a window the dark man disappeared completely, while he was standing in the outer courtyard. I informed the woman that she would not see this intruder again and that she could finally sleep peacefully.

God had called us to move to Africa to serve him. That was exactly what we were doing but the primary mission was not healing and deliverance, it was the Widows' Help Center. The gifts I had of the Holy Spirit, also served for the advancement of the Kingdom of God and I loved to serve this way, but I also had to think of working for our primary purpose of this journey - the widows.

To do this, we had to have the legal document of the land, which would be used to build the Windows' Help Center. The application for this document had been filed at the tax offices. The agent who had our case called to inform us that everything was ready. We went there and he gave us the whole file and informed us that we had to go to the Town Hall to have this document signed by the man the mayor had presented to us last time. We decided to wait until the next day to do so since the day was already very advanced.

On Wednesday morning we went to the Town Hall to have the document signed and finalized. The man in question was surprised to see us arrive with the document in our hand. He began to insult us, "Who do you think you are? You can't just come to my office like that. There are procedures to follow. You can't skip the steps."

"But explain to me what steps we skipped?" I asked.

"It is not because you are Canadian that you have to go in front of everyone. Return this document to the tax office and they will come to bring it to me. You cannot bring the document yourself."

"Where is the difference?" I retorted, "Whether it's us or them, the document will be in your hands."

"I don't have time to talk to you anymore! Bring it back to the tax people and they will bring it to me. After that there's a two-week deadline for me to put my signature on."

He was furious with us. I could not believe that a man can act like this, especially when he is the official representative of the Town Hall of Dedougou.

Rosalie quietly explained the situation to the man outside the Town Hall. "Let me explain. It was God himself who sent us here to do his work. Moreover, the mayor himself had asked you to do it quickly because he was very happy with this project for the widows."

"You always talk about God but I believe in God too. When I sacrifice chickens, I do it for God!"

What a strange answer! Since when does a man need to sacrifice chickens for God? This kind of sacrifice is for Satan and those who work with the devil are the sorcerers. So this man was definitely one of them!

"No, I imply that what pagans sacrifice they offer to demons and not to God. I do not want you to be participants with demons. You cannot drink the cup of the Lord and the cup of demons. You cannot partake of the table of the Lord and the table of demons."

-1 Corinthians 10:20-21 (ESV)

The people who were around us had clearly heard this satanic reply. A friend who worked at the Town Hall came to me and asked what was going on. I answered him loudly, so that everyone could hear. "This man refuses to sign the documents and then he starts to insult us! It's a real shame for the Town Hall." We left without any signature on the document.

During the day, one of our close neighbors came to visit us at home. He was a Muslim who worked at the Town Hall and he had noticed us during the altercation outside in the courtyard, in front of the offices. He was intrigued and asked us why we were in this state. We explained everything to him in every detail.

He was devastated by what he heard and confirmed what we thought, "This man has the reputation of being a sorcerer. Everyone in town is afraid of him." Following the reply at the Town Hall about the sacrifices, we were suspicious that he was a servant of the enemy. Now we had confirmation.

The Muslim informed us that he knew the sorcerer's superior and that he could have an appointment with him. We accepted without hesitation and he left our home to call his contact.

In the evening, the Muslim came to the house to take us to see the superior, who I will not name in this book. We met at the personal residence of this man and he had greeted us with respect. After attentively listening to our story, he asked us to return the document to the tax people the next morning and he will speak with to this man so that he may sign the document as soon as possible. "Don't worry, he said, I'm taking care of all tomorrow morning." We left his residence with a sense of victory in us. Since our arrival in Burkina Faso, God has put many Muslims on our path to help us in our journey. It was proof that the Creator used whoever he wanted, when he wanted.

"Our God is in the heavens; he does all that he pleases."
-Psalm 115:3 (ESV)

The next morning, we were handing over the document very early in the morning to the tax people and quickly explaining the reason for this return. Afterwards, I went to the morning prayer of deliverance at the church. A couple accepted Christ as Lord and Savior, a woman was cured of belly aches; a powerful deliverance took place, etc.

My cell phone rang between two prayers. It was the tax people who told me that the man from the Town Hall had come to sign the documents in person in their office. I informed the other intercessors that I had to leave urgently and I headed straight to the tax offices. The agent behind his desk asked me what I had done to force this man to leave his desk to sign a document. He had never seen this since he was in this office. "It was God himself who had managed everything, I replied. He wanted to insult God with his stories of sacrifices, so my Lord put shame on his shoulders."

The agent handed me the signed document and I finally let out a sigh of relief. I could now start funding requests from non-governmental organizations, embassies and other support.

At the exit of the tax building, I ran into the woman who had a ghost walking around her house. She told me that she slept very well since I put the oil on the walls of the house. The presence was no longer there and her children slept very well, without being disturbed during the night. She thanked me again but I explained her to thank the Lord every day because this miracle came from his hand and not from mine.

Since I came to this country, I had accomplished several deliverances by chasing satanic spirits, demonic possessions, and sorcerers' spells. I knew that someday they would all seek revenge, so I always asked for divine protection on my family. I commanded the Christian's Armor and the blood of the Lamb on me, my wife, and my son. Despite all this, I felt that the enemy was preparing a vicious blow against a member of my family.

I was right to worry. On Saturday, May 5, 2018, Rosalie and I were at the market to buy some necessary stuff when my phone rang. I knew this number; it was Emmanuel's cell phone. I took the call but it was not my son. The man asked me, "Is that Emmanuel's dad?"

"Yes I replied!"

"Emmanuel just had an accident right in front of my business. You should come as soon as possible. I think he's badly hurt and he's crying a lot."

It was the young man who had a small business next door to me. Panic invaded me in a fraction of a second. My heart was beating very fast. When you receive a call like that, you always imagine the worst. Pictures of horrors passed through my head. Is he seriously hurt? Was he losing all his blood to the point of rendering the soul very slowly? Was he suffering from a broken arm or leg? Or, maybe it was the fractured spine? I got a hold of myself and informed my wife that we had to leave urgently.

While I was driving the bike, she was praying sitting in the back and I was just answering "Amen" to all her sentences. That day, I am sure I had broken motorcycle speed records.

When we arrived at the shopkeeper, he informed me that my son was now at home. Indeed, when we entered the courtyard, we saw Emmanuel sitting on the terrace with a stranger.

I inspected his body in search of a trace of blood, some bruises or a signs of fracture but there was nothing. The stranger presented himself and told me that he witnessed the accident.

"Your son was riding normally on his bicycle when a madman, who was driving too fast with his motorcycle, rushed in from behind. Your son had no chance of avoiding him since he had not even seen him coming. This madman went straight at him without trying to avoid him. Your son flew into the air and fell on his back. He stayed a few minutes on the ground, before he started screaming and crying. The madman lost the balance and fell with his motorcycle. I was able to get his name and phone number."

He handed me a piece of paper containing information about this crazy motorcycle driver. Emmanuel was still lamenting the pain, but after such a violent shock, it was normal. I thanked the man by also taking his personal information. He added a very important detail, "Really, it is God who has protected your son because he has no wounds or scratches on him. I have seen several accidents in my life but this is the first time I see a person get away with no serious injury or death."

I wanted to give him money for his gesture towards my son but he refused and just left my home after saying goodbye to us. I had never seen this man before and I do not remember seeing him later. I know it was an angel of God who had taken care of my son while waiting for us to return home. As he had said - God had protected my son!

I let my son rest a little and I walked to the shopkeeper because his bicycle was still at the scene of the accident. I could not imagine all the force of the impact but, when I saw the terrible condition of the bike, I understood why Emmanuel was still afraid to leave the house. There was nothing left of the bike. It was a total loss. All the pieces were bent and some were missing.

I could see parts from the bike all over the place, as well as traces of circles in the sand that showed that the motorbike had rolled down sideways after the accident.

That madman was going way too fast. God had really protected my son. I picked up the bicycle and I brought it to a repairman. I was carrying the bike on my shoulder because it was no longer rolling. At the sight of the damage, the repairman asked me if the cyclist was dead. "No," I replied. "My son doesn't even have a scratch on him."

"That's impossible!"

"No, it is a miracle of God."

"That's for sure!" he replied.

He and his acolytes couldn't believe that the cyclist had survived this accident. He agreed to fix it because I didn't want my son to see his bike all bent out of shape. He had to forget this accident and get back on the bike as fast as he could, otherwise he will always refuse to get on his bike all his life. I went back to see the repairman with my son after waiting a few hours. The bike was no longer a new bike but the most important thing was that it was rolling again. They had reworked the bent pieces to make them take their original form. The man asked me if my son was the cyclist. "Yes, that's him."

"You little boy, you are lucky to have survived this."

Emmanuel did not respond, but simply made a nod of the head to say "yes". My son left on his bike to the house while I walked. I was still happy that he had taken up the bike so quickly after the accident.

I knew that this accident had been provoked by the enemy himself because of some details in this story - the motorbike was going too fast, the madman had not tried to avoid my son, he had charged directly at him, by hitting him from the back and, if the motorbike had not fallen to the ground, he would have left the scene as fast as he had come.

Since it was a shot of the enemy, I did not enter into communication with the driver of the motorbike. It was quite possible that this man had not even acted voluntarily, but that he was controlled by a spirit seeking revenge. For my part, everything was forgiven! Material damage is nothing compared to a human life.

On the following Tuesday, I went again to the Church's prayer of deliverance. I received a lot of people, but Sandrine never came. I stayed until the end hoping to see her but I was very disappointed. But then Sandrine presented herself to the prayers on the following Thursday. I met her personally enthusiastically, with the idea that I would finally discover the reasons for her sadness. She had a paper in her hand and showed it to me - there was nothing written.

I was really disappointed in her. She had just shown me beyond a doubt that she did not have the will to get out of it. "Sandrine, it's enough! It is now several weeks since you come to me for help but you are not doing anything to help yourself. You do not show any will, so I prefer to receive people who want to get out of it, rather than a woman who does not want to do anything. This is the last chance I'll give you. Next Tuesday, you're going to come here with a full sheet of paper. I want all the details or I transfer your case to somebody else. I don't want to waste my time anymore."

She looked at me again without saying anything and then left the premises. I know that many people might judge me after saying such a thing but here's what I'm saying to them - "Some people have to get a good kick in the ... to move!" That's just what I did with her. I totally confronted her, so she can find the strength to get out of it. Unfortunately, it was the last day I saw Sandrine. She never came back to church...

The following Sunday, after the morning service, some women came to my place to ask for prayers. The first woman had heart pain; she said that she often dreamed that her heart was completely closed. The second woman also felt pain in the chest because of the intense stress she was experiencing in the last few days. We prayed for the first two women who immediately had divine healing. They didn't feel pain anymore.

The third woman explained her problem, "My boyfriend sent me a summons to court because I broke his mirror. He always insulted and denigrated me. When I learned that he had deceived me with another woman, in a rage, I threw his mirror on the floor to chase him out of my house."

She was really nervous and was terribly afraid to go see a judge. Her boyfriend used to denigrate her all the time, so she imagined that whatever she would do, she would always fail. She kept saying that she was going to lose in court. I started praying for her and when I put my hand on her head and asked the Holy Spirit to fill her with fire, she fell to the ground in incredible jolts. She was constantly moving, so I kept praying more intensely. At the end of the prayer, we sat on a chair and I told her by the name of Jesus, "You have just received the fire of the Holy Spirit in you and, with his presence; you will not be able to fail. You are now more than victorious."

She smiled and I knew that she was beginning to trust in herself. During the prayer, God had shown me things about this woman so I told her, "The Lord saw that your sorrow is very great and he heard your cries. In court, he'll be by your side and you'll be the winner of this case. Your boyfriend's lies will all be revealed to the judge. You will have to tell the truth and only the truth. No lie must come out of your mouth and the truth will win." These few words had fortified her so much that she began to glorify the name of Jesus. We felt the fire of the Holy Spirit burning in her. We were all happy for this great divine manifestation.

To be able to come to Burkina Faso, we had taken visas of up to six months and, unfortunately, they all expired in mid-June. I had filed applications for citizenship in Burkina Faso for me and my son, in the justice court of Dedougou. Rosalie already had her nationality, since she was born in Burkina and could stay in this country even if her visa expired. But for me and my son, we had to file these requests to make sure we would be not be illegal in an African country. I had no desire to visit one of the African prisons, especially after hearing several horrific stories about them.

After filing the applications in court, they asked me to come back and pick up the citizenship certificates on June 6th. After leaving the court, I went to the High Commission to file a request to create an association. We wanted to have a Burkina Faso association so that we could act and work legally, in this country that was welcoming us. In order to be able to receive subsidies or foreign financing, this step was an obligation. Foreign organizations did not like to give money if there was no evidence that this funding would go to humanitarian work and not to the hands of a fraudster. The receipt of an association demonstrated the seriousness of the project.

I had done several searches on the Internet in order to know how to complete all the necessary formalities for the creation of the Association of "Moisson de Christ." I contacted several people to be members in good standing of this new association and we held a first official meeting in order to vote for the statutes and the rules of procedure. Everything went as planned and the new members of the board all signed the document of the meeting, in addition to handing me a legalized copy of their identity card Burkina Faso. All I had to do was to attach all the documents together and bring them to the High Commission.

The man behind the Office of the High Commissioner looked at the documents carefully and looked up at me. He said to me, "Your documents are not conforming. Your request for an association will be refused." I asked him to explain me in more detail and he told me in all honesty that there were several important points missing in the three official documents, the memorandum, the statutes, and the rules of procedure.

I had worked for several days to finally realize that this work had been useless. The man behind the desk noticed the disappointment on my face and told me that he knew someone who could show me how to complete the documents in question. With his help, the demand for creation would be much more likely to be accepted. I thanked this man for his sincerity and I left home carrying my disappointment on my shoulders.

In the evening, a man called on my cell phone and asked me if I wanted his help to complete the association documents. I replied yes, and a few minutes later, he sat before me to discuss the important points. He was a very elegant man who knew the laws of the country and the paperwork very well. He showed me everything I needed to change in my documents and told me all the errors to be corrected. I really learned a lot with this really nice man. He had just given me confidence and, as soon as he left my home, I started working on this request to create an association.

On Thursday, May 17th, the third woman, for whom we had prayed because her boyfriend had summoned her to court, returned to visit us at home. She absolutely wanted to give us news.

She said, "First, I prayed before I met a mediator, who was actually a constable. My boyfriend explained his version of the facts first, but he was always lying. He was accusing me of almost every problem on the planet. He was trying to make me feel like the worst woman in the world. He asks for reimbursement of the broken mirror, damages and interest, payment of the loss of a day of work, and even more. The amount required was really huge. I was really worried because I didn't have the money to pay for everything he asked for. What worried me even more was when the constable turned to look at me; he always had a furious look. I had the impression that he believed my boyfriend."

"I did what you told me - I declared the truth. No lie was coming out of my mouth. I told the constable that I was really sorry to have destroyed the mirror, but my boyfriend had greatly disappointed me. I wanted to spend the rest of my life with him, but he destroyed my dreams. I did not ask for any money, I wanted only one thing - for him to leave me alone."

"The constable looked at the evidence of both parties and told my boyfriend that he had lied from beginning to end. All his statements were completely destroyed by the evidence I had brought. My boyfriend still tried to lie and the constable, now very angry, ordered him to shut up immediately or he will put him in jail."

He told him – "Trust me, you are lucky that this woman does not want to go before the judge, because you would have lost your case and you would have been obliged to pay a huge sum to that woman you mistreated."

"I was really happy. I had just won my case before the mediator and my boyfriend signed a statement of guilt, so he cannot do anything against me. He does not even have the right to enter into communication with me."

"I told you that God would be present," I replied. "Truth always triumphs over falsehood."

We prayed together to thank the Lord for finally giving peace in the heart of my sister in Christ. She cried with joy because the Holy Spirit was still burning in her heart. It was obvious that she would win by declaring only the truth.

"Jesus said to him: I am the way, and the truth, and the life."

-John 14:6 (ESV)

"When he (Satan) lies, he speaks out of his own character, for he is a liar and the father of lies."

-John 8:44 (ESV)

"For everyone who has been born of God overcomes the world. And this is the victory that has overcome the world—our faith."

-1 John 5:4 (ESV)

Jesus himself said he is the truth and the Bible shows us that the devil is the father of lies, so if the truth always triumphs over lies, we are more than victorious in Jesus Christ. My sister in Christ could not lose against this man full of lies. She was more than victorious!

On Friday night, when the moon was already in the sky, Gilbert, called me to ask for prayer. He told me that Christians from Ouagadougou were at his garage right now and need prayer urgently. Me and my wife jumped on the bike and drove to the garage.

Gilbert and his assistants were in the process of dismantling a white pickup into pieces. I approached to find more about the problem.

Gilbert said to me, "The men are disciples of Pastor Mamadou Karambiri from Ouagadougou. They have been in a village not far from here and they all have to go back to the capital tonight. Along the way, between the village and Dedougou, a snake appeared on the dashboard of the pickup and crawled on the driver's hand to provoke an accident. The driver quickly shook his hand without losing control of the car, but failed to see where the snake fell.

They stopped on the edge of the road to look for this snake, but never found it. Having thought that it had come out by itself, they decided to go back on the road. They crossed Dedougou and then, when they arrived at the first police checkpoint at the exit of the city, the snake reappeared on the dashboard. They stopped again, but the beast remained untraceable. They decided to turn around and came here so I could find the snake in the pickup."

This story was amazing but this snake was not real, it was the enemy who wanted to attack men of God. I introduced myself to the men of God and I informed them that I was going to pray that this serpent would not return.

I walked around the pickup praying and sometimes throwing oil on some parts of the vehicle. I didn't feel any satanic presence. I told Gilbert, "You are dismantling this vehicle for nothing; the serpent is not here right now".

I then approached the men of God to explain to them what the Lord had just shown me. Comfortably seated before them, I said to them, "This accursed serpent will not harass you again tonight. You can go back to Ouagadougou without any worries. But, tomorrow will be another day." The men thanked me for my gesture and I said goodbye to them, before going home. Gilbert had already begun to put the parts of the pickup to their respective places.

On Sunday, after the service, Gilbert had come to give me the rest of this snake story. He said, "You were right from the beginning. They left and never saw the snake again."

"The driver was so nervous to get back in the driver's seat after the snake touched his hand, that they were forced to take another driver. The serpent never manifested itself between Dedougou and Ouagadougou. Yesterday morning, when the man of God, the one whose hand the serpent had touched, took the steering wheel to go to work; the beast reappeared on the dashboard again. The man stopped the vehicle right in the centre of the main road in Ouagadougou without worrying about traffic and got out without hesitation leaving the door open. The snake tried to follow him outside but the man closed the door on the snake. The beast died stuck in the door."

He showed me a picture that the man of God had sent him on his cell phone. I could clearly see the dead snake with half the body outside and the other half inside the pickup. Gilbert continued, "You were right when you told them that he would not see the serpent that night, but the next day would be another story."

"It wasn't me; it was God who told me. I didn't quite understand why he said - Tomorrow would be another day. Now I understand everything!"

"Clearly," replied Gilbert, "This serpent really wanted to attack this man of God, in particular. The enemy is very cunning."

We continued a bit to talk about this incredible story until a brother came to me to ask if I could come to his high school to do maintenance on computers. I agreed and we made an appointment for the next morning. After the service, I went back home to prepare some USB keys with antivirus software, protections against malware and other specialized software for computer maintenance.

The next morning, I returned, as agreed, at the Bethel High School of Dedougou. It was a private high school and the Brother in Christ was the principal. He came to me and explained that he would like all the laptops to be formatted to make sure that all the student's personal files were deleted. He showed me twenty-two Lenovo laptops. They were all identical so I just had to do a reset of the factory settings.

I spent two days rebooting a few computers but the laptops were so contaminated with computer viruses that I had no choice but to reformat everything. As soon as I used my flash drive, my software was contaminated and I couldn't use it anymore. I informed the principal that I would return next Monday to do this work. I went go back home and I started downloading software and drivers on the Internet.

On Sunday, May 27th, in the afternoon, Emmanuel, a Christian Brother from another church, came to our house to ask for prayer. He had been suffering for several years and still felt very weak physically and mentally. Doctors told him it was Hepatitis B, but other doctors said he had absolutely nothing. He showed me the diagnostics signed by the doctors. They had done a test for Hepatitis, but the results were negative. Emmanuel admitted to me that it was almost 12 years since he was working.

He was constantly exhausted and had almost no physical strength. I asked him to sit in the chair while we were going to pray for him. I decided to intercede to ask that the fire of the Holy Spirit invade him and consume all this lethargy that does not come from God, especially that spirit of extreme fatigue.

As soon as I started praying in tongues, the Christian Brother also started speaking in tongues.

Suddenly he got up in one shot and began to jump all over the place. He was praying in tongues, jumping everywhere without exhaustion. My wife and I felt the presence of the Holy Spirit mightily. He jumped and jumped while shouting the name of Jesus. He finally fell on his knees to cry while glorifying the Lord. I put oil on his forehead and declared that the spirit of fatigue that was in his body had been driven out by the Holy Spirit. We thanked the Lord for this divine healing and the Brother confessed to us that he had never felt so good for years. He felt like he had become a young school boy again. Such a passion for the Lord was truly magnificent to see.

Meanwhile, we had to file several requests for funding to international organizations before the deadline of May 31, 2018.

To do this, all our documents for the creation of association had to be delivered at the High Commission on Monday, May 28th, Attacks to prevent us from having the receipt on time, appeared slowly before our eyes. A big black cloud was forming and the wind was starting to blow very hard. Moreover, they had a blackout in the entire town of Dedougou due to bad weather. Nothing was right for us.

We had to legalize our documents with 200 FCFA (local money) tax stamps, but there were a lot of contests for government jobs, a strike at the Treasury Department and a huge shortage of tax stamps like never before. We went to the High Commission to explain the situation, but the offices were closed because of the government's job contests. We tried the Town Hall, the courthouse, the police station, and some small shops but the stamps were not found. So we tried the Treasury Department, but they closed several services because of the strike

I asked the woman to call the director because it was really urgent and when the man arrived, we recognized him immediately. A friend of ours worked as a director but had been transferred to Gaoua, southern Burkina Faso. Before he left, he had come to our home to introduce us to the new director who would replace him.

He didn't know why, but he knew he had to introduce us. He was right to do it. The new director brought us into his office and we explained him the urgency of the situation. He agreed to make us a payment receipt for the creation of the association.

We were really happy because it was an important document that we had to add to the file. Now that we had this receipt, all that remained was to have the others legalized. I started searching and discovered that there was some tax stamps left in Douroula, a village a few kilometers outside Dedougou. I called the person in charge of the tax stamps at the Town Hall of Douroula and he asked me to come on Wednesday morning because he was on a mission outside. I found that the deadlines were very tight, as we had to apply for funding at the Canadian Embassy in Ouagadougou by May 31st before 4 pm. We returned home soaked in rain, shaken by the winds and soiled by mud on the roads. A good shower was necessary.

The next morning, I went to Bethel High School to do the maintenance of their laptops. I had previously prepared some USB sticks to be able to install three or four at same time. Everything was going very well and I had managed to restore more than twelve laptops. Then I went back to my home to fill out the forms for the Canadian Embassy funding application. It was a very busy day and, in the evening, Brother Emmanuel, who always jumped with joy, came home to ask for prayer for his wife. She told me that she often felt a presence behind her shoulder and had pain in her belly.

I started praying for her, thinking that her case was not so bad, but after putting my hand on her head, she bent over forwards. She stood up and bent again, and again. The spirit in her manifested itself, so I took authority over him by ordering him to leave this body because he was not the owner. The woman began to cough, as if she had something in her throat. She started to vomit a strange whitish liquid. I kept yelling for it to leave her and then she came back to herself. She was liberated! The woman felt so good now!

"A spirit seizes it, and immediately it cries, and the spirit agitates it with violence, makes it foam, and has trouble to withdraw from it, after having broken it all."
-Luke 9:39 (ESV)

Wednesday morning was the special day because we had to go to Douroula to have documents legalized. We woke up very early and left on a motorcycle. The road was paved with compacted fine stones which made the road a bit dangerous because, when a big truck was passing by, its tires were sending small rocks everywhere. We had to slow down and let the truck go forward a good distance ahead of us. Finally, we arrived to Douroula, and the Town Hall was very easy to find since it was the first building at the entrance of the village. The man at the front desk told me that the legalization officer had been in Dedougou for a few days.

He had still not returned to Douroula. I thought we had made all this trip for nothing, so I called the manager. He told me that he was at the hotel in Dedougou and that he immediately got on the road to come and meet us. We had to wait for him there.

Fortunately, there were several grape vines in the courtyard of the Town Hall, so Rosalie and I had fun climbing trees to pick the grapes and eat them. People must have laughed at the sight of the white man who climbed like a monkey just for grapes.

The officer of the Town Hall finally arrived on his motorcycle. He was a jovial and very amusing man. He always made jokes with everyone around him. We felt an incredible joy of life coming from this man. He looked at the documents and told us that there were no more stamps of 200 FCFA but there were only 500 FCFA. I absolutely had to have these documents, so I accepted even if it would cost me more. He legalized the whole thing and then we went back to Dedougou on a motorbike to drop the file off at the High Commission.

The men we had given the full file told us that they thought we would never succeed. "This is the work of God!" I replied. "Will I get the document by 5 pm tomorrow?"

"There should be no problems." he replied.

Finally, everything was done! Rosalie and I were so happy that we stopped in a small restaurant to eat some pieces of pork cooked in the oven. After this relaxing little break, I dropped Rosalie off at home and returned to complete maintenance on the laptops at Bethel High School. All of them were now fully functional.

At night, at home, a Muslim neighbor came to see us. He sat on a chair in front of us and told us a story about his wife. This man's father had taken possession of the newly built house for his son. This house was supposed to be the family home for the son, his wife, and his children but the father had confiscated it for himself. The wife was very upset to see that her husband was letting his father do whatever he wanted, so she returned to her family in Ivory Coast. The man became very sad. His father noticed the sadness and all the pain he had provoked. He decided to give back the house to his son, but it was too late - his wife had left him. The son regularly communicated with his wife and always asked her to come back to him but she was constantly refusing, until recently.

She had finally asked her husband if he could send her money to pay for transportation back to Dedougou. The Muslim man was desperate because he did not have that amount on him. He needed 50,000 FCFA in order to be able to see his wife again, but did not know how to get the money. So, he came to ask us to help him. I explained to the man that I would love to help him but I could not do it, because no Canadian church was funding our project and we had not yet received any grant from any international organization. We only lived with what God gave us and we had just enough for us. He had left disappointed, but we had no choice. As I knew my wife's heart very well, as soon as the man left our court, she tried to convince me to give him the money. "I don't want to and I can't!"

Thursday, May 31st the deadline for deposit the request for funding to the Canadian embassy in Ouagadougou. I went to the High Commission to take the signed document. When the officer behind the desk handed me the document, I noticed a small mistake.

On the receipt, they had entered "Moisson du Christ" instead of putting "Moisson de Christ".

This little mistake could prevent me from getting the funding because the name of the association was not the right one. The man was so uncomfortable with this mistake, that he quickly got up and said, "I must quickly catch the Commissioner to sign the new document because he is about to leave for the day." He left the room quickly and returned after a few minutes with a new document in his hands.

He had printed a corrected copy and had ran to obtain the necessary signatures. Now everything was consistent and I could send my funding request.

I thanked the agent of the High Commission and went back home. The request for the embassy was to be sent by email. I had already filled out the application forms and I had scanned copies of all the documents of the association. The whole thing was sent directly to the embassy and they confirmed the receipt of the forms. Now we had to wait for their final decision that would come out in a few months.

Brother Emmanuel's mother-in-law came home to ask us to pray for her. She had hip pains and couldn't sleep. I started praying for her and she felt that the pain was slowly fading away. At the end of the prayer, she informed us that she no longer felt any pain in the hips.

"You will have a remarkable night," I replied. "You'll sleep like a baby. Don't forget to thank the Lord every morning for what he has done on you." She left in joy.

On Friday morning, I went back to Bethel High school to hand over a personalized USB stick with all the software they would need in the event of a new installation of laptops. He was happy to see how I had taken care of this contract. I also gave him a document that included the steps for maintenance or reinstallation of the laptops.

On Saturday morning, Brother Emmanuel's mother-in-law had returned to give us news about her healing. She was still limping a little bit but felt no pain and she had spent a very restful night. Nothing could wake her up since there was no more pain.

After she left, my wife began to harass me again, to give the 50,000 FCFA to the Muslim man. Although I doubted the truth of his story, I asked my son to go and tell him that we wanted to see him. He came back and sat in front of us. I said to him, "We have thought a long time, since we are in the Lenten of Muslims, we will give you this gift. It is not good for man to be alone, while others are celebrating. Here's the money you asked for." I gave him five bills of 10,000 FCFA and I saw tears in his eyes. He kept thanking us. I continued to doubt him, even though he had tears in his eyes. He rose to leave and I sent him a little subtle message, "I look forward to meeting your wife!" My wife had full confidence in him, but deep inside me, doubt was always present.

CITIZENS OF BURKINA

The six-month visas we had taken to enter Burkina Faso were soon to expire. I filed applications for Burkinabe citizenship in the justice court as the husband and son of a woman born in Burkina and I had to return to court on Wednesday June 6th to pick up the nationality certificates. The woman who took care of this kind of request had not yet arrived. So, I waited a bit and then she passed me to go to her office. I followed her and, once inside the office, she asked me the reason for my visit. "I come to pick up our certificates of nationality." She looked at her desk and explained that they had not yet been signed.

She was going to work on it today and asked me to come back next Friday to pick them up. I thanked her and went back home. I was a little worried because, without these certificates, I would have to extend my visa by going to Ouagadougou, which would be very expensive, or on the border of Mali, which was very dangerous for a Canadian white man, because of terrorists. Even if the risk of attack or abduction was very high on the border of Mali, this option remained the best because I could apply for a one-month visa for 10,000 FCFA only. A trip to Ouagadougou would cost more in transport, accommodation, and taxis. In addition, visas are at least three months. Honestly, I didn't want to get close to the border, but if I had to, I would, because if God is for us, who can be against us? Right now, I just had to wait.

The following Friday, I went back to court to pick up the certificates. The woman in the office informed me that there was a small problem with my personal request. My son's was already accepted and signed. A man entered the office with my request in hand and showed me the problem - on my application for nationality, I wrote that my name was Martin Falardeau while on my birth certificate it stated Joseph-Jean-Claude Martin Falardeau.

I explained them, "In the past, in Quebec, when a child was born, they added Joseph for the boys and Mary for the girls. They also put the name of the child's godfather, in my case; it was my uncle Jean-Claude Falardeau, who was my godfather. However, my real name is Martin Falardeau. Government realized that this kind of birth certificate provoked a lot of problems, so they stopped making multiple-name certificates. If you look at my son's certificate, it doesn't have that kind of thing on his. Also, look at my passport and all the other official documents, it's always written as Martin Falardeau only."

The man seemed to think about how to correct this problem quickly and then asked me to follow him in the judge's office and explain the same thing to him. In this new office, there were several boxes filled with documents on the floor and a man was sitting behind a large desk. I repeated the same explanation and I showed him my driver's license, my social insurance card, and my passport. He saw that I was telling the truth, so he asked me to go out and wait for the result. Wait for the result, I wondered, "Was I not clear enough in my explanations?"

A judge will always be a judge, and I knew that he should not be contradicted, so I obeyed his request and I went out to wait outside. Time went by and I wondered why it was that long. He only had to put a signature on the certificate, but it took forever. I was beginning to imagine a plan B in my head, in case the judge refused to sign. I already saw myself driving the motorbike to the border of Mali to extend my visa. It's amazing the things that can pass through the mind of a person who is anxiously waiting for an answer. We always imagine the worst. I even called Rosalie to tell her the story.

The woman who took care of the certificate applications sometimes passed me and I finally decided to ask her what the latest news about my case was. She said, "Don't worry, they'll accept it." I could not say if this reply had really encouraged me or not. Finally, a man approached me and asked me to follow him in the woman's office. They took out the certificates and handed them to me. Finally, my son and I were citizens of Burkina Faso. From that day, I had officially the right to work freely in this beautiful country of humble men. Thank you, Lord.

The next day, Brother Emmanuel, the one who leaped with joy, and his wife came home. He wanted to ask me to follow him to Soury, a village not far from Dedougou, in order to pray for his wife's sister. I began to wonder if there was a bigger problem with Brother Emmanuel's in-laws - a mother who suffered from hip pain, a wife who had vomited a whitish liquid because of a spirit and now the sister who had also a problem linked to an evil spirit.

Brother Emmanuel explained to me the problems of his sister-in-law, "An evil spirit invaded her 15 years ago. She often walks naked in the village and yelling nonsense. A pastor took her to his home and often prays for her. Prayers calm her but she always starts her manifestations again."

I wondered why they had never tried anything to deliver her in 15 years. Now the spirit had to be firmly attached to her. It would be very difficult to deliver her. I still followed them on a motorbike to the village of Soury. They lead me to the small church of the International Union of Christians of this village since she lived with the pastor. The woman was sitting outside, a little frightened by my presence. I introduced myself to the pastor, who did not speak much French or English so Emmanuel's wife translated the discussions.

I decided to prepare the site by praying on the four corners of the pastor's court while pouring oil. In order to be far from the indiscreet glances, we settled inside the small church. I also poured oil into the four corners of this church. Emmanuel's sister-in-law was on a wooden bench. I walked around her looking into her eyes.

She was terribly afraid of me and admitted it to me several times. I began to pray few minutes for her by putting my hand on her head but she did not show any spiritual reaction. So, I sat by her side but she was always trying to get away from me.

I then asked her to lie down on the bench. She started undressing. "No, I said! You don't have to take off your clothes. I just want you to lie on your back on that bench." Once again, she began to try to remove her clothes.

The pastor spoke in Bwamu (local language) and ordered her to lie on her back without undressing. She obeyed him. I finally managed to resume my deliverance prayers on her.

This time, I felt that there was another presence with us, an unhealthy presence. So, I started asking her a few questions to find out more about her. I found out that she was a student at Gorom-Gorom, a city in Southern Burkina, and wanted to pass her BPC (important school diploma in that country). She wanted to put every chance on her side so she had been to see a marabout, to do satanic rituals for her success. The sorcerer put a spell on her in order to be able to sleep with her, instead of helping her with the final test of the school.

The young woman became pregnant with this sorcerer and had a daughter. Her problems did not stop there. She was very scared of this man and decided to leave him to return to her family in Dedougou. It was then that madness had invaded this young woman. The marabout had bewitched her, so that no other man could touch her. She had become so crazy, that she would hit the first person she saw, start running naked in the village and insulting bystanders and neighbors for no reason.

It was now more than 15 years that she was in this state of madness. She gave me the name of this marabout of Gorom-Gorom - Paul Souleyman. She kept saying that he was still there with her and that he was watching her every night. Seeing that she was still sunk in madness, I took her by the hand and took her outside the church away from the presence of others. We were just the two of us.

I asked her to look away, to look at the scenery and the people in their backyards. "Look at all these people over there I said. You see how happy they look. They're in families. Wouldn't you like to have a happy family, too?"

"Yes." she said to me.

"You can have all this. If you cut the ties with this marabout of Gorom-Gorom."

She always looked attentively at the distant people in their yards. I knew that the woman who was alone with me outside the church was not crazy. We were talking normally together and I saw no sign of madness. On the contrary, she used intelligent words. I realized she was acting crazy in front of some people. For what reason, I am not sure, but alone with me, she was the very intelligent woman she had been in her youth. We returned inside the small church where I explained to others what I believed about this woman. "She's not that crazy. She is still attached to that marabout and she's so scared that she pretends to be crazy."

"Why she had been acting so for more than 15 years?" asked Emmanuel's wife.

"She's the only one who knows why, but fear can lead people to do strange unexplainable things. Maybe she wants to protect the girl she had with this marabout."

The woman just sat, listened to us, and said nothing. I turned to her and told her, "Now I want you to pray every day with the pastor and attend the church service. Only prayer can free you from the fear you have. Here's a little gift for you - it's a Bible. I want you to read it every day because you'll need the double-edged sword to defend yourself against the enemy. This sword is the Word, so read it regularly. If I learn that you do not do what I ask, I will come back with a prayer team and, believe me, they are more intense than me in prayer of deliverance. If you've been afraid of me, you'll be even more afraid of them."

She had listened to everything and she firmly held her new Bible in her hands. We all came out of the church and, after saying my goodbyes to everyone, I reminded the woman, "Don't forget to do what I asked you, or I'll come back and see you with a team." She still held her Bible with both hands and indicated to me she would do everything. I rode on my motorbike to go home.

In the evening, Brother Emmanuel came back to my house and asked me to pray also for another of his sisters-in-law. "Another one?" I thought, "There was a real problem with this family."

I sat in front of this woman and asked her several questions to understand what the problem was in this family. She explained to me that she often saw shadows at night in her room. Sometimes these shadows came to haunt her and harass her while she was sleeping. She often woke up with stomach aches. She believed that it was because of their father, who worked regularly with marabouts and that she thought that the curses had all fallen upon the children. Now I understand! When a family man decides to ask for help from these sorcerers, he must give something back.

The sorcerers always asked for money, but were never satisfied with money - they wanted more. They acted without their client's knowledge and came to create spiritual bonds for future generations. The children were then faced with spells that they had never asked for because of the father who had not thought, before consulting a disciple of Satan. This was also the case in the Old Testament with the Jewish people.

"You shall not bow down to them or serve them, for I the LORD your God am a jealous God, visiting the iniquity of the fathers on the children to the third and the fourth generation of those who hate me."

-Exodus 20:5 (ESV)

I stood up and prayed for this woman. Putting my hand on her head, she collapsed on her knees screaming incessantly. I put my hand on her head again and she collapsed on the ground, rolling in every direction and screaming.

I continued to pray to chase away that malicious spirit that was in her body. The spirit left her and she was definitively liberated from this demonic grasp. I helped her sit on a chair because she was completely overwhelmed by what had just happened. She had never lived such a thing in her whole life. She often saw people collapsing on the ground during prayers at the church, but never thought that this kind of reaction could happen to her as well. She was really confused and lost.

I tried to encourage by talking to her about some of the cases I had with brothers and sisters in Christ, to show her that she was not the only one in this situation. "Jesus just delivered you," I said. "Now be in joy. The ties that attached you to your father's marabouts are now broken. Every morning, thank the Lord for what he has just done in you. Do not forget to read the Word regularly because it is the perfect weapon to repel the enemy. Jesus too, had repelled the enemy by using the Word as a weapon." She thanked me and left me more joyful than before.

"And the tempter came and said to him: If you are the Son of God, command these stones to become loaves of bread. But he answered: It is written, Man shall not live by bread alone, but by every word that comes from the mouth of God. Then the devil took him to the holy city and set him on the pinnacle of the temple and said to him: If you are the Son of God, throw yourself down, for it is written, He will command his angels concerning you, and on their hands they will bear you up, lest you strike your foot against a stone. Jesus said to him: Again it is written: You shall not put the Lord your God to the test. Again, the devil took him to a very high mountain and showed him all the kingdoms of the world and their glory. And he said to him: All these I will give you, if you will fall down and worship me. Then Jesus said to him: Be gone, Satan! For it is written, you shall worship the Lord your God and him only shall

you serve. Then the devil left him, and behold, angels came and were ministering to him."

-Matthew 4:3-11 (ESV)

PASTOR AT THE MAQUIS

On Monday, June 11th, Rosalie left very early in the morning to take the bus towards the capital Ouagadougou. She brought with her the document of the association, in order to publish it in the Official Gazette of Burkina Faso. This step was essential for the creation of an association. Arriving at his destination, she took a taxi and immediately went to the General Secretariat of the Government. Rosalie saw several people in the courtyard of this official building and she went to share with them about the Lord. The man near her was actually the one who dealt with the publications in the Official Gazette. He informed Rosalie that he had been a Christian for several years and that he was going to the Church of Pastor Mamadou Karambiri.

They went up to his office and Rosalie told him how God had sent us to Burkina for the advancement of his kingdom. The man was really impressed by the association we created and the work we wanted to do. He declared that there was a delay of several weeks before the publication but, since it is for a work of God, he would make things go faster. He also left his business card with my wife, so that we would come to meet him at his biological breeding center of several hectares. He wanted to show us his center and inform us about how to take care of it and manage it all. Rosalie was really happy with this new encounter. She returned to Dedougou the next morning with the first available bus.

Behind our residence, just on the other side of the empty land, there was a small Maquis (small outdoor bar) run by a man from France, named Samuel. I was sometimes sitting at a table and chatting a little with the regular customers of this place. They explained to me that the mother of this French man was working here in Burkina Faso in her own NGO, which was helping orphans.

Her son spent several years as a musician in Mali and then moved to Dedougou. He had never left Burkina Faso since.

I did not know for what reason, but I felt that I had to get closer to this man in order to bring him slowly in the light of the Lord. So, I began to visit his Maquis in order to gain his trust. Unfortunately it triggered all the tongues of vipers, who talked about my presence in a drinking establishment. They told everyone that they were outraged because they had seen me drinking beer, comfortably seated at a table in the Maquis.

I know that many pastors falsely preach that it is forbidden to take alcohol, but I would like to ask all these pastors to quote me the verse that forbids this. I can answer for them - there is none! It is the drunkenness that is prohibited and not the reasonable taking of alcohol. Pastors, stop putting rules and laws within your churches because, by doing this, you become exactly like the Pharisees of the Bible. These men believed themselves to be above the rest of the population because they knew the law word by word and they judged disobedient people.

"Woe to you lawyers also! For you load people with burdens hard to bear, and you yourselves do not touch the burdens with one of your fingers."

Luke 11:46 (ESV)

"Therefore let no one pass judgment on you in questions of food and drink, or with regard to a festival or a new moon or a Sabbath. These are a shadow of the things to come, but the substance belongs to Christ."

-Colossians 2:16-17 (ESV)

After a few days in the Maquis, Samuel came to chat with me. He had already heard of the work that the Lord was doing through my hands. My house keeper had already told me the same thing. He told me that the people of Dedougou told him that a white man from Canada was healing and delivering all those who came to his home and that God was working with power with him. Some stated that if I opened a church, everyone would come to the worship the Lord.

The problem was that God did not sent me to Dedougou to open a church. So I began to explain several miracles that God had done, without giving too much detail to the spiritual level, because Samuel did not yet know the Lord. He would not understand the gifts of the Holy Spirit and the mysteries of the Kingdom of God.

"And he answered them: To you it has been given to know the secrets of the kingdom of heaven, but to them it has not been given."
-Matthew 13:11 (ESV)

"Even the Spirit of truth, whom the world cannot receive, because it neither sees him nor knows him. You know him, for he dwells with you and will be in you."
-John 14:17 (ESV)

I already knew the bad reputation that Samuel had among the majority of the population, but I never trusted what people said. Some said he was very bad with the people around him, that he insulted everyone, or that he did not pay his employees - the list went on and on. But these tongues of vipers were all seemed to forget a very important thing that Jesus himself said...

"Those who are well have no need of a physician, but those who are sick. I came not to call the righteous, but sinners."
-Marc 2:17 (ESV)

This man really needed the light of the Lord in his life. I spoke to him regularly about Jesus and I felt that he sincerely appreciated my presence. He opened up more and more and told me a lot of confidential things that I would not put in this book out of respect for this man. He also testified to me all his past and how he ended up in Burkina Faso. Today he was carrying several demons connected to his past, which made him drink a lot of alcohol. He was trying to forget the dark days of his life. Unfortunately for him, alcohol had never helped solve anything. On the contrary, it aggravated the sadness in the body of a man who carried a heavy past. One day I had seen him empty a large bottle of whiskey in just 2 hours.

Samuel had confessed to me that he would love to have a great relationship with the Lord but was afraid to lose everything he loved to do. "Like what?" I asked him. He was looking for an answer other than drinking alcohol or wasting his time in the Maquis, but couldn't find it. He had just realized that his life was going nowhere. This simple question had completely demolished the wall he had forged to hide all his woes in the depths of himself.

One day he introduced me to his wife Mathilde, from Burkina Faso. When we first met, I felt a strong sadness. She never smiled and always looked discouraged. I realized that she did not like her husband's way of life. I felt that this story would soon end in divorce, if Samuel continued like this. He always came home completely drunk and always drove his motorcycle under the influence of alcohol.

One night, when there was a heavy rain falling on Dedougou, Samuel still took the bike to return home. It was a very dangerous mix - alcohol, motorcycle and rain storm. He lost control in a big puddle of water and fell to the side with the bike. His shoulder struck a huge stone. Again, under the influence of alcohol, he lifted himself up painfully and tried to raise his bike without succeeding.

He had realized that he could no longer use his arm after hitting the stone with his shoulder. So, he called his Maquis employee to come and help him get home. It was just this kind of bad event that was discouraging his wife. I knew that alcohol was destroying him, so I wanted to move him away from this Maquis. He would never agree because he was the owner, so I had to find another solution to make sure he would stop living near the bottles.

Following his motorcycle accident, Samuel always had intense shoulder pain. He had made the decision to consult a marabout, who manipulated his shoulder in several strange ways and gave him a dubious medicine. The man always came out with more pain. I kept telling him that he was making a big mistake when he went to see that kind of person, but he didn't listen to me. He spent almost two weeks with this sorcerer, who was not able to cure anything.

Finally, we invited Samuel and his wife for a friendly dinner at home, the evening of Sunday, June 24th, after enjoying a good meal prepared by my dear wife, Samuel and his wife both asked us for prayer.

I was delighted to see that Samuel had finally realized that healing came only from the Lord and not from a sorcerer, who simply wanted to extract the maximum amount of money from him. His wife was a Catholic. I stood up and prayed for Samuel by putting the oil on his forehead. I felt the fire and the power of the Holy Spirit inside me.

When I put my hand on his shoulder, my eyes became like x-rays and I could see through his skin. I found that the clavicle was broken at the ligament of his arm. After completing the prayer, I explained to him that his clavicle was broken, but he replied that the marabout had said otherwise.

"Then we shall see which one of you is telling the truth," he replied to me. The result was very obvious since I had the God of Truth with me and the marabout had the father of lies with him. Who would you bet on? Samuel confessed to me that he was already feeling much better, that the pain seemed to leave him slowly. I confessed to him, that he would have a remarkably peaceful night, without pain or strange dreams to awaken him. He still doubted, but it was normal from a man, who had never seen the Holy Spirit at work.

I was surprised to see Mathilde rise and ask for prayer, as she did not feel very well. Many Catholics did not believe in the works of the Holy Spirit like the Evangelists, but she seemed open to prayer in tongues. She confessed that she felt a lot of discouragement in her life. We took care to remove all the chairs around her because I felt she had a malicious spirit that was lurking in her body. I started praying for her then, like all other times, when I put my hand on her head, she collapsed to the ground and her body had irregular tremors.

Samuel jaw dropped at the manifestation of an unclean spirit, right in front of his eyes. I put oil on the forehead of the woman on the ground, and I continued the prayer of deliverance. I used the authority given by Christ to expel this intruder from her body.

When she came back to herself, we helped her sit on a chair to regain her strength. I asked her how she was felt and she replied, "I feel free!"

Sure, she was free, free from the grasp of that intruder who controlled her.

I turned to Samuel and said, "You see what happens when the Holy Spirit acts on a person. Your wife fell on the ground by the power of the Holy Spirit. It was not me who pushed her and she is not an actress paid to play a role in order to convince you. It's your own wife!" He had no choice but to admit that what he had just seen far exceeded anything he believed. He had already seen this kind of thing on television, but still thought that the pastors were liars and that the people who fell, were paid to do so in order to convince everybody else, so they could receive larger tithes and offerings.

We were talking about his own wife. She was not there to convince her husband, she was not paid, and I did not do it to receive tithes or offerings, since I had never asked money from anyone. God gave me free gifts; I had to share them for free to the people around me for the advancement of his kingdom.

"One gives freely, yet grows all the richer; another withholds what he should give, and only suffers want. Whoever brings blessing will be enriched, and one who waters will himself be watered."

-Proverbs 11:24-25 (ESV)

I had a short vision about the future of the Maquis, so I made a proposition to Samuel, "We should show Christian movies at your Maquis." He looked at me attentively and seemed a little interested. So, I continued, "Imagine, we will show a Christian movie and if there are more people in your Maquis than during the broadcasts of other movies with violence and action, we will continue to broadcast Christian films."

"Okay so let's try it tomorrow night," he replied.

On Monday night, people do not go out much, so Samuel did not give me much chance to prove to him, that it was God who wanted to transform his Maquis. Since I had full confidence in my Lord, I accepted his offer without hesitation. There is nothing impossible to my God and, if it is really his will, he will fill this Maquis. Samuel will even need extra chairs!

It was getting late, so the couple stood up to hit the road. We could already notice a little change in Mathilde's face. After the usual goodbyes, they left together and went straight to their home. Rosalie and I spoke for a long time about Samuel's wife and her powerful deliverance. We were still laughing at the face that her husband had when he saw her fall. His eyes were wide open and his lower jaw seemed to fall to the ground. He was completely overwhelmed by the events. The vision of the power of the Holy Spirit would probably help him believe in Jesus as his Lord and Savior. We were hoping for it wholeheartedly. We prayed for this before we closed our eyes.

Monday evening finally arrived and I was very anxious to prove to Samuel that God would fill his Maquis if we broadcast a Christian movie, instead of movie with violence, filled with blood and scenes of nudity, which are often totally useless in a movie. I had brought the Bible film, which lasted more than three hours. It was the complete history of the entire Old Testament. I thought I would broadcast that one first and then show the film about Jesus later, after the owner realized that the Christian movies were attracting more audiences.

When we started the movie, there were only a few regular customers. The more the film progressed, the more people came. They walked on the road near the Maquis and heard the names of the patriarchs of the movie - "Abraham, Isaac, Jacob and others." They turned their gaze towards the Maquis and saw that it was really a movie about the Bible.

They all came to sit and watch this wonderful movie. Halfway through the film, there were no more available chairs in the Maquis but people kept coming and sat down on the ground, not wanting to miss anything. God had answered with strength and power.

Samuel was obliged to admit that my God really existed.

The spectators often shouted when seeing spectacular scenes like the destruction of Sodom, the sea separated in two by the stick of Moses, the collapse of the wall of Jericho, David against Goliath, etc. We had even heard a few people applaud at the end of the movie. Others came to see Samuel to ask for a copy of this movie, so that they could show it to their family.

I told Samuel not to copy this movie but rather to rebroadcast it next time to attract even more people. If a movie is copied, in just a few days, all the inhabitants would have the file in their possession and no one would come to watch it in the Maquis. "We mustn't copy any more film," I told Samuel. He was so happy to see all these people in his Maquis and confessed to me that he had never seen so many since the official opening of his Maquis. I replied ironically, "Then we will be forced to broadcast the film on Jesus!"

"For sure!"

Three days later, Rosalie and I were in the Maquis to talk a little bit with Samuel when his wife arrived. She was so beautiful because her new smile was wonderful. She was totally in the joy of the Lord. She explained to us all the details of her joy, "This morning I was in the kitchen, and I felt a fire invade me. I started to sing Christian songs and praise Jesus without being able to stop. Something in me pushed me to do this and I raised my arms in the air to praise even more intensely. I felt my heart was burning with passion. Then I started crying like a baby. I could not stop and I kept saying – Thank you Jesus! Samuel looked at me and called me crazy, but I told him that I was crazy about the Lord."

We immediately jumped with joy since she had just received the Holy Spirit. Only the fire of the Holy Spirit could push a person to do so, in the love of Our Lord. When I had received the promised comforter, I too, had cried like a baby and I could not stop. It was before the brother and sister during a prayer of intercession. Everyone had noticed me. Some knew it was the power of the Holy Spirit but others had also called me crazy.

My wife went to sit with Mathilde, while I stayed with Samuel to chat with him. I asked him how his shoulder was. "I can't feel any more pain and I think it's cured," he replied.

"You know, I would very much like to see X-rays because your clavicle is broken at the shoulder level."

"How can you know that?" he asked me.

"I saw it when I prayed for your healing."

"Now, you are going too far, I do not believe that! My clavicle is good because I do not feel any pain."

To quickly change the subject, he told me something that really surprised me, "The evangelists really scare me!"

"Why?" I asked him.

"With their stories of speaking in tongues, screaming and dancing like crazy. There is nothing serious in all this."

"When the Holy Spirit will come in you, as he did for your wife, you will understand. But at this moment you only understand the physical things of this world. Later, you will see the spiritual things and you will hear the voice of God."

He was still being the tough guy and his pride made him resist any Word of God. I did not worry because I was like him before becoming a servant of the Living God. I felt that the Lord was going to act on him and that he would come personally to the church and worship the Lord.

The next afternoon, I went to the Maquis to chat with the owner. God had shown me a wonderful project that could earn him a lot more money than his drinking establishment. In West Africa, the Maquis had the bad reputation of being a place of prostitution, but Samuel never hired women to work as a waitress or, worse, as a prostitute.

But many men came during the night with women who were not their wives, engaged in extramarital affairs. I often saw this kind of thing happening in this place.

It was not a very attractive place; it was a place of sin. When I was alone with the French man, I explained to him the vision I had for his Maquis, "It will no longer be a Maquis, but it will become a family center where there will be joy every day. There will be no sale of alcohol but it will be juices and healthy snacks for families."

"Children would be able to play several games and physical activities every day. In the evening, movies will be shown but only movies for the family or Christians."

The next evening, we were surprised to see Samuel and Mathilde come over to ask for more prayer. The woman always had a smile on her face and spoke with enthusiasm. We could feel all the joy in his heart. The husband wanted me to pray again for his shoulder, as he felt a slight pain in his shoulder again.

"Are you going to have x-rays?" I asked him.

"No, it's not broken!"

"You know that the longer you wait, the more the infection can spread in your body and that can be very dangerous."

"What? Your God cannot heal that?"

"Bless the Lord, O my soul, and forget not all his benefits, who forgives all your iniquity, who heals all your diseases."
- Psalm 103:2-3 (ESV)

I did not like the mocking tone he was taking, so I decided not to talk about it anymore. Samuel did not understand anything about the spiritual world.

"He has made everything beautiful in its time. Also, he has put eternity into man's heart, yet so that he cannot find out what God has done from the beginning to the end."
- Ecclesiastes 3:11 (ESV)

I began to pray again for him but I felt deep inside me that this prayer was useless. I put oil on his forehead as the Word asked to do for the sick. Subsequently, we turned to Mathilde who was simply asking for a thanksgiving prayer for all that the Lord had done in her. She was free and happy! We had prayed with joy and Mathilde had embarked on our prayer to thank the only Living God.

The following Sunday, Pastor Tiken from the International Center for Evangelization at Dedougou asked me to come forward and talk a bit about the work I was doing in the French Maquis. Many people were speaking a lot against me because I was drinking beer in a place of sin. They forgot, or did not want to understand, what Jesus Himself had bequeathed to us as a mission.

"The harvest is plentiful, but the laborers are few. Therefore pray earnestly to the Lord of the harvest to send out laborers into his harvest. Go your way; behold, I am sending you out as lambs in the midst of wolves."

- Luke 10:2-3 (ESV)

I got up and took the microphone to give the real truth about my presence in a Maquis. I found it a little insulting to have to justify myself this way, but I had to do it to silence the tongues of vipers of this church. So I said, "As many people know, I often visit the Maquis owned by the French man named Samuel that is right behind my place, on the other side of the empty land. I'm evangelizing him because he carries a lot of demons with him."

In saying this last line, several people who knew him, began to sneer mockingly. The vipers had just come out in public. I continued without worrying about them, "He needs the light of the Lord just like anyone else. He and his wife came twice to ask for prayer at our home. His wife received the Holy Spirit with power but Samuel continued to resist. We broadcast the Bible movie to his Maquis and he had more customers than he ever had before. He now wants to broadcast the Jesus movie."

"I know that God will turn this place of sin into a family place where alcohol will no longer be sold. I believe that Samuel will be sitting here one day because he will give his life to the Lord. I'm sure of it."

The people all applauded, because they knew nothing of God's plan in the life of this white man. I handed the microphone to a sister in the church and went back to sit on my chair next to my wife.

The pastor also asked my wife to come forward to talk about her ministry of evangelism. She approached and explained in details all that the evangelization team had accomplished since the beginning of this ministry. When she declared the incredible number of conversions many of whom were in the church, all were surprised. The Lord was moving with power in Burkina Faso and it was normal because God is in Africa!

When Rosalie returned to sit down, I explained to her a word I had heard from God. "The month of July will be a month of surprise," I explained. "We are going to have a lot of surprises since we have been in Burkina for seven months and the month of July is the seventh month of the year. In addition, it's the month of my birthday. I feel that God is going to surprise us greatly."

THE FIGHT

When I came to Burkina Faso, I knew that I would have a lot of physical, but mostly spiritual fight. I was prepared for it, at least I thought I was, but we are never fully prepared to face these extremely risky battles. The enemy will do anything to stop the advancement of the Kingdom of God.

"Because we wanted to come to you, I, Paul, again and again but Satan hindered us."
-1 Thessalonians 2:18 (ESV)

On the evening of the first day of July, two young women came to the house to ask for prayer. It was Franceline, 15 years old, and Prisca, 24. Prisca was Catholic and often had strange dreams during the night. These dreams bothered her a lot during the day. I asked her to stand up and I started praying for her with having a hand on her head. Franceline was sitting on a chair behind us and waiting patiently for her turn. When I began to take authority to expel from the body of Prisca all that was not from God, she fell to the ground.

To my surprise, Franceline also fell to the ground behind us and I had not touched her. I now had to make two deliverances at the same time, since the two women were on the ground. I kneeled down and moved between the two to expel the unclean spirits that were in them. When the deliverance was completed, we helped the women to sit down, and then I had a vision about Prisca - she would be a school teacher. She confirmed that this was what she wanted to do. Afterwards, I turned to Franceline, who explained to me that she had felt something in her belly while I was praying for Prisca.

When she heard me screaming, "I command you to get out in the name of Jesus," she totally lost control of her body. She confessed to me that a marabout had given her a "magic" pencil that would help her to succeed in school but, contrary to her expectations, she had failed three times. Now she felt she was under the curse of this marabout.

I explained to her that marabouts did not work to help people, but rather to bring fresh souls to their boss Satan. After several minutes of regaining their strength, the women felt freed.

On the following Monday, my wife Rosalie met Franceline, who told her that during the night after the deliverance, she saw a shadow coming out through her belly and leaving. She had slept so well afterwards, she felt at peace. Rosalie prayed with her to thank the Lord for this act of deliverance.

The next morning, I went to the prayer of deliverance at the church. A 15-year-old girl named Flavie came with her mother, to ask me to chase a spirit out of her. Her mother told me that she had been acting so strangely for a long time. I felt that it was a spirit that I already knew; the spirit that came out of Rita had found another body. I started praying for her, but every time I said, "Let her go!" the spirit immediately shouted "No!" The deliverance lasted several minutes and the spirit finally left her. She looked all around her, wondering where she was. She seemed totally lost. I asked her what was the last thing she remembered and she replied, "I saw a dark man coming out of my body."

"You are now liberated" I replied. "You will not see this dark man again if you thank the Lord every day for what he has done for you."

We still prayed for few minutes to thank the Lord and then the mother and daughter left in joy.

On Thursday, a friend of Rosalie's came to visit us with her two sons, so that they could play with Emmanuel. They were going to stay with us for a few days. As is the tradition in Burkina Faso, when we have visitors, we feed them and provide them with a means of transport. I did not like this situation, because many times we had lent our motorbike, it was always returned damaged or completely empty of fuel, and without our knowledge.

Even my son's small P50 motorbike had the same problem. We had lent it to Rosalie's nephews and they had brought it back quickly, without telling us anything.

They had left as fast as they had come. I had a feeling, so I had risen to go see the bike - the rear suspension was completely screwed! That's why they had left so quickly. Of course, it was always us who had to pay for the repairs, never the ones that broke it. We always took great care of our bikes, but those who borrowed them did not give a damn about damaging them, because they were not theirs. We decided never to lend our bikes to anyone again.

But Rosalie kept telling me that she was her childhood friend, so we could not stop her from taking ours, especially as she arrived from Ouagadougou and had no means of transportation. I really did not agree with her and I reminded her that whenever we had lent something to someone, we always had to pay for repairs.

On Saturday morning, the eldest son of my wife's friend was very ill. He had stomach aches, intense fatigue and sometimes vomited a greenish liquid. It was the signs of malaria, so I prayed for him. The Lord, in His grace and kindness, allowed this child to have healing. All the pain he felt dissipated. He started playing football with my son and the other kids in the neighborhood. Fatigue and exhaustion were gone.

During the Sunday morning service, several people received the deliverance. After the pastor's message, he called the fire of the Holy

Spirit on all the faithful who were in the church and several people began to react in a strange way. Some shouted, others shook vigorously, and others fell, etc. I stood up to help the people who prayed for the deliverance or for the fire to burn mightily in the body of those who had reacted to the pastor's call. I noticed that two women were acting abnormally. I came closer to hear what they were whispering. The first one said incessantly, "Thank you Jesus!" Then, without warning, she set to jump all over with her arms in the air, hanging onto the faithful around her. So she didn't need prayer but I kept an eye on her.

Now she was not saying "Thank you Jesus!" She was screaming "Thank You Jesus!" I took her by her left arm and a brother of the church came to help me by taking her right arm.

We sat her on a chair. I then turned to the second woman who kept muttering, "Help me Lord!" She cried intensely, so I understood that she needed prayer of deliverance. With the help of the Brother in Christ, we laid on our hands and she fell on the ground shaking in every direction. She was nonetheless delivered and we helped her to get up. I was glad that the service was in progress, so the friend of Rosalie was able to see all the power of the Holy Spirit within this church.

Because we only had one motorbike, Rosalie was riding with her friend on the bike, while I was walking back home. When I arrived at my house, I found that Rosalie had lent my son's P50 to her friend's child. I looked at her and said, "It will come back to us broken again." Later, the young man came home with the P50 and, as I had predicted, the bike was damaged. The engine smoked a lot and the oil was dripping on the ground. It had certainly been driven so hard, by keeping the accelerator at full throttle, without stopping. Our son loved his bike and it was his first bike so he took great care of it. Sadly, the others never took care of our things.

Since the beginning of July, I did not know why, but I felt continually discouraged. I was getting up in the morning always exhausted. I slept poorly at night and I always turned from left to right, right to left on the mattress, for no reason. It was like I knew something serious was going to happen. After all, as a laborer of deliverance, I chased several demons and unclean spirits, so many of them blamed me. Maybe they would try to go after me, or even worse, a member of my family. One thing was certain, something was going to happen, and it prevented me from sleeping well at night, despite my prayers during the day.

Rosalie's childhood friend and her children left our home on Wednesday morning. But the next day, another family came home. This was Nicole, another childhood friend of my wife. She had to go to a village few kilometers away from Dedougou and had arrived with her huge sport utility vehicle, filled with people and luggage. There were two adult women, one teenage girl, and three young girls, for a grand total of six people.

My son was happy to see Nicole again because, the last time she had come to our house, she had brought him sweet gifts, bought in Ouagadougou that we could not find in Dedougou.

She pulled out a big bag filled with gifts from the back of her car and handed it to us. We invited them all to come and sit on the terrace, after thanking them for the bag. She was only passing through quickly, since she had to go to the village before nightfall. We discussed briefly then Nicole asked us to pray for their trip. We stood up and started praying for these women.

I saw something about a little girl who was sitting. I couldn't hold back, so I explained the vision I had had. "You will fall ill after accepting and eating something," I explained to the girl. "Someone will show you foods, by asking you to taste it because it is really delicious. Don't do it. Ask your mother first. This thing is going to make you sick." I turned to Nicole and asked, "Is she allergic? Because I see she'll have an allergy attack on what she's going to eat."

"I don't know," she replied. "Often, she eats and then complains of belly aches afterwards but we do not know why."

"I'm telling you, she is allergic to something. Watch what she eats in your village. For the trip, everything will be great; you will have no problem on the road."

I asked the little girl to stand up because I wanted to pray for the belly aches she had regularly after she ate. I also asked her not to be afraid and to close her eyes since we will pray for her. So, I have interceded for the healing and protection of this small child, so that she never has an allergy problem again. I put the oil on her forehead and I put my hand on her head to ask the Lord to put angels constantly around her, who protect her every day. The night began to fall, so the women asked us to walk with them to the road. We accompanied them outside the courtyard and, after brief goodbyes; they left aboard their big vehicle.

That night and the next night, were extremely tormenting. I managed to sleep only a few hours. Something bothered me during sleep, but I couldn't find what it was. All these torments made me extremely exhausted to face the Saturday. Two women came in unannounced to ask for prayer. Despite the fatigue, I agreed to receive them. The first one told me that her husband was a very aggressive man and that he often beat her. She had already made a pact with a marabout and, since then, she often had stomach aches. I asked her to stand up, and then I prayed with authority over her. I was chasing that spirit of maraboutism that was in her.

When I put oil on her forehead, I felt that something was coming out of her belly to leave her. Afterwards, I put my hand on her head to ask for the presence of the angels around her, so that she would be protected from the attacks of her husband.

I also asked the Lord to touch her husband's heart, so that he could see that every time he hit her, it causes a very serious injury, not only physically, but also emotionally. After the prayer, she confessed that she had no stomach ache and that she had joy in her. I told her that one day her husband will come back to her and he will sincerely ask for forgiveness for everything he has done to her. His heart will be sincere and he will cry like a baby. She did not believe that her husband could cry, because she had never saw a single tear on his face.

I told her how she could do to ask the Lord to touch the heart of her violent husband. I explained her to do like Rosalie did for me when I was not a Christian. She had written a letter to God, and every night she prayed that everything in this letter would be realized by the name of Jesus. Her first request in the letter was that the LORD touches my heart and turns me into a better man. A few weeks later, the Lord touched me and I accepted him as my Savior. The woman agreed to write a letter and pray daily for all her requests.

Then I turned to the second woman who was waiting. She just told me that she was there for exactly the same reasons as the first woman. I watched her a bit and then I said, "There's something you don't want to tell me. I know there's something else."

I noticed that she was very uncomfortable, so I didn't insist, and I immediately started praying for the same reasons as the first woman. On the other hand, since she was not sincere with the Lord, she felt no change inside her body. Her face clearly demonstrated all the disappointment she had. I sat down in front of the two women and then I talked a little bit with them. I heard a word about the second woman, "Her husband is unfaithful!" Then, looking at the first woman, the voice said to me, "Her husband adores Satan!" I did not want to talk about this to the two women, so I kept the secret until they left.

Rosalie explained to me, that she knew the husband of the first woman very well. The husband and his close relatives worked a lot with the enemy through spells and marabouts. Many would say that he was very involved in a satanic sect and would proudly wear an enormous inverted cross on his neck. I knew there was a satanic church in Dedougou, but I didn't know anyone who was in this evil place.

Now, I understood how this man could attack a woman, so fragile, for no apparent reason. It was not him, but rather the spirit in him, that pushed him to beat this Catholic believer simply for personal pleasure. This spirit only put rage and hatred in his heart. Love for his wife had no place in him. I had to prepare for everything now because he would certainly seek revenge for my prayers.

On Sunday, July 15th, as the sun disappeared slowly on the horizon, my family and I had an excellent supper. Driven by fatigue, we decided to go to bed very early. I locked the front door of the courtyard and turned off all the outside lights. I was heading for the kitchen through the side of the house when I heard my wife screaming, "I am chasing you in the name of Jesus!"

Without thinking, I ran to join her and see what was going on. A completely black salamander had entered the kitchen and hidden behind the cupboards. It was impossible to reach it, so I asked my wife to leave it there, and I would take care of it the next morning. We locked the outside door of the kitchen, turned off the light, and closed the door that overlooked the dining room, to prevent this black critter from walking around in every room of the house.

I took care to check a second time that all the lights of the courtyard were off and that all the accesses were secure, since our keeper, Prosper, would not be there to monitor during the night. Sunday was his day off for rest. I double locked the front door of the house that was in the living room.

My son had already showered himself and was lying on his mattress under the mosquito net, so I entered our master bedroom. Rosalie had just come out of the shower, so I took her place to wash myself too. Afterwards, I joined my wife under the mosquito net to pray together to thank the Lord for this wonderful day. We turned off the light and our eyes closed to spend the night.

Shortly after midnight, an evil presence entered our room with one purpose - to attack me physically. This dark creature gently entered under the mosquito net without waking us up. Then she jumped on me and attacked me like a rabid dog thirsting for human blood. My eyes immediately opened and I saw the creature on me. It was a dark silhouette almost invisible because of the darkness in the room. I could see her dark eyes looking at me with such hatred, that it was now clear that this creature was there to kill me. It had huge eyes and incredible strength. This inhumane thing shook me savagely, in every way.

My body was shivering, like I was inside a freezer. All my nerves were vibrating without me being able to do anything to control them. In spite of the shivering, the sweat was dripping all over my skin; my face was covered in sweat. I tried to scream, but she put her hands on my throat to the point of choking me. I was trying to wake up my wife, but the creature blocked all my attempts. I thought it was the end for me. I saw the creature putting its hand inside my torso and I felt my heart being crushed to the point that I was losing my breath. I was trying to gasp for air but nothing worked. I was crying, because I could see that my end was close.

At that moment, I remembered the promise that my heavenly father had made me when my son was born, "Thou shall not leave this world before thy eyes have seen thy son become a pastor!"

This promise gave me strength to fight this thing. God had confessed to me, that I would not leave this world until my son was a pastor. He was not yet a pastor, so this beast could not kill me. I had to resist it, as best I could. Since it controlled my legs and arms, all I had left was the tongue. The creature had taken away the ability to shout the name of Jesus but I could whisper. So, I began to whisper the same sentence incessantly, "May the blood of the lamb cover me and protect me! May the blood of the Lamb cover me and protect me!"

I closed my eyes because I did not want to see this satanic being. I kept repeating the same sentence, "May the blood of the lamb cover me and protect me!" The tears continued to flow down my face, as the beast jostled me again and again. The struggle was so brutal, that I felt intense pain all over my body. But my mouth continued to repeat, "May the blood of the Lamb cover me and protect me!" The beast knew that I did not look at it anymore, so it started to growl hatred towards me. Its voice caused me to believe that it was a dog from hell. I opened an eye to see if Rosalie had heard the growl of this beast, but she continued to sleep.

Probably, I was the only one to see it and hear it. I closed my eye and I continued to resist the creature. I had just understood what it was looking for; it wanted me to abandon the fight at all costs. I would never let it win; it would never win the battle in the name of Jesus. Even if I had to spend whole days to endure these attacks, I would be victorious.

Finally, the creature stopped shaking me in all directions. I didn't feel it on me anymore, so I slowly opened my eyes. She was gone, she had left, and she had given up first. I still had shivers and muscle spasms that kept me from moving normally. I looked at the time - it was 5 o'clock in the morning. I had just fought a battle of about 5 hours against this morbid and sadistic creature. I wanted to get up but I couldn't do it, I was in total shock. I heard a voice talking beside me. "Hello, darling." My wife had just woken up.

"Is there anything wrong?" she asked me.

She could see all the shaking and spasms in my body. When she saw my face, the anxiety invaded her. "What happened?" she asked me again. I was trying to talk, but the intense pain made me cry. Moreover, the sounds that came out of my mouth were very weak and hoarse because of the weakness of my body. I still managed to explain to her that I had just been savagely attacked by a powerful demon for almost 5 hours. When I told her that I really thought it was my end, I started to cry again in shock.

I could see that she had a hard time believing all this, because she was right beside me and nothing had awakened her. Rosalie prayed several minutes for me, and then I told her I wanted to stand up to see if I could still walk. My knees were hurting terribly, so much that I had to put my hands on the walls, so I wouldn't fall. All the members of my body were no longer functioning normally. I could barely control my movements just to get around. I couldn't yet explain the reason for this vicious attack on my own person. It was certain that many of Burkina's Satanists were very angry at me for having faced them on their territory, but the question was which one had perpetrated this attack?

I noticed when I left the bedroom, that the door between the dining room and the kitchen was wide open while we had taken care to close it the day before. I could see the light coming from the kitchen. As I approached a little more, I noticed that the door that was going outside was open. But it was locked from the inside. These clues showed us that a person or an unclean being did indeed escape by this route. Rosalie now had evidence before her eyes that an intruder was in the house and had fled through the kitchen. It had entered in the form of a black salamander, which we had not seen since, and had escaped in the form of human or some kind of humanoid.

"For, behold, the darkness shall cover the earth, and gross darkness the people: but the Lord shall arise upon thee, and his glory shall be seen upon thee."

- Isaiah 60:2 (ESV)

This was one of the most painful days of my life.

I felt like a very old person whose painful joints making it difficult to move normally. Not to mention an intense headache, tummy ache and an extreme fatigue. I spent several hours sitting there doing nothing but thinking about this unfortunate event of the last night. I was not talking to anybody. I was just trying to remember all my actions of the last few days to figure out who could have done this kind of feat on my own territory. Who had enough power to do this offense in my private life? Rosalie took care of me all day, since I was barely able to move alone. I must admit that it was rather nice to be pampered as well, but the fact of not being able to do anything by myself gave me the feeling of being useless.

Joint pain lasted two days before I could move easily, but on the following Wednesday, I got another spiritual attack. The fear I had felt during the cruel attack had come back for no reason in my body. I think it was a shock of this tragic night. For an hour, my body was constantly shaking, as if I was too cold and I had very intense muscle spasms. I had temporarily lost control of my body but then everything was back to normal. Rosalie and I both came to the same conclusion - this attack was the fruit of the Satanist husband of the woman, for whom I had prayed a few days before. This was not a coincidence since I had prayed for the woman last Saturday and the attack had taken place the next night.

Unfortunately, the spiritual attacks did not stop there. On Thursday, when I woke up, I felt that something was not right. I was very dizzy with stomach pain. If I turned my head too fast, the stun could make me lose my balance and fall to the ground. I had nausea and painful pains in my nose and skull. On the eve of my birthday, I was getting malaria mixed with sinusitis. Rosalie left early in the morning to buy some Quinine to fight this malaria. Despite this medication, dizziness was always present and I had to constantly pay attention to each movement, so as not to lose balance. I was also very tired, so I spent almost every day in bed. Even the day of my birthday was a big disappointment - in bed all day.

On Saturday afternoon, Rita and her aunt came to visit us at home. We discussed several things and I was happy to see this little 15-year-old teen, who shone with joy in the Lord. After their departure, three young men came accompanied by the wife of the satanic husband. She asked us to pray for these young people. Though I was feeling bad, I took a chair and sat down in front of the three young people.

The former was named Jean-Eudes and admitted that he had failed his school tests four times. He did not understand why because he studied a lot and worked very hard but once before the test, he forgot everything he had studied. "You also have strange dreams at night," I said. "I also see you have a lot of stomach aches." I saw that he wondered how I could know these things before he had time to tell me. "Your problem is spiritual," I continued. "Don't worry, we'll pray for you."

The second, named Jacques also had the same kind of problem that made him forget everything he had studied for the tests. "You're a very nervous and stressed young man," I said. "Your problem is not spiritual because you have no stomach ache but you lack confidence. When you come in front of the copy of your test, you tremble with nervousness and you forget everything." He confirmed all my statements about him with an anxious glance. "Do not worry; it is the Holy Spirit who tells me things about you. We also will pray to correct this problem."

The third young man, named Abraham, simply wanted prayer for the Lord to show him the direction he should take for his studies. "We will pray for you too," I replied.

So, I asked Jean-Eudes to stand up so that Rosalie and I could pray for his problem. We began by interceding with authority, in order to drive away that spirit that disturbed him in his sleep. When I put one hand on his head and the other on his belly, his belly began to move very quickly, as if the nerves of the belly were receiving several uncontrolled electrical impulses. Rosalie put the oil on his forehead and we completed praying that he successfully passes his next test. His stomach aches were gone.

Then Jacques stood up for prayer. We asked the Lord to fill him with confidence in himself, that the angels accompany him every day of his life and that the Holy Spirit invades him with strength and power. At the end of the prayer, I received a few words from the Lord. I announced them to Jacques, "You study in administration."

"Yes!"

"You want to be a business manager and also have your own business," I said.

"Yes, it is true."

"Then do not worry about anything because the Lord will accompany you and you shall succeed. You will have your own company and it will be very prosperous."

The young man returned to sit down, without understanding how I had managed to guess so much about him. Then came the great Abraham, who wanted to know the will of God over his life. We asked the Lord to reveal his glory to him and to inform him on the direction he should take in his life. Again, at the end of the prayer, God showed me things about this man. "You're an expert in mathematics."

"Yes, that's right!"

"I'm not sure what kind of work you're going to do, but I know that this job will bring you to travel often around the world. I believe that you will be at the United Nations and that you will be a leader with people in your department, maybe as a computer specialist or in the communication department."

"I study in computer science." he replied.

Rosalie went to speak with the woman, while I stayed with the three young men. They were all very impressed with what I had told them.

They asked me several questions about the Holy Spirit and I loved to answer them because I saw that a passion had just been born in them. They wanted to be closer to Jesus. They all went away in joy and Rosalie came to see me and shared the discussion she had had with the woman.

Rosalie had told her about the sordid attack I had experienced and the woman confirmed to her, that it was certainly the work of her satanic husband. She had not lived with him since last January because he had tried to kill her several times. She had missed more than a month of work, because of the wounds that this man had inflicted on her.

One day, he had dragged her outside by pulling her hair, to punch her in the face, in front of everyone. Her face was covered with blood. No one had intervened, since they were all afraid of this sorcerer. He then looked at everyone, shouting, "That's the way to treat a woman who does not obey." He then dragged her by the hair again, back inside the house. Even his family were followers of the enemy; she was the only Christian in this pack of bloodthirsty wolves. When she heard the details of the night attack, the black salamander, the dark silhouette, and the fight for hours, she immediately said that this was exactly the family's way of acting. They all had to be frustrated that I had broken the ties that connected her to them. Vengeance was the primary purpose of their attack.

The next morning, when I woke up, I was still feeling a disturbing new sensation in my body. Both hands and my upper lip were always irritating me. Plus, I had a lot of itching all over my body. I entered the bathroom and looked in the mirror; my hands were completely swollen, as well as my upper lip. I had reddish patches all over the body, as well as some skin bumps in some places, like water blisters, but without the liquid inside.

I realized that I was having a severe allergic reaction to Quinine, since it was the only new product I had recently. It was no longer an option for me to take another Quinine pill so I didn't aggravate my situation. We decided not to go to church that morning because my health did not allow it.

Moreover, I did not want to answer the millions of questions of the curious people. I had made the decision to wait, before taking any new medications.

I was hoping that the whole thing would shrink by itself during the day, but at night when we were about to go to bed, the swellings were so intense. I had a lot of trouble sleeping because I was worried about my throat. I had already seen and heard of allergic reactions that went wrong after the throat started to swell. I was trying not to think about it, but I was not able to stop thinking about it. The doubt always hovered in my head. "What if my throat swelled during my sleep...?" I thought. Unfortunately, the doubts I had were affecting my faith so much.

"And whatever you ask in prayer, you will receive, if you have faith."

-Matthew 21:22 (ESV)

On Monday morning, since my condition had not improved,

Rosalie jumped on the motorbike and went to the drugstore to buy anti-allergic medications, anti-inflammatory drugs and a new, less strong and less risky, antimalarial treatment for my health. She returned after a few minutes with three boxes of medication. I started with anti-allergic and anti-inflammatory in order to get rid of that swollen lip that distorted my face. I attended to the malaria, after winning against this allergy crisis. This medication was very powerful and made me sleep all day. On the other hand, its effectiveness was incredible because, in just two days, everything was back to normal. No signs of any swelling were visible on my body.

I started the malaria treatment, though I only felt a faint dizziness. Africans are very resistant to this disease, spread by mosquitoes, because they grew up in this medium and their body solidified against this blood intruder. On the other hand, a white man had to be very careful about this disease because he could easily die. It was a matter of prevention that I had started the treatment again. No more Quinine this time.

"Where there is no guidance, a people falls..."
-Proverbs 11:14 (ESV)

RETURN TO CANADA

For several days now, Rosalie and I regularly discussed our finances in African land. We had come to follow God's call, but funding for the Widows Help Project was still waiting. Even the construction of the Help Center could not start due to lack of money. In all sincerity, we had left Canada without any financial assistance or promise of funding, hiring, or anything.

Only our faith in God allowed us to follow the will of the father. We had just spent seven months in Burkina Faso without the help of any Canadian or African Church, without the help of any national or international organization and no government assistance whatsoever. Only God the father had helped us financially since our arrival.

Now we wanted to start building the Help Centre wholeheartedly, but the funding was slow to come. So, I threw a kind of ultimatum to God - if the funds did not come in before the end of July, we would all go back to Canada and work to find funding.

Normally, I sent all my grants and funding requests by email, but, as in many cases, the recipients of these messages did not take the time to read and just delete the messages from their inbox. The best thing was to go to the field, in this case - Canada, to knock on the doors ourselves and explain the details of this project directly face-to-face. They would have no choice but to listen to what we had to say.

Our stay in Burkina would has not been in vain, since we were now a legal association in the province of Mouhoun and we had official documents and ownership of the half a hectare of land. In addition, we were able to transport all the material and equipment inside a container by boat to Burkina Faso, Togo, or Ivory Coast, without having to pay clearance fees, since it would be for an association.

Our stay allowed us to legalize everything. We all became citizens of Burkina Faso. Now we had to go back to Canada for some government formalities, such as completing the forms that would determine our status as a Canadian resident, extend Medicare, etc.

Rosalie had to get a few customers from her company, who hadn't placed any orders since we left the country. Thinking about it, our return to Canada was practically an obligation, not an option. We also thought of stopping in Quebec City to see my family for a few days before continuing to Edmonton to stay for about a year.

If we were to get funding sooner than expected, we would send it to Rosalie's brother in Burkina. Gilbert would be able to pay and oversee the construction work of the Help Center. So when we were ready to return to Burkina, we would already have our own home and Help Center built and functional. We could then start direct assistance to widows.

The critical date of July 31st was approaching quickly and we had not yet, received any funding. The Canadian embassy in Ouagadougou had not yet told us anything about the request for funding that I had sent them in the previous months. In this silence, it became more and more clear, that we will go back to Canada. So, we made a list of everything we wanted to sell before leaving. There was no option of leaving with several suitcases, as we did not want to spend too much on the trip.

The money would be very important when we arrived in the country, in order to get ourselves settled again. I was always a person who liked to prepare everything in advance, so as not to have any unpleasant surprises along the way. With God, things are the opposite; we do not anticipate in advance, because the Heavenly Father asks us not to worry about anything and constantly trust him every day.

"Therefore I tell you, do not be anxious about your life, what you will eat or what you will drink, nor about your body, what you will put on. Is not life more than food, and the body more than clothing? Look at the birds of the air: they neither sow nor reap nor gather into barns, and yet your heavenly Father feeds them. Are you not of more value than they?"
-Matthew 6:25-26 (ESV)

I contacted a good friend from Edmonton, who was looking for a tenant for the basement of his house. I told him about our plan to come back directly to Canada for funding, but to keep it private at this moment, since the decision was not final yet. He was very happy to be able to see us again and above all, to be able to rent his basement. I also told Pastor Blaire Clinton of Church in the Vine, in Edmonton, also asking him not to tell anyone.

This pastor was a great man of God, who had helped me a lot spiritually before I left for Burkina. I was already seeing how the reunion was going to take place in Edmonton. I could see the surprised face of all of our brothers and sisters in Edmonton, who did not expect to see us again, anytime soon. These reunions were just a picture in my head, since we didn't know yet whether we would return to Canada or not. Everything was in the hands of God; we were putting ourselves in his will, for our future, and for our lives.

The last few months before we came back to Canada, God acted in a very interesting way with me. I asked him to tell me his will personally, because I wanted to know without doubts if he would have us return to Canada to seek funding, or if he wanted us to stay in Burkina. He did not say anything to me, but whenever there was doubt in me, or I was wondering if he was always with us, he would send people who needed prayer to us and we could feel his presence by the deliverances and the healings he performed, through our hands. He showed us that he was always with us and that no matter what decision we would make, he would always be there with us.

It reminds me of when Catherine, a friend very close to us, had sent a young woman to inform us that she badly needed prayer because she was sick. Rosalie and I knew Catherine well and she was not the kind of woman to send a third person to ask for prayer. If she had done so, it meant that the situation was serious. So we went without further delay to her residence, to see with our eyes the problem of our friend. When we arrived, she was lying on an old bed in the living room watching television. She painfully sat up on the bed to chat with us.

After a few small discussions on various topics, we finally learned that she had malaria and jaundice, at the same time. I noticed that the tips of her nails were all unusually yellow. Catherine had no appetite and, if she swallowed something, her body immediately rejected it, by vomiting what she had taken. She had lost the strength to stand up for us to pray for her so we asked her to stay sit. The prayer began smoothly and we had finished with strength and authority to chase these diseases from her body. I still felt that the Lord was present because he had shown me something very important about our friend.

During the prayer, I had a vision that showed me that all of our friend's problems came from someone around her who did not like her, who was probably jealous of her and who was trying to hurt her. After the prayer, Catherine confessed that she felt much better already and she was even able to get up alone, from her bed. She told us that she wanted to see her husband in Gaoua, a town south of Ouagadougou, several hours away from Dedougou, but there was always something that prevented her from leaving for the trip.

This time illness prevented her from taking the bus to spend a few days with her husband. I realized that my vision was real; somebody around her was trying to hurt her. I decided not to talk to her for the moment so that she could rest and regain strength. I just told her, "By tomorrow morning you will feel much better and you will be able to dance to praise the Lord." Afterwards, we let her rest and, walking to our house, I informed Rosalie on the vision that the Lord had shown me about Catherine and all her problems.

She absolutely wanted to inform her friend immediately, but I had recommended her to wait until the next day. She agreed and we went back home. In the evening, Rosalie had prepared Tô, mashed sorghum or millet, a traditional dish in Burkina. She had sent a big plate filled with Tô, with a sauce from the leaves of the tree that we called the "the miraculous tree."

In reality, this tree was called Moringa tree. The great advantage of this broadleaf, besides its exceptional properties, was that everything was consumed in this tree, from roots to flowers through the bark. Each part of the plant had distinct benefits. Roots treated arthritis, rheumatism, epilepsy, kidney stones, cystitis, bladder disorders, ear and toothache, foot edema and inflammation, liver disorders, infections and spleen, besides being a laxative, which also fought against fibroids, myomas, or cysts. The barks treated wounds, skin infections and tumors, dental and ophthalmological pain, lack of appetite and kidney stones. The leaves relieved the headaches and stopped bleeding.

They had an antibacterial and anti-inflammatory effect when applied to a wound or an insect bite. In infusion, the leaves treated gastric ulcers and diarrhea, fought anemia, hypertension, hypotension, herpes, nerve and cellular degeneration and regulated blood sugar. The seeds gave a fine, light yellow and odorless oil which was used in cosmetics but also in the cure of the following diseases: inflammatory pain, constipation, eye infections, hypertension and hypotension, diabetes, digestive disorders, disorder bladder, preventive protection of the prostate, sexual weakness, general fatigue. In conclusion, this tree was aptly named as a miraculous tree.

The next afternoon, after church Sunday worship, Rosalie called Catherine for news of her condition. She informed her that she felt much better and that she could move safely around the house. She had devoured the Tô dish that Rosalie had sent her and no longer felt exhausted. When my wife told her about someone close to her who wanted to hurt her, Catherine admitted that she knew it too. All clues and signs pointed to a person very close to her. For days she had felt that this person had changed and that she had become jealous enough to want to hurt her personally. Maybe this person was going to a sorcerer's house to hurt Catherine.

One thing was certain - she had managed to prevent Catherine from joining her husband in Gaoua. Catherine was going to investigate further, to obtain evidence before making a decision about this person. She could not act on mere doubts, but wanted to have real evidence. It was a wise decision on her part. God had again shown us, that he was always acting through our hands and our prayers. The good shepherd never gave up his sheep, even if his sheep were too far away from him. The shepherd was going to get them and bring them back to the flock. That was what we called a good father who took care of his children.

On the evening of July 31, 2018, the deadline for the decision to leave Canada or not finally arrived. The hours passed very slowly since we were all hoping to see a miracle happen. Unfortunately, 5 o'clock arrived and there were no financial surprises or miracles that could have made us change our minds. The decision had now become official - we had to go back to Canada to look for funding for the Widow Help Project ourselves. I looked at airline ticket prices for this time of year and noticed that it was more advantageous to leave before August 15th. After this date, prices increased considerably, almost double the price.

So we had only two weeks to sell everything we had and sort out what we would bring to Canada, from what we would leave with Rosalie's mother to pick them up when we returned to Burkina. Only two weeks, I did not expect to get there because we still had a lot of things to do. We had asked a man, whom Rosalie knew very well, to help us sell everything. He was happy to do so, since we offered him a good percentage of sales as a thank you. He had gotten to work very quickly since he had already started selling several things the next morning. We were very impressed to see him working for us. The fact that he would get percentages on the price of each sale made him sell faster. At this rate, we would most certainly have the amount needed to purchase the tickets within a few days.

On the Wednesday of the first day of August, a man named Serge came to visit us at home. It was not the first time he came to see us, but that morning he wanted to thank God.

Serge was a close bodyguard to former President Thomas Sankara who had been assassinated following a putsch. Under Blaise Compaore's regime, all other bodyguards had also been murdered except for Serge, who had managed to flee and hide in remote villages. He had spent many years wandering from village to village, for his own safety. He was able to walk freely after the fall of President Campaore but he could no longer be a soldier like before. He had been forced to do odd jobs everywhere to be able to feed himself.

The first time I met this remarkable man, I had asked him to write a book about his life because, the fact that he was the one and only survivor of Thomas Sankara's bodyguards, his story would become a huge success. I felt he did not want to bring his past back to the surface because he still feared retaliation. I respected and understood his decision very well. That day, he told us that a very rich woman, who was driving in a luxury car near the market, noticed Serge and immediately stopped to ask him to join her. He did not understand what this woman wanted from him, so he walked towards her warily. She had recognized that he was a well-known soldier and asked if he wanted to work for her.

Serge answered that he was looking for a job so the woman asked him to come to her house to discuss it. Serge went on site with his bicycle. She offered to work as a security manager for all her businesses. He would not be a simple security guard, but she wanted to offer him the position of supervisor of security guards. He would be the boss and executive chief of all other security employees. Serge was overjoyed to see how God answered his prayers. Rosalie and I had also prayed for the Lord to give him a job worthy of his qualifications.

He had come to us to pray together to thank the King of Kings, who had heard his tears and responded to his requests. May the God of Abraham, Isaac, and Jacob be glorified forever for all the blessings he gives to his children!

That evening Catherine had come home to discuss her situation. First, she was completely cured of her malaria and jaundice since we prayed for her recovery.

We thanked the Lord for this miracle. Secondly, she asked me to repeat the vision I had about the attacks that still prevented her from going to join her husband in Gaoua.

So I told her, "I saw that a woman, who works for you or close to you, was constantly trying to hurt you and prevent you from going to Gaoua. I also feel that there is a story of infidelity in all this."

"You are absolutely right," she replied. "I know who this person is and it is true that she is trying to harm me. She is the young woman who works for my husband in Gaoua. A friend also had the same vision as you, which confirms that it's the truth."

She went on to explain to us where this young woman came from and she informed us that her father was a great marabout. Catherine had therefore made the decision to go as quickly as possible to Gaoua and to clarify this whole story once and for all. If this woman wanted to have her own husband, despite all that Catherine had done for her, she would be immediately fired without notice.

And if there had been infidelity with her husband, she was going to crack down on him too. She had suspected for a long time since he was no longer calling home to get news of his wife and always seemed to hide things when they were talking on the phone. She felt very distant and felt that he was changing a lot. She needed to clarify everything, to know the depths of this story, before making her final decision about this young employee and her husband. Rosalie and I, had prayed for her, so that the Lord gave her the wisdom to make the right decisions.

The next day, August 2, 2018, one of the two women who had come home on July 14th, had come back again to tell us something incredible that had happened in her life. It was the woman whose husband was a very aggressive man and that he often beat her. She told us that this man had already taken her out of the house by pulling her hair, punching and kicking her and then dragging her inside again by her hair.

She thought she would never get through with such violence. She had lost a lot of blood that day. She feared so much for her life that she had separated from him.

She told us that after praying for her and advising her to write a letter to God, she wrote the letter with all her heart and prayed every night for all that was written in the name of Jesus. A week later, her husband had called to ask for forgiveness for all the harm he had done to her. She could hear in the sound of his voice that he had changed.

She agreed to meet him in a public place and they had connected as if they were young, newly engaged couple. She felt that her husband was sincere and that he really wanted to become a new man. He did not want to lose the one he loved because of his stupid actions and his inner rage. Her husband was now on the path of change, to get closer to the light of our Lord. We all knew that he would soon give his life to the Lord and he would go from deep darkness to bright light.

In the evening, Pascaline, an elderly woman whom Rosalie knew well, came to ask us for prayer for several reasons. She said that a curse rested on her family. One of her sons had gone to work in Mauritania and Mali, but they had not heard from him for 3 years. He had completely disappeared, and when they tried to call him on his phone, there was always the same automated message telling us that his phone was off. I felt deep inside me that this man was still alive and that he wanted to go to Senegal, but had a serious problem along the way.

His case worried me a lot, because I often heard the words "Help!" in my head. He needed help, but could not reach anyone, either because of the loss of his phone and he no longer had the numbers, or because someone or something was preventing him from calling his family, or that he had become mentally affected by a serious accident and that he no longer remembered his past. I could not determine the exact cause but I always heard "Help!" At least one thing was certain in my mind - he was still alive. So we asked Pascaline to stand up and we started praying for her.

During the prayer, something told me, that she had not told us everything about herself. I was very disturbed.

The Holy Spirit prompted me suddenly to pray for her because she had spiritual connections with the enemy, ties that prevented her from acting freely, that deprived her of praying easily and harmed her faith in Jesus Christ.

At this moment, I screamed - "Something is wrong and I do not like it!" Then I immediately put one hand on her belly and the other hand on her head. I saw that she had pain in her lower back and hips and I noticed that she had heavy chains that held her down. A form of curse had invaded this family. When I began to take authority to chase and completely wipe out her satanic bonds, Pascaline fell to the ground crying incessantly. Rosalie felt that the Holy Spirit was freeing her of all these demonic attachments and that the Lord was healing her physically and spiritually.

I dropped to my knees to put my hand on her head but she moved slowly from left to right, as if something was in her and was trying to avoid my hand. I screamed, "I chase you in the name of Jesus Christ my Lord and Savior. I command that all ties of witchcraft, fetishist, or any demonic link be completely destroyed in the name of Jesus!" She began to cry even more intensely then she slowly opened her eyes. We helped her to sit on a chair to regain her strength. I looked into her eyes and told her she would not have any bad dreams with dark people. She asked me how I'd known she had such night dreams. I replied, "It was the Holy Spirit who showed it to me while I was praying. Plus, you will not have any more pain in your hips and lower back."

"I never told you about these pains. How did you do to find out?"

"This is the work of the Holy Spirit. Your next night will be very relaxing and peaceful. From today, I want you to thank the Lord every morning for all he has done for you and for all he will do for you."

"I will!" she replied.

"All witchcraft links have just been wiped out so you and all your kids will get better. Some of your children will give their lives to the Lord. Do not worry about anything and, above all, never doubt God. Doubt comes from Satan, have certainty and self-assurance. The Lord has heard your tears and he will answer all your requests."

She thanked us warmly and Rosalie prayed a little for her to strengthen her faith. After leaving, I continued to talk to my wife about this missing man in Mali.

I was very worried about him, though I knew he was alive. The words "Help!" kept looping in my head. I had to put his name in my prayers, so that his family could trace him and help him. With all those Islamist terrorists hiding in Mali, it was not the best place to work. May God protect this young man and bring him back healthy to his family. Amen!

Other majestic divine interventions still took place on the terrace of our house in Dedougou. This concrete deck with decorative tile covering was used for the rescue and healing of many people seeking spiritual help. This was the case of Flavie, a young woman of 22 years old, who had always finished first in all school tests. She was very smart and was destined for a bright future. But, for some unknown reason, her father had taken her to a sorcerer's house to make sure that she would pass her last academic test with success, that she would finish the best of her school.

He had taken her to his village to meet an evil marabout, who made several satanic incantations on this young woman. The sorcerer had given her a canary, filled with fetishes supposed to help her succeed. We all knew that these marabouts had only one intention - to guide misguided souls into the hands of Satan himself. This was exactly the main clause of their contract with the enemy. They were not there to help, but to harm and destroy. Flavie had obeyed her father and had accepted this canary of fetishes.

Of course, the result was the exact opposite of what her father was hoping for, because she had failed miserably.

Moreover, she was now seeing black shadows, which constantly harassed her during her sleep. She was scared for her own life because these dark shadows prevented her from reading the Word of God. As soon as she opened her Bible, her eyesight became confused for no apparent reason and she could not read anything.

When she went to church to listen to the pastor's preaching, her concentration was affected and she could no longer understand the message. Her own mother worried a lot because she had noticed a very negative change on her daughter.

Not knowing what to do, her mother decided to bring her daughter to the prayers of deliverance on Tuesday and Thursday morning and Friday night Holy Spirit evenings at the International Center of Evangelization Center in Dedougou. Unfortunately, there was no change on her daughter - she was always sad and lost in thought. On the night of Friday, August 3, 2018, Flavie had a dream where she saw, that after meeting a white man named Martin, a light would cover her completely and she would be released from all links of witchcraft in her life. God had just shown her how to get rid of her satanic chains that prevented her from being free.

The next morning we received a phone call from this family asking for prayer. They had tried everything to help the young woman and decided to follow the instruction of Flavie's dream. We accepted without hesitation, especially since it was clearly the will of God. They arrived at our house only few minutes after the call, which really showed their despair. After some discussion about the main reason for their presence here, I asked Flavie to stand in the center of the terrace because I knew she would fall to the ground because of the spirit of marabout she carried in her body.

Rosalie and I had started praying for her, and after only a few minutes, the spirit had manifested itself and the young woman fell to the ground. I knelt down to have one hand on her belly and the other hand on her head, to order that malevolent spirit to leave her in the name of Jesus. Rosalie put oil on her feet, hands, and forehead while I continued to pray with authority for her deliverance.

After several minutes, she suddenly opened her eyes and looked around, like a woman who did not know where she was. I asked her name and she answered, "Flavie! then she exclaimed, I saw a light!"

"Did that light come into you?" I asked her.

"Yes, it entered my body."

"How are you feeling now?"

"I feel free!"

Rosalie and I knew that Jesus himself had come to deliver her because he was the light of the world that chases away the darkness.

"Again Jesus spoke to them, saying: I am the light of the world. Whoever follows me will not walk in darkness, but will have the light of life."

- John 8:12 (ESV)

This 22 year old woman had just been freed from all her demonic holdings by Jesus himself. She had not seen the face of this Savior, but we all knew that it was the Son of God himself who had intervened to free her. Flavie now felt free. We had asked her to read a few verses in the Bible and she had done so without any problem.

She could now read and understand the Word, without an evil spirit disturbing her vision. She was delivered and still had a wonderful smile of joy. She had received the peace of the Lord.

"Peace I leave with you; my peace I give to you."
- John 14:27 (ESV)

Flavie had seen the Lord act in her life, so I asked her to make sure to thank the Lord every day. She also had to read the Word of God daily and put all her trust in Jesus. She was so beautiful, with her wonderful smile that shone all the joy she had in her heart. Her mother, who was there, noticed that her daughter's desperation was now gone. The love of God had filled her daughter's heart and she was rejoicing at this great blessing of God.

Our Lord never abandoned his sheep who needed help. He always acted in his time and not in the time of men. May all glory and honor come to him in the name of Jesus!

Two hours later, a Muslim woman arrived at our residence to ask for prayer. She had a health problem that doctors could not heal. She told us that, according to the x-rays and the neurologist's diagnosis, she had two vertebrae that were completely black due to a strange infection. This problem caused intense irritation of the sciatic nerve in the lower back, which prevented her from walking easily. She suffered a lot in the buttocks and legs. These irritations prevented her from sleeping peacefully during the night.

Rosalie and I prayed for this woman. I had noticed that she did not like to hear "In the name of Jesus" during our prayers. I knew that Muslims did not recognize the divinity of Jesus. For them, he was just a prophet and not the Son of the Living God, as presented in the Bible of the Christians. Unfortunately for her, I could not pray using the name of Allah or Muhammad, so I continued to use the name of Jesus even though she did not like it.

Many Muslims desired to receive the blessings of Jesus, but

refuse to believe that he was the Son of God having received all the powers of the Father. When I put my hand on her head, I felt that the Lord wanted to heal her. I told her that all the pain would disappear in three days. Afterward, she could leap for joy to praise and thank the Lord. She replied, "Amina!" I was not the kind of person who preached that the Gentiles did not have access to Heavenly Father. I did not accept those who said we needed the baptism of water and the baptism of the Holy Spirit to be saved. Let's just look at what the Bible tells us about this topic. What did Jesus say about what we need to be saved?

"Jesus said to him, "I am the way, and the truth, and the life. No one comes to the Father except through me."
- John 14:6 (ESV)

Jesus himself had said that no one could go to the Father except those who passed through him.

In other words, no one could go to God without having a personal relationship with Jesus, without accepting Jesus as Lord and Savior. He is our free ticket to eternal life. He did not say that we had to be baptized with water or fire before being saved. He had simply said that we had to believe in him.

If you want better proof, read the story of the first person who was saved by Jesus himself - he was the crucified criminal next to Jesus. He was not a Christian. He was not baptized. He never received the Holy Spirit, since the Comforter had begun to fill people days later, at Pentecost and the days that followed. Here is the full text that confirms it.

"One of the criminals who were hanged railed at him, saying: Are you not the Christ? Save yourself and us! But the other rebuked him, saying: Do you not fear God, since you are under the same sentence of condemnation? And we indeed justly, for we are receiving the due reward of our deeds; but this

man has done nothing wrong. And he said: Jesus, remember me when you come into your kingdom. And he said to him: Truly, I say to you, today you will be with me in paradise."

- Luke 23:39-43 (ESV)

If you need more proof, think of the second man to recognize Jesus as the Son of God. Not a Jew, not a Christian, not a baptized man, not a person who had the Holy Spirit, but a Roman centurion.

"And when the centurion, who stood facing him, saw that in this way he breathed his last, he said: Truly this man was the Son of God!"

- Mark 15:39 (ESV)

The first two people to recognize Jesus as Lord and Savior were a criminal guilty of the death penalty and a Roman centurion hated by the people of God. They were both saved because they recognized who this sinless man was on the cross. They had seen that he was the Son of God.

Also, to all those who say we receive the Holy Spirit only after being baptized with water, here's a Bible verse that completely destroy all your false claims.

"While Peter was still saying these things, the Holy Spirit fell on all who heard the word. And the believers from among the circumcised who had come with Peter were amazed, because the gift of the Holy Spirit was poured out even on the Gentiles. For they were hearing them speaking in tongues and extolling God. Then Peter declared: Can anyone withhold water for baptizing these people, who have received the Holy Spirit just as we have?"

- Acts 10:44-47 (ESV)

The God I know is a loving God who has asked us to love our neighbor as ourselves. Is this neighbor only a Christian? No, our neighbor can be a Christian, a Muslim, a Buddhist, an atheist, etc. Our neighbor represents all humans on the planet.

"Or is God the God of Jews only? Is he not the God of Gentiles also? Yes, of Gentiles also, since God is one who will justify the circumcised by faith and the uncircumcised through faith."

- Romans 3:29-30 (ESV)

I'm not denying the baptism of water, far from it. It is only those who are baptized with water and the Holy Spirit, who access Heaven. Water baptism is a powerful symbol of obedience and submission to Jesus. It demonstrates that our old body full of sins then becomes a new creature without spots by total immersion in the water.

"Go therefore and make disciples of all nations, baptizing them in the name of the Father and of the Son and of the Holy Spirit"

- Matthew 28:19 (ESV)

It was also for all these reasons that I firmly believed that this Muslim woman could be healed by the divine glory of our Lord, that she could receive the seed that would allow her to flourish in faith in Jesus Christ our Lord and Savior. After all, many of the ancient Muslims who accepted Christ became Christians powerfully filled with the Holy Spirit. Men like Pastor Mamadou Karambiri who was a Muslim firmly rooted in Islam, before the Lord came to tear him away from the darkness to lead him powerfully to the light. Today, he is one of the most recognized and appreciated pastors in West Africa. God had worked hard on him for the advancement of his kingdom. I also knew that God would act in the same way with this Muslim woman.

"Judge not, that you be not judged."

- Matthew 7:1 (ESV)

The next day, during Sunday worship at the church, I noticed that little Flavie was just few seats behind us. She praised the Lord with all her heart and she still shone the joy and love of Christ. To see her so warmed my heart. It made me so happy to see all these people delivered from their satanic hold. These ancient captives shone ever more brightly than any other Christian in the church. How could one know all the beauty of light, if he had never known darkness? How could one know the pleasure of freedom, if he had never known captivity? That is why the delivered ones shone always more than the others.

The decision to leave Burkina and return to Canada to seek funding to fulfill God's plan, still bothered me a lot while sleeping. I often woke up at night wondering if I was really following God's will or whether my heart was pushing me back to see the ones I knew in Canada. I had a hard time differentiating between the voice of God and my own inner will. I regularly asked the Father to show me any sign that would prove to me beyond doubt that he was behind this decision to leave West Africa. I did not want to act against the will of my Father.

Sunday, August 12th was a memorable day. Several new converts to Christ were going to be baptized in front of the International Center Church in Dedougou.

I went there because a particular person would also be baptized. The one I fondly called "my little Rita" was going to be baptized and entering the big family of God. I had tears in my eyes to see her so happy. She, who once ran barefoot on the empty lands and hit her head to kill herself, was now going to give her life to Jesus. I had even brought my camera to not miss anything at this unforgettable moment.

I loved this girl so much, that I considered her to be like my own daughter. After a few baptized people, she finally entered the water. A brother in Christ made a short prayer for her and then plunged her completely into the water. She came out completely changed, she was now a new creature. She shone with happiness; I was so happy that I will always remember this remarkable day.

We had fought the devil together and we had been more than victorious with Jesus. All the newly baptized entered the Church and the host of the ceremony, asked a person to sing a Christian song for the occasion. Rita got up first and began to sing. I was totally stunned when I heard this beautiful voice. She sang very well and had a beautiful voice. I thought I heard an angel singing. A tear fell on my cheek. At the end of the ceremony, Rita came to join me. She still jumped on my neck and said, "I thank you for everything Uncle!" I smiled at her and she understood that my heart was in joy.

Rita was not the only one to be delivered, because, without knowing it, she strengthened me enormously in the work that I carried out for the Lord. No one deliverance had marked me as much as this little Rita. Everyone had given up on her because of the power of this demon - people did not want to pray for her deliverance. The very one, that frightened many Christians, was showing all the Christians of Dedougou that there was nothing impossible for our God. I told her that her personal testimony would be a great force of evangelization for all the desperate people of the world and all those who had given up on the trials. Thank you my dear Rita, you will always be in my heart!

On Wednesday, August 15th, we still had not accumulated the amount necessary to buy the plane tickets so we had postponed the date of our departure by a few weeks.

That same evening, a brother of the International Center for Evangelization came home to discuss about his project to help needy children. He did not want to ask me to help him financially, but he just wanted help to find out more about how to file financial aid applications. We had a good discussion on the subject and I gave him several tips for this kind of file.

At the end of the evening, we prayed for him and his organization to help needy children. During this prayer, I saw three angels standing before me and watching me intently. They were the same angels who were in many of my visions, while I was in Edmonton, Canada. I realized immediately that God wanted us to return to Canada since we had all the documents needed to apply for funding. This vision had really pleased me since I had not seen these angels for several months. They had just shown me that they were always with us.

In the evening, before going to bed, I prayed to the Lord to show me another sign, which would confirm that I am acting entirely according to his will.

The next morning, I dropped Rosalie at the bus station because we had agreed that she would go to the Royal Air Maroc agency in Ouagadougou to buy flight tickets. We were supposed to leave in August, but had not managed to raise the money needed to buy tickets. Now we had just the amount needed for our flight home. We checked the price several times on the airline's website to make sure the price would not change and then Rosalie left with all the money we had on hand. Later that day, I went to the Maquis behind my home to evangelize to two Muslim men who were there.

At the same time, a man on his motorcycle came to join me. I had never seen this man before. He stopped by our table and greeted everyone who was seated. I thought he had come to speak with one of the Muslim men, but when he came to my side he said, "Martin, I came here to see you." I was quite surprised that this person knew my name even though I knew that many people in Dedougou knew me very well. Some locals called me the "rebellious pastor." The man informed me that God had put on his heart to give me something. He handed me an envelope containing not less than 100,000 FCFA.

I almost burst into tears in front of this stranger because I knew that he was sent by God himself. The man got on his motorcycle and drove away. Was he an angel? Probably!

At the same time, my wife called me to tell me that she was

running out of money. Since we did not buy the tickets over the Internet, there were additional fees added. It was about 46,000 FCFA to buy all the plane tickets we needed. Rosalie asked me if she should return to Dedougou, since we had no more money. She praised the Lord after hearing the story of this mysterious man on the bike. I did not believe in chance, I knew very well that God had used this man to fill our lack of money. I thanked the Lord wholeheartedly for this gesture and I immediately went to an Orange office to transfer the money to Rosalie. God did another miracle, the Orange office was just facing Royal Air Maroc agency in Ouagadougou. Rosalie just had to cross the street to get the money.

With this amount, she managed to buy our tickets and take the first bus which returned to Dedougou. She arrived earlier than expected at home. God had again answered my prayer to confirm that we were acting according to his divine will.

On Monday, August 20th, Officer Coulibaly came over to buy my mini-projector. He had great difficulty walking and informed us that he had a herniated disc, but the doctors refused to operate. He suffered terribly and this problem had prevented him from being promoted to Chief Warrant Officer. We offered to sit down, as he could barely stand. Rosalie asked him if he wanted us to pray for him, but he replied that he was a Muslim. "If you do not see any problem with the fact that we pray in the name of Jesus," I replied, "I do not see any problem praying for a Muslim who needs it." He smiles at us after this response.

He began to ask us several questions about the Bible of Christians and the life of Jesus. I was literally stunned by this thirst for knowledge from a Muslim. He wanted to know more about the one that Christians called "the Savior." After several questions, he was completely surprised to see that we had answered all these questions. He admitted that some Catholics priests had never answered all his questions.

He finally agreed that we pray for his divine healing. We have involved the name of Jesus in each of our requests, so that this man can see the glory and power of Jesus. After the prayer, I had a word for this Muslim man, "This night will be a wonderful night without pain. You will sleep like a baby and you will not want to wake up. Tomorrow you will feel a lot of changes in your body. The healing will begin tomorrow and will end in three days. You will be fully healed in only three days. Do not forget to thank Jesus for this miraculous healing."

"You can trust me, I will thank him!"

The officer left our residence in joy. He was happy to have met us and wanted to come back the next day to continue our discussion of the Word of God. We accepted without hesitation and then he left on his motorcycle.

The next day, around noon, Rosalie called Officer Coulibaly for news about his recovery. She woke him up! He was still sleeping and admitted that he no longer felt any pain. He still had some minor problems to walk properly, but he was already much better. Rosalie prayed with him on the phone.

On the second day, the Officer came to see us at home to show us that he could now walk without difficulty. He had decided to leave the bike at home and come to our house walking because it had been a long time since he had walked that way. He sat on a chair and we spent the whole evening talking about Jesus. He still demonstrated an incredible thirst for the Word of God. I knew that he would give his life to Christ and that he would become a powerful man of God. On the third day, the Officer could finally run without any pain. He was totally healed and confessed that he would continue to thank the Lord for this wonderful healing. He was now free from the evil that prevented him from moving freely in life.

The following Monday, Gilbert and his wife came to visit us. We sat down on the terrace to talk together. When I looked at Rachel, Gilbert's wife, I had a vision. I told her, "You're pregnant!"

She was immediately surprised and wondering how I guessed it, since she had not spoken to anyone. I told her it was the Holy Spirit who showed it to me. Gilbert was just as surprised as his wife. God would fill them because he was, he is, and he will always be the Father who hears and responds to his children.

The young pastor David called me on Tuesday, August 28th, to ask if he could come by with a very serious case. Because it was a request from this pastor, I accepted without hesitation. He arrived home a few hours later, accompanied by a tall man. They sat on the deck chairs and the stranger explained his problem down to the smallest detail. He had been a police officer for many years and everything was fine. Then, without warning, spirits of sadness and depression entered his heart. He now wanted only one thing - to commit suicide. He heard a voice telling him to shoot himself in the head with his own weapon. He admitted that he had tried twice to kill himself with his gun but had missed.

With all this disappointment, he went to the police station to pick up an AK-47 automatic weapon and try to commit suicide again. A colleague saw him and stopped him. His superior, informed of the situation, decided to temporarily suspend him so that he could take care of himself. He no longer had access to guns but the depression was still getting stronger. He saw black shadows that harassed him every night. Tears ran down his cheeks as he told us his story. I said to him, "This depression is spiritual and not mental." I also saw two dark spirits lurking around the policeman. They seemed to be preparing to reply, as soon as deliverance began. I asked the man to sit in his chair and we started the deliverance.

David took control of the prayer, as I supported him, interceding. I still saw the two dark spirits behind the man but there were also three angels waiting behind the shadows. The angels waited for the right moment to intervene and chase the intruders. Suddenly, the policeman shrieked a monstrous loud grunt and fell to the ground. I hastened to remove the chair so we put oil on his forehead, hands and feet. He moved slowly in all directions, as if he felt an intense pain in him. We continued the prayer, and then he let out another powerful grunt and stopped moving.

I asked him what his name was and he answered me correctly. We helped him to sit on the chair. He was completely exhausted, drained of all his energy. He could barely speak, but managed to admit that he was feeling very good. He admitted he had felt that something very heavy had left him. Now he felt very light and only wanted to sleep. David and I smiled a little, while telling him that it was perfectly normal to have that feeling. "This night will be the best night of your life." I told him. We had continued talking for several minutes and then the man left with Pastor David. We knew he was totally free from these evil intruders. He did not want to commit suicide anymore, but felt a joy of life. He felt that his heart had started beating again.

A few days later, Pastor David called me back to give me news about this policeman. He admitted that he had completely changed. He loved life and his marriage was much better. Even his superior had noticed the positive changes in the life of this policeman and thought to rehire him.

The policeman thanked David for taking him to my residence. May God be glorified for this miraculous gesture!

On September 6th, Rosalie had a call from her friend Nicole who lived in Ouagadougou. She seemed sad and informed my wife that she had strange pains in her left breast. She had an appointment at the hospital to do some tests, but she feared it was a breast cancer. She asked to pray for her. Rosalie told me the problem and the Lord showed me that she should not worry. "It is not cancer," I replied, "It is just stress that causes pain. She should take a few days of vacation. The pains will go away on their own after a few days." Rosalie told Nicole everything I had shared. Of course, she had a hard time believing what I was saying, so I advised her to go to the hospital to do the tests. I knew she would feel much better after having confirmation from the doctors.

On September 12th, we woke up very early in the morning to move all the equipment we had decided not to bring back to Canada. All these things would be stored at my wife's mother's house so we could pick them up when we come back to West Africa.

Subsequently, we went to the station to board the bus that

would take us to the capital. My son was excited because he was finally going to see his friends back in Canada. The trip between Dedougou and Ouagadougou took place without any problem.

At the capital's station, Nicole, Rosalie's friend, came with her big vehicle to join us because she knew we had several suitcases. She wanted to drive us to the airport. During the trip, she confessed to my wife that the results of the medical tests were all negative. She did not have breast cancer and the doctors admitted that stress could cause this kind of painful sensation. In front of the airport gate, she gave an envelope to Rosalie. Without opening the gift, we thanked her and she left the place. We entered the airport to wait for our flight with Royal Air Maroc. We had a stopover in Casablanca and another flight would take us directly to Montreal.

This return allowed us to see my family again in Quebec City before taking the bus to bring us to our final destination - Edmonton.

Currently, we are working to raise funds for the construction of the help center for widows of Mouhoun and we are preparing our return to Burkina Faso. The Lord will tell us when the time has come to return to this wonderful country. In the meantime, God accompanies us every day and he will always accompany us because he is faithful. He never abandons those he loves.

When he calls a person to do his will for the advancement of his kingdom, he does not take detours, he informs directly. After that, it is up to us to respond positively and work constantly by following his instructions. He is here for our happiness, not for our misfortune. Thank you Lord for having chosen us to fulfill your mission and to gather your harvest. May all glory come to you in the name of Jesus. Amen.

CONCLUSION

To obey the will of God, the call of the Father or the voice of the Creator is always a challenge. Jesus never told us that it would be easy to follow him. Instead, he mentioned that if we obey the call to follow him, we would be hated by all.

"Behold, I am sending you out as sheep in the midst of wolves, so be wise as serpents and innocent as doves. Beware of men, for they will deliver you over to courts and flog you in their synagogues, and you will be dragged before governors and kings for my sake, to bear witness before them and the Gentiles."

- Matthew 10:16-18 (ESV)

"You will be hated by all for my name's sake. But the one who endures to the end will be saved."

- Matthew 10:22 (ESV)

On one hand we have the Lord himself, who lets us know his plans for our life. But, on the other side, there are the walls that are formed by the enemy, for the sole purpose of preventing us from accepting this request of our Father. There can be different categories of walls, all equally daunting. The wall of conscience is probably one of the worst, since it causes us to totally question everything we know about the reality in which we live. Jesus, who had asked one of his disciples to leave his deceased father and follow him, is an excellent example of the wall of conscience.

"Another of the disciples said to him: Lord, let me first go and bury my father. And Jesus said to him: Follow me, and leave the dead to bury their own dead."
- Matthew 8:21-22 (ESV)

How would you react if the Lord asks you to drop the funeral of your own earthly father to follow the will of your heavenly Father?

Our conscience would certainly tell us to go quickly to bury our earthly father out of respect for our family, and after all the formalities related to the family funeral, to leave everything to follow the Lord.

Another very powerful wall can stand before us to prevent us from doing the will of God. This is the wall of finance. This kind of wall is one of the most complicated. It is not always the reality of the personal finance that causes problem, but rather the entourage (peer pressure) around us, who seek to discourage us by using this wall of the finance against us. On a personal level, we can quote the young man who had asked Jesus what he had to do to obtain eternal life.

"Jesus said to him: If you would be perfect, go, sell what you possess and give to the poor, and you will have treasure in heaven; and come, follow me. When the young man heard this he went away sorrowful, for he had great possessions."
- Matthew 19:21-22 (ESV)

This young man had many goods and was probably very rich, but when the Lord asked him to sell everything and give everything to the poor, he went away sad. He did not follow the Lord because he had great material possessions which he was very fond of. His wealth had removed him from the call of the Lord.

If Paul of Tarsus had worried about the financial means to undertake his many travels, we would probably not be Christians today. He had just grabbed his shoulder bag, a stick in his hand and his old shoes to walk for days and days to bring the gospel to the Gentiles. He was not worried about the money since God was with him. He knew beyond any doubt that his heavenly Father would provide for all his needs because he was doing his will. That's having faith!

Unfortunately, the wall of finance can be used by our immediate entourage, such as family and friends. I cannot even count the number of times a person close to me asked me, "How are you going to live?" Worse still, using personal feelings regarding my own son, "Have you thought about your son's school?" These questions may seem trivial, but they are very detrimental to our decision of whether or not to follow God's call. That's what I classify as the wall of the entourage.

This new wall includes family and friends, especially those who, by their often misleading words and without any faith in God, will do everything to turn us away from God's plan.

"Therefore whoever wishes to be a friend of the world makes himself an enemy of God."

- James 4:4 (ESV)

"Abraham believed God, and it was counted to him as righteousness and he was called a friend of God."

- James 2:23 (ESV)

"But I have called you friends, for all that I have heard from my Father I have made known to you."

- John 15:15 (ESV)

I do not know about you, but personally I prefer to call myself friend of God, rather than friend of the world. I much prefer to follow my heavenly Father, leaving behind all the deceptive words of these tongues of vipers, which dictate only what the enemy asks them to do.

"Get behind me, Satan! You are a hindrance to me. For you are not setting your mind on the things of God, but on the things of man."

- Matthew 16:23 (ESV)

These tongues of vipers can reject us publicly, using personal insults. I still remember a pastor who had insulted me in front of several brothers and sisters inside the church by calling me a demon. He added, "If God used a man for his work, it surely would not be with a man like you." He even had the audacity to make all this public during a preaching at the church. This message was actually a personal attack. He used a passage from Titus' book to pass his judgement against me.

"For there are many who are insubordinate, empty talkers and deceivers, especially those of the circumcision party. They must be silenced, since they are upsetting whole families by teaching for shameful gain what they ought not to teach."

- Titus 1:10-11 (ESV)

All the friends I had in this church had all turned against me. They had all understood that the pastor was talking about me. This situation had placed immense discouragement in my heart. But, I preferred to follow the voice of God and not the voices of men. Men can be wrong but God is never wrong! The following Sunday, I returned to this church to greet the hypocrites who called themselves "friends", one last time, before I shook the dust off my shoes, going out proudly through the front door.

I felt deep inside me that I was fulfilling the will of God in my life. I was happy to have made this last gesture since I followed the call of God in my life. Do not forget that all the Jews had rejected Jesus except some valiant heroes who had decided to abandon everything to follow him. They abandoned family, friends, and work to follow "the way, the truth, and the life."

The wall of doubt is another obstacle to obeying the call of God. Satan himself uses this kind of wall to block us in our relationship with the Lord. He has become an expert in implanting doubt into people's hearts, in order to better control and divert them from the truth. He had done it with Eve to get her to bite the forbidden fruit.

"And the woman said to the serpent: We may eat of the fruit of the trees in the garden, but God said: You shall not eat of the fruit of the tree that is in the midst of the garden, neither shall you touch it, lest you die. But the serpent said to the woman: You will not surely die. For God knows that when you eat of it your eyes will be opened, and you will be like God, knowing good and evil."

- Genesis 3:2-5 (ESV)

The enemy had succeeded in putting doubt in the heart of the woman, to the point that she no longer believed the truth that God had said about the fruit of this tree, in the middle of the garden. First, he contradicted the order of God that stipulated not to eat it. Second, he made her believe the effects of the fruit were very wonderful, since she would become like God. Of course, he deliberately omitted the fact this choice was going to put a separation between her and God, and that she would be driven out of the garden.

It was exactly the same lie Satan had used to deceive the third of angels, before the creation of the world. He had deceived the angels into believing that they had to rebel against God, in order to seize power. All the while neglecting to tell them that they all risked being chased out of heaven and separated from the Creator's divine presence. Satan became so expert at sowing doubt in hearts, that he used the same strategy against Jesus as he fasted in the wilderness.

"And the tempter came and said to him: If you are the Son of God, command these stones to become loaves of bread."
- Matthew 4:3 (ESV)

He was trying to put doubt in Jesus' head in order to manipulate him and push him to turn the stones into loaves. By doing so, Jesus would have destroyed his fast in the desert. But he had not fallen into the trap of the enemy since God himself had told him that he was indeed his Son at his baptism of water by John.

"This is my beloved Son, with whom I am well pleased."
- Matthew 3:17 (ESV)

There are many other walls that can form to block our path, to prevent us from following God's call. Walls, such as the discouragement makes us back away from his call, the laziness that always slows us down, the jealousy all around us, the fear of what can happen, etc. But one thing is certain - we can recognize a true servant of God, when he overcomes all the walls that come before him. One thought gives him the strength to overcome everything - faith in the one who sent him.

If you receive a call from God himself, I urge you to listen to him and follow him with all your heart. If this call comes from God, do not worry about anything because he will always be at your side. Never doubt God because, as you have read, doubt comes from the enemy to distract you from the truth. If God tells you He will move, He will move! If you remain in him continuously, he will also be your most faithful friend. On the other hand, if another person makes a prophecy about you, do not hesitate to ask the Lord for confirmation.

"And thereby put me to the test, says the Lord of hosts, if I will not open the windows of heaven for you and pour down for you a blessing until there is no more need."

- Malachi 3:10 (ESV)

I knew a brother in Christ in Africa that supposed prophets in his church had told him, "God wants you to leave your job to serve him every day." He had blindly listened to what the false prophets told him and quit his job. He had been waiting more than 11 years for God to show him how he could serve him. During all these years, he did not work; to align with what he thought was God's will for his life. These false prophets even had the audacity to say the same thing to his wife. They wanted her to quit her job too. Fortunately, she totally refused. She was the only source of income in the family.

In our churches today, many people say "God said" but they do not distinguish between the voice of God and their own thoughts. We must be very careful and clearly know what comes from God and what comes from men. Never forget what Jesus said to Peter.

"...For you are not setting your mind on the things of God, but on the things of man."

- Matthew 16:23 (ESV)

This shows us that error is human and that only God can boast of never being mistaken.

"It is better to take refuge in the Lord than to trust in man."

- Psalm 118:8 (ESV)

"Stop regarding man in whose nostrils is breath, for of what account is he?"

- Isaiah 2:22 (ESV)

Do not rely on men, but always ask the Lord for confirmation. If my family and I had listened to the men, and especially the men of God, we would never have set foot in Burkina Faso. We would never have seen the Holy Spirit at work through the gifts that he gave us and we would never have done the will of God in our lives. Do you realize what we would have missed if we trusted men rather than God? The truth is in one place - the Word. This Word is Jesus! Let's put all our trust in God the Father, God the Son and God the Holy Spirit!

"In the beginning was the Word, and the Word was with God, and the Word was God. He was in the beginning with God. All things were made through him, and without him was not any thing made that was made. In him was life, and the life was the light of men. The light shines in the darkness, and the darkness has not overcome it."

- John 1: 1-5 (ESV)

You will be severely persecuted, rejected, even by your loved ones and hated by the vast majority because you will bring the light that the world does not know, and that they repeatedly refused, for lack of knowledge or spiritual blindness. But do not worry about anything, the Lord will support you daily in all the trials.

"And that night the angel of the Lord went out and struck down 185,000 in the camp of the Assyrians. And when people arose early in the morning, behold, these were all dead bodies."

- 2 Kings 19:35 (ESV)

If only one angel has managed to do an exploit like this and eliminate one hundred and eighty-five thousand men in one night, imagine what can do the complete army of angels of the Lord.

"The Son of Man will send his angels, and they will gather out of his kingdom all causes of sin and all law-breakers, and throw them into the fiery furnace. In that place there will be weeping and gnashing of teeth. Then the righteous will shine like the sun in the kingdom of their Father. He who has ears, let him hear."

- Matthew 13:41-43 (ESV)

If the Lord communicates to you his divine will for your lives, if these requests are in order with the Word, do not hesitate, and go to your destiny. If it is the Lord who sends you, you will not fail, but if men send you, failure is assured. Imagine, if God calls you and then lets you down, he would be a disastrous witness for the advancement of his kingdom. So he would never do that because he provides for all our needs, if we remain in his will.

"You whom I took from the ends of the earth, and called from its farthest corners, saying to you: You are my servant, I have chosen you and not cast you off; fear not, for I am with you; be not dismayed, for I am your God; I will strengthen you, I will help you, I will uphold you with my righteous right hand."

- Isaiah 41:9-10 (ESV)

"The sun shall be no more your light by day, nor for brightness shall the moon give you light; but the Lord will be your everlasting light, and your God will be your glory."

- Isaiah 60:19 (ESV)

PRAYER BY ROSALIE

God of all the Universe
From the earth and the heavens
Hallowed be thy name on earth as in heaven
No one is comparable to you Heavenly Father

You are the only true God, there is no other
Neither the past century
Neither the present century
Neither the century to come

God of salvation, Father of our Lord Jesus Christ
Our Father to us through Jesus Christ
Saint, Saint, Saint is your Holy Name
You predict things, You are watching to fulfill
You are God

Thank you for Jesus Christ
Thank you for the cross of Jesus
Thank you for the death of Jesus, for humanity
Thank you for the blood of Jesus who reconciles us to God

Many people in the world still make sacrifices
Sheep, goats, oxen even human sacrifices
Which cannot save them, nor give them the salvation
The insurance, joy and peace of heart

Drop the sacrifices and come to the Living God
Who gave us his only Son for the sacrifice of the whole world

Come and repent today is the day of salvation
The arms of the heavenly Father are open
The heart of the Father is waiting for you
Reconcile with your Creator by recognizing Jesus

Born of a virgin named Mary, God became flesh on earth
Recognize the cross, death, resurrection
His ascension to heaven with the Father
And his return to take us

Glory to the glorious Holy Spirit
Who is with us until the end of the world
You live in us, you are the Spirit of life
You are the Spirit of wisdom

You are the Spirit of grace
You are the great Comforter
You are the great Intercessor by excellence
You know Heavenly Father's thoughts

Thank you Holy Spirit for your fire
Your gifts, your joy, your life in us, your peace
Thank you for the oil that abounds in our vases
Thank you for the fire that does not go out
Thank you for helping us prepare
Our meeting with the husband Jesus Christ

To you all Glory
Wonderful and glorious Holy Spirit
Thank you for talking to us
To reveal to us the hidden things
Thank you Spirit of Grace

Worldwide, receive Jesus Christ like your Lord and Savior
He paid the price for us, let's be grateful
The sacrifice of his person
Jesus Christ returns.

AMEN

43478469R00141

Made in the USA
Middletown, DE
25 April 2019